In Flanders Fields

IN
FLANDERS
FIELDS

THE 1917 CAMPAIGN

by Leon Wolff

With an Introduction by B.H. Liddell Hart

 TIME Reading Program Special Edition
Time-Life Books Inc. Alexandria, Virginia

Time-Life Books Inc.
is a wholly owned subsidiary of
TIME INCORPORATED

TIME Reading Program: *Editor*, Max Gissen

Library of Congress CIP data following page 455.

For information about any Time-Life book, please write:
Reader Information, Time-Life Books,
541 North Fairbanks Court, Chicago, Illinois 60611

TO LILLIAN

In Flanders fields the poppies blow
Between the crosses, row on row,
    That mark our place; and in the sky
    The larks, still bravely singing, fly
Scarce heard amid the guns below.

We are the Dead. Short days ago
We lived, felt dawn, saw sunset glow,
    Loved and were loved, and now we lie
    In Flanders fields.
Take up our quarrel with the foe:
To you from failing hands we throw
    The torch; be yours to hold it high.
    If ye break faith with us who die
We shall not sleep, though poppies grow
    In Flanders fields.

—John McCrae

Contents

Illustrations & Maps

If there is a theme to the work of Leon Wolff it would seem to be war, and anger at war and the men who conduct war. It is not surprising, therefore, that some critics have sought to classify him as one of America's angry young men. It is an epithet that Wolff does not reject, although his age belies it—he was old enough to be an Air Force officer during World War II. "Of course I am an angry man," he says, "but I believe I am protesting properly, always in behalf of right and decency." He has protested, with considerable success, three times between the covers of notably eloquent books: *Low Level Mission,* the story of the costly and debatable American air strike at the Romanian oil fields of Ploesti in 1943; *Little Brown Brother,* a documentary account of America's brutal war against the Philippine natives in 1898, for which Wolff won the Society of American Historians' 1961 Francis Parkman prize; and *In Flanders Fields.*

In Flanders Fields is the history of Britain's 1917 campaign in Belgium in which Field Marshal Sir Douglas Haig expended some 300,000 men to gain—and later lose —a few hundred yards of meaningless, blood-soaked mud.

Published in 1958, this book was the curtain raiser on a period of intensive literary soul-searching about the First World War. To many of a later generation, this conflict conjures up little more than a generalized picture of muddy trenches, ceaseless bombardments, periodic waves of poison gas and flimsy aircraft fighting D'Artagnan-like duels in the skies overhead. In Wolff's book, many readers saw that war for the first time for what it really was: one of history's most dreadful, bloody and senseless conflicts, a war in which stupidity played an equal role with bravery, in which frustration raged as destructively in the hearts and minds of generals as it did blindly in the dulled emotions of front-line soldiers; a war in which military tactics came to a dead stop in the nightmare landscape of no man's land and simple attrition became a philosophy of battle.

Other books have since illuminated other aspects of this first of all modern world conflicts. Barbara Tuchman in *The Guns of August* told how it began; the British writer Alastair Horne in *The Price of Glory* reviewed the 10-month horror of the battle for Verdun; Richard Watt in *Dare Call It Treason* disclosed the full story of the mutiny in the exhausted French armies following that fruitless campaign; and Alan Clark in *Donkeys* caustically described the kind of leadership which could bring such things to pass—in this case, the British Command in the first two crucial years of the war.

Leon Wolff's story of the campaign which Haig launched from the Ypres salient in 1917 combines aspects of all of these. Wolff himself has characterized his work as always being born of some historical incident which smacked to him of "the unbelievable and the unfair"—and this battle was the epitome of both. *"In Flanders Fields,"* he says, "began as a violent adolescent prejudice. The campaign was a caricature of war. It is preposterous and impossible that a military campaign could be conducted in that way. It was unfairly and brutally conducted up to the highest level."

This note of anger is not explicit in the book. It does not have to be. It suffices for Wolff to set down, in page after carefully documented page, just what happened—how the plan was conceived by Haig in his headquarters in Belgium; how reluctant consent for it was wrung from David Lloyd George, the British prime minister, and other political leaders in London; how the weeks and months of preparation crept by until the rainy season broke, which turned the Flanders fields into a vast expanse of stinking, shell-torn, all but impassable mud; how the troops, exhausted, exposed, betrayed by security leaks, slogged forward time after time under unremitting shellfire to capture a few yards of ground; and how it all ended, finally, in futility. Never was a battle fought under more dreadful conditions; never did a single military leader inflict his will so fixedly on soldier and politician alike for a more ephemeral or foredoomed cause. This was tragedy of the most appalling order.

Captain B. H. Liddell Hart, the eminent British military historian who has written the Introduction to this special edition of the book, calls *In Flanders Fields* "a campaign which was the quintessence of the conduct and experience of the First World War." So, indeed, it was. This war, which began so bravely with flying banners and the widely held conviction that it would be over by Christmas, proved to be a turning point which changed the world forever. And in this one campaign all of the significant developments of the war as a whole emerge sharply: how weapons had outrun tactics and the ability of commanders to cope with them. In the deadly stalemate which inevitably followed, the military leaders on both sides, blankly turning the pages of their histories, could find no other solution than to hurl wave after wave of men against machine guns and artillery in search of the breakthrough that could not possibly come. There was only one way such warfare could end, as Major General J. F. C. Fuller points out in his introduction to the original edition: in sheer exhaustion—and that story is told here too, the pitiful story of the frontline soldier who, knee-deep in clinging mud, could only fight and bleed and die.

This is the story Leon Wolff tells. It is a tale of war that will be long read and remembered.

—THE EDITORS

Leon Wolff's book *In Flanders Fields* deals with the 1917 campaign on the Western Front, a campaign which was the quintessence of the conduct and experience of the First World War. It is, in my judgment, the best account of that campaign that has appeared in this generation, and one of the outstanding books on that war. But I would also rate it among the most illuminating studies of war published anywhere at any time.

Written by an American, and one who was too young to see service in that war, it has the advantage of freedom from bias in examining the course of the French and British operations, and in threading a way through the tangled thickets of controversy that developed at the time and continued to grow during the postwar decades. Leon Wolff has penetrated the tangle, in search of the truth, with remarkable skill and success. His book brings out the drama, the illusions and the wrangles of the period, along with their ghastly results, so effectively as to make that time extraordinarily vivid in the mind of the reader—and make readers who had personal experience of the war feel that they are living through it again.

The year 1916 had closed in gloom for the Allies. The simultaneous offensive on all fronts, planned a year before, had misfired. The French were suffering from exhaustion,

the British had lost the flower of their new armies in the
four months' offensive on the Somme without achieving
any visible result proportionate to the cost, the Russians
were on the verge of collapse after colossal losses and another fresh ally, Romania, had been overrun by the enemy
—like Serbia in 1915. America's entry into the war on April
6, 1917, was a great moral tonic to the Allies, but it would
be another year before American reinforcements would
begin to tilt the military balance in the Allies' favor.

It was at this point that the British commander in chief
on the Western Front, Douglas Haig, eager to win the war
with his own British forces before the Americans could
arrive and snatch the credit, pressed home his long-
cherished desire for an offensive in Flanders. Despite the
grave doubts of Prime Minister David Lloyd George,
which soon hardened into outright opposition, and in dis-
regard of information indicating that the Flanders region
would revert to swamp under prolonged bombardment
and the usual rainy weather of August, Haig insisted on
launching the campaign. For an early breakthrough such
as he was aiming at, surprise was of vital importance, but
in choosing to attack in the bare Flanders plain, all Haig's
immense preparations were displayed to the eyes of the
German observers. A fortnight's bombardment gave them
further warning. The weather turned bad and the ground
became a quagmire, as predicted.

Leon Wolff recounts the story of this offensive, one of
the most costly and useless of the war, in a deeply moving
book with a wealth of striking detail. While soberly factual, the story amounts to a tremendous indictment of the
High Command, and particularly of Haig. But the evidence is presented in a very fair-minded way; indeed, at

times it may even err on the charitable side in weighing some of the assertions and excuses propagated by partisan apologists in later years.

Long before the massed bombardments of 1917, any front-line soldier who served in the Ypres sector was well aware that it soon turned into a morass during the rainy period. Even when I was there in the autumn of 1915, the fire trenches were often so deeply filled with muddy water that it lapped over the tops of our rubber boots. Many of the communications trenches were flooded to the brim, so that the only way of reaching the front line was "overland" and under cover of darkness, by roads and tracks. Along many of these the mud was thick, and every step was tiring. Flanders mud was the most gluey I have ever known —and it felt all the more so when one was caught in the light of a flare or star shell, and the consequent burst of fire.

So it was a certainty that if the elaborate drainage system created by generations of Flemish farmers was to be destroyed by heavy bombardment, an offensive then would become bogged down in any rainy spell, even before the autumn. The creation of such a barrier was ensured by Haig's plan of preparing the way for his attack by a 10-day bombardment with 3,000 guns—a gun to every six yards of front, and nearly five tons of high explosive to the yard.

How was it possible for Haig and his staff to be so blind to the inevitable and frustrating consequences? The Tank Corps staff had warned G.H.Q. that summer, and the engineers' staff had pointed out the drainage factor earlier. But the heads of his General Staff, his immediate operational advisers, did not go up to see the front for themselves. Even when they had qualms, they were so much in awe of Haig that they hesitated to voice their doubts—being aware that these would be unwelcome once he had set his mind and heart on the Flanders offensive—while he was too self-contained and reserved to encourage them to do so. The essential clue to Passchendaele, as the campaign is sometimes known, lies in Haig's personality.

He was typical of the soldiers of his time in the too-simple black-and-white way he saw things and in his intemperate way of expressing his views. He was typical, too, in his prejudices, particularly against "politicians." But he also had a tremendous sense of a God-given mission —to lead the British Army to victory. The sense of a divine call easily produces a sense of divine right. This had enabled Haig to push himself to the top by steps that could hardly be justified by ordinary standards. It is remarkable what a basically honorable man can do under the influence of such a religious conviction—though it is not uncommon in history.

The war deepened his religious tendency, and with it grew the sense of divine inspiration, as shown in numerous comments in his personal diary. Even when he beat the French generals in an argument, he ascribed it to a special power he possessed. Sometimes, to be sure, events cast a doubt on his certainty as to the source of his inspiration. On the eve of the Somme offensive in 1916 he wrote, "I feel that every step in my plan has been taken with divine help." The tragic opening day of that offensive brought the heaviest day's loss in the history of the British Army— 67,000 casualties for hardly any gain.

Haig's diary is of special value in showing the outlook with which he approached his problems. Here a discerning reader can trace the sources of his failures as well as of his strength. What he saw, he saw so clearly that he found it difficult to appreciate that there was anything beyond. That tendency, combined with his self-confidence, made it difficult for him to see another point of view. He appeared so ready to assume that others were agreeing with him that he did not detect their reservations.

His self-confessed habit of optimism might well account for miscalculations. But it was his own official biographer who provided a further explanation—in a passage which indicated that "with him it was not merely a sentiment but a policy," and quoted a letter of his which "reveals his deliberate intention to give pre-eminence to the more favorable aspects of any situation." Obviously this is a very serious admission. It goes further than anything in Mr. Lloyd George's memoirs to justify the charge that the Cabinet's reluctant approval of Haig's plans at Passchendaele was gained by deception. We can see now, as Haig could not, that the end did not justify the means. Good intentions paved the path to Passchendaele.

The self-revelation of character that Haig's diary provides is more than sufficient to explain his clashes with Lloyd George and their inevitability. In temperament the two men were poles apart. Moreover, the instinctive antipathy to "the Politician" which the diary reveals, long before he met "L.G.," clearly shows what a difficult man Haig was bound to be as a servant of government whenever broad considerations of policy conflicted with the narrower view of strategy. Even Sir William Robertson, the government's chief military adviser and Haig's stanchest supporter, was castigated in the diary when he cautioned Haig about the grave danger to the Britain of 1917 of undertaking "large and costly attacks."

In trying to restrain Haig from such exhausting ventures, Lloyd George was handicapped by having only just
become prime minister, and in owing his position to the
support of the Conservative party, his former political opponents. A further handicap was that many of these men
instinctively supported Haig in any conflict of view, while
the king himself was in "close alliance" with Haig and assuring him privately of support "through thick and thin."
(In World War II, by comparison, Winston Churchill was
far better placed, enjoying almost unanimous political
support. Yet even so, he had quite a lot of difficulty in
dealing with the military chiefs, although they were more
amenable and more ready to recognize the policy factors
affecting strategy than Haig had been.)

Leon Wolff's account of the events of 1917 is much more
than an objective analysis of a campaign. It attains a
superlative degree of insight and understanding in dealing
with the conditions of that war and with the human factors
that affected the course of the struggle. *In Flanders Fields*
will have a permanent place in the library of war as a
fine combination of sound history, brilliant writing and
reflection.

—B. H. LIDDELL HART

Introduction

This is an outstanding book, the most fascinating I have read on the period reviewed. It is much more than a military history, rather an invocation which summons out from the depths of the past the catastrophic year 1917—the progenitor of the age in which we live. Here is brought to light again all its many facets, its antagonisms, its blunders, its horrors and its heroism, and also their repercussions on politics and social life.

The sources drawn upon are multitudinous and varied, ranging from official histories and the memoirs of statesmen and generals to obscure articles and long-forgotten newspaper reports. The participants come strikingly to life: Lloyd George, the mercurial, who says one thing one day and another thing the next; Haig, the man of gunmetal, who says nothing and does the same thing day after day; Nivelle, the cocksure; Pétain, the cautious; Foch, the oracle of the offensive; Henry Wilson, the military harlequin; Robertson, the baiter of politicians; and Repington, the curtained intriguer. These and a host of others play their parts, and as the author says—although he tried to avoid saying it—the play itself unrolls before the reader "with the inevitability of a Greek tragedy."

During this "carnival of death," as Chief of the Tank

Corps General Staff, I met most of the leading participants, and took part in all the British battles mentioned in
this book; and what astonishes me is not so much the author's insight and devotion to facts but the extraordinary
way in which he has recaptured the atmosphere of forty-
one years ago, and made facts live again as they were then
lived. Two are outstanding: the inability of the politicians
to win a profitable peace, and the incapacity of the generals to win profitable battles.

As regards the first, the author writes, "Early 1917
would have been a splendid time to stop the war." With
this I full-heartedly agree, and it was the only time. Until
then the fighting had been largely experimental; the battles of Verdun and the Somme, in which 1,800,000 men of
both sides were killed and wounded, had exhausted the
belligerents, and had shown that frontal assaults on entrenched positions were unable to solve the stalemate.
These massacres and the famous Lansdowne peace proposal of November 14, 1916, led to the fall of the Asquith
administration, and Lloyd George, who succeeded Asquith, was pledged to a more vigorous prosecution of the
war. His policy, as the author points out, was to hit and hit
again with all our strength until the Germans cracked,
and although later he anathematized Haig's Flanders campaign as "this insane enterprise," politically he was responsible for it.

Early in 1917, the sole sane alternative to negotiated
peace—the only type of peace which, as history has again
and again shown, can lead to profit—was to put great battles into cold storage, and rely on the blockade to starve
Germany into submission—that is, to win the war by sea

power instead of land power. Three months later America entered the war, and a negotiated peace became impossible. April 6 was the black day in European history.

As regards the incapacity of the generals to win profitable battles, because the author—perhaps wisely—does not discuss tactical developments prior to the war, I think it is of importance for the reader that I should make clear what was at the bottom of their failures.

It was the rifle bullet, which had rendered the defense stronger than the attack: it begot the rifle-pit and the trench, it sheathed the bayonet, it blunted the sword, it drove back the cannon, and it dismounted the horseman. Fifty years before 1914, in the American Civil War, when the muzzle-loading rifle prevailed, a participant wrote, "Our infantry were tired of charging earthworks. The ordinary enlisted men assert that one good man behind an earthwork was equal to three good men outside of it." Summed up, the rifle bullet was lord of the battlefield.

Although between then and 1914 the breech-loading magazine rifle and the machine gun had been introduced, with fire power a hundred-fold greater than in 1861–1865, so conservative were armies that all, there are no exceptions, adhered in essentials to the tactics of the flintlock musket, which took a minute to load, and had an effective range of less than 100 yards. It may astonish the reader to learn that the only man who accurately forecast what happened in 1914 was a Polish banker, Mr. Bloch of Warsaw, who in 1899, in his book *Is War Impossible?* wrote:

The war, instead of being a hand-to-hand contest . . . will become a kind of stalemate. . . . Everybody will be entrenched in the next war. It will be a great war of entrenchments. The spade will be as indispensable to the soldier as his rifle. . . . All wars will of necessity partake of the character of siege operations. . . . Your soldiers may fight as they please; the ultimate decision is in the hands of famine. . . . That is the future of war . . . the bankruptcy of nations and the break-up of the whole social organization.

And in 1918 it was famine, the dividend of the blockade, more so than battles, which brought the Central Powers to ruin.

All this was miles beyond Haig's mental horizon, and the author's estimate of him closely tallies with my own. He lived and worked like a clock; every day he did the same kind of thing at the same moment; his routine never varied. In character he was stubborn and intolerant, in speech inarticulate, in argument dumb. But he was not an uneducated soldier. Unlike so many cavalrymen of his day, he had studied war, and, strange to say, this was to be his undoing, because he was so unimaginative that he could not see that the tactics of the past were as dead as mutton. We are told he held that the "role of cavalry on the battlefield will always go on increasing," and that he believed bullets had "little stopping power against the horse." This was never true, as an intelligent glance at past battles would have made clear to him. Yet it had to be true, otherwise how could he employ his cavalry? Thus, in spite of fire, wire, and mire, cavalry figured in all his battles, and to the detriment of the other arms, because they and their enormous forage trains blocked communications. Further, General Charteris, his Chief of Intelligence, tells us he considered himself "the predestined instrument of Providence for the achievement of victory for the British armies." "British" should be noted, because he was congenitally anti-French.

His Chief of Staff, General Kiggell, a tall, gloomy, and erudite soldier, was Commandant of the Staff College when I was a student there in 1914, and the only thing I distinctly remember his saying was, "In the next war we must be prepared for very heavy casualties." His theory of war was to mass every available man, horse, and gun on a single battlefield, and by the process of slow attrition wear down the enemy until his last reserves were exhausted, and then annihilate him.

Within the walls of the old Vauban fortress of Montreuil, where GHQ were established, Kiggell meditated like a Buddhist bhikku; revolved the prayer wheel of his doctrines, and out of them concocted Napoleonic battles on paper, which on the ground turned out to be slaughterhouse dramas. He was essentially a cloistered soldier; he never went near a battle, and—if reports are correct—only once visited a battlefield, and then long after the battle had been fought. Spiritually he was the twin brother of Flecker's Mandarin general in the "Golden Journey to Samarkand,"

Who never left his palace gates before,
But hath grown blind reading great books on war.

The remaining members of GHQ General Staff were nonentities; but they should not altogether be blamed for being so, for to serve a projection of the deity is apt to make the most prominent feel small. All were, as they had to be, yes-men, and the only one who had any influence with Haig was General Charteris, a hale and hearty back-slapping fellow, as optimistic as Candide, who conjured forth resounding victories from each bloody hundred yards' advance like rabbits from a hat; he fed Haig on false news—anyhow false to the men at the front—and completely misled the press and British public. It was he who, to pep up the troops, invented the German corpse factory, which, although it did not add to the prestige of his office, certainly made the front line rock with laughter.

The battles examined in this book form two pairs of Siamese twins; the one, those of Arras and Aisne II in the spring, and the other, those of Messines and Ypres III in the summer and autumn; and their origins and the politico-military wranglings which shaped them will greatly intrigue the reader. He should, however, bear in mind that the first two coincided with the entrance of the United States into the war and the outbreak of revolution in Russia; the one meant enormous eventual additional strength for Great Britain and France, and the other pointed to the release of a large number of German divisions on the eastern front and their transference to the western.

The battle of Arras, which opened on April 9, led to an advance of 7,000 yards at the cost of 160,000 casualties. That of Aisne II, under Nivelle—of whom the author has much to say—was begun eight days later. It resulted in a severe French repulse and the loss of 180,000 in killed, wounded, and missing—and worse still, in mutinies in the French Army. These prohibited a resumption of a French offensive for several months.

Haig had objected to both these battles, for ever since he had succeeded Sir John French in December 1915 his eyes had been glued on Flanders, and with him a battle in that region had become an obsession.

Next, on June 7, came the battle of Messines, which is particularly well described. Its aim was to flatten out the salient south of Ypres, so as to facilitate the launching of Haig's master battle eastward of that city. It came as a tactical surprise—a novelty in this war—and because of this and because its objective was a limited one it was a great but costly success.

Meanwhile, from the battle of Arras onward, an acrimonious wrangle between Lloyd George and Haig had been going on. The former, in spite of his hit-and-hit-again policy, was violently opposed to the latter's stubborn adherence to a battle in the Ypres area. At length, to force the Prime Minister's hands, Admiral Jellicoe was roped in to say that, because of the U-boat menace, "if the Army cannot get the Belgian ports, the Navy cannot hold the channel and the war is as good as lost." Haig knew this to be bunkum. Charteris has a note on what he said about it: "No one really believed this rather amazing view, but it had sufficient weight to make the Cabinet agree to our attack." Later, the plea put forward that in order to reduce pressure on the French Haig was compelled to attack, was a postwar afterthought to justify his battle. He did not fight at Ypres for submarine bases or for the French; he fought because he was confident of victory. He did what Napoleon said was the worst thing a general could do—paint an imaginary picture of a situation and accept it as real.

Haig knew the Ypres area well; he had fought over it in 1914 and, although the mud had not then been excessive, he must have known that the level of the surface water was so high that in many places parapets had to replace trenches; incidentally, the original tank was designed to surmount them. This should have made it clear to him that were the ground and its drainage dikes heavily shelled, irrespective of rain, the battlefield would become a bog; this had actually happened during the battle of Messines.

As more than half of this book is devoted to the Third Battle of Ypres, all that space allows me is to reinforce the author's illuminating analysis with a few observations of my own.

In the preparatory bombardment 4,283,550 shells, weighing 107,000 tons, were hurled onto the reclaimed bogland of Ypres, and in the opinion of the official historian "the British Army . . . by its own bombardment and barrages created in front of itself its own obstacle." This I can vouch for, because on August 2, the third day of the battle, I went forward to look at the battlefield. The ground was shattered beyond recognition, and in many places slush was two feet deep. On my return, my general, Hugh Elles, asked me, "How are things going?" to which I replied, "Look at me!" I was plastered with mud from head to foot. The next day I put in a report, a line or two of which the author quotes in Chapter Nine; in it I suggested that the Tank Corps be withdrawn from the battle and, in order to distract the enemy, be employed in the French St. Quentin area. After reading it, Elles remarked that Haig would never cooperate with the French; thereon I suggested instead the British Front facing Cambrai—we little suspected, at the time, this was the seed which was to sprout into the first great tank battle in history.

By the night of July 31, the first day of the battle, heavy rain was then falling. Haig's project of massed infantry assaults followed by massed cavalry pursuits had foundered in the slough created by his massed artillery bombardments, and automatically Kiggell's theory of attrition came into play. It led to such slaughter that GHQ calculated that by October reinforcements would be 100,000 men short. On August 21 a conference was assembled to discuss what could be done to keep the battle going until November. Every department was to be depleted of men; work on roads, railways, and hutting was to cease, and the Director General of Medical Services considered it would be possible to get a certain number of men from the venereal class, though this might spread infection.

Reader, note the date—only three weeks after the battle had opened. Next, note another date. On October 2, by when pack mules were being used to supply the forward guns, and it was taking fourteen hours to bring a wounded man back from the front line, Haig assembled another conference to set before it his views on how the successes gained could be exploited. Preparations were to be made to launch a general offensive on the heels of the retreating enemy. Behind it the Cavalry Corps was to advance, and when the moment was favorable the enemy was to be pursued and annihilated. Yet, in actual fact, had the entire German Army volatilized, it would have been impossible for troops to pursue, because on account of the mud it would have been impossible to supply and feed them.

On November 10, the battle ended four and a half miles from its starting line. Ten days later came the battle of Cambrai. There was no preparatory bombardment; instead 376 tanks led the infantry assault over unbroken ground and through the toughest trench system in France at negligible cost. Although lack of reserves led to failure, the battle proved to all who could see that the stalemate was not an unsolvable problem, and that the answer to the bullet was a sheet of half-inch armor plate; the solution was as simple as that!

With a brief mention of this revolutionary battle, except for the author's final comments, this remarkable book on 1917 ends.

—J. F. C. FULLER

Author's Preface

In the beginning, Neolithic intertribal rivalries had gradually blended into coherent European history. Thousands of years came and went. The people, the kingdoms, the quarrels, the modes of conflict changed; but the causes of the wars remained as irrational as ever. In 1871 a routine incident took place: Alsace and part of Lorraine were annexed by Germany as part of her price for having won the Franco-Prussian War. While this technical transfer caused little change in the lives of the inhabitants of the area (except possibly for the better), they became properly incensed nonetheless, and their former French compatriots promised revenge.

German military power continued to grow, though now Bismarck took care to inform the world that his country's conscription system, broadened militarism, and accentuated navalism were only defensive. "Germany is surfeited," he insisted, and was arming only to withstand evil powers which might try to deprive her of legal rights and possessions.

But other nations did not understand this, and considered the increasing strength of the *Reich* a threat to their own security. The two giants, Russia and France, drew even closer together when Germany and Austria (in reflexive fear of the Russian-French friendship) banded together in their military alliance of 1879. This was expanded into the Triple Alliance a few years later when Italy joined it. Its purpose was at least frank; it was directed flatly and by name against the defensive Franco-Russian coalition, which in turn was directed against the defensive Austro-German combination.

Thus far, all the alarums and excursions caused primarily by Bismarck's attempts to keep Germany supreme on the Continent had at least been confined to Europe. But now a new and more ambitious personality entered the scene—Emperor William II of Germany. He had a larger ax to grind, for it was his youthful dream to expand German trade, colonies, and prestige throughout the world. While the blessings of such a program, even if successful, might have trickled down only microscopically to the more humble occupants of his realm, they reacted to it with such enthusiasm as to suggest that they envisioned the achievement of heaven on earth thereby. But in commencing to build the necessary navy the Germans brought forth a new and formerly aloof antagonist—Great Britain.

The watchful English had no intention of being preempted, and began to lay down even a bigger and better navy. Secondly they entered into defensive combination with France and Russia. Thus was born the Triple Entente.

Now the Germans in great indignation accused Edward VII of "encirclement," and proceeded to strengthen their ties not only with Austria-Hungary and Italy but with Turkey. All the last-named three had designs, meanwhile, on the Balkans, for ponderous reasons having to do with Serbian designs on Austria and Bulgarian designs on Turkey, to name only two such designs. There was a great Balkan crisis in 1908, followed by a sudden, nasty squabble in 1912, in which all the small countries ganged up on the helpless remnant of the Ottoman Empire and swallowed its European portion. Italy, Bulgaria, Serbia, Greece, Rumania, and Turkey were involved in this affair, which came and went with such callousness as to bring a twinge of fear to the Great Powers. However, instead of trying to remove the basic causes of tension they proceeded to intensify them by still more desperate military measures.

A last-minute arms and naval race followed—"militarism run wild"—and in their fear the people, statesmen, and kings turned to their generals and admirals for protection. The power of the military clique became enormous in all nations balancing on the brink. The symbols used to justify the drive to war grew apace, and were exaggerated into quasi-religious articles of faith.

Austria-Hungary furnished a classic example of such phobias and slogans. She was determined to maintain the Dual Monarchy. She was provoked over losses of political power and prestige in the Balkans. She was hateful of the gains won by her Serbian rival. She was determined to expand her sphere of influence eastward. And when Archduke Francis Ferdinand, heir to the Austro-Hungarian throne, was killed at Sarajevo by Serb patriots as bemused as those of other lands, Vienna found a pretext for crushing her rival once and for all. Germany backed Austria reluctantly.

What followed was as swift, as purposeful, as inevitable as though it made sense. For when Austria attacked Serbia, Russia (protector of the Slavic states) could not stand by. And Germany had to support her main ally in deeds as well as words. Yet France was committed to

Russia on the basis of the Triple Entente, for tangible reasons of economics, and by a Premier who welcomed war. For similar reasons Britain had to support France and Russia. On the other side, Italy was theoretically obligated to fight beside Germany and Austria. Within a week almost everybody in Europe was fighting, and in time practically the whole world joined in.

In the fourth year of this war there occurred one of many military cataclysms: the Third Battle of Ypres, often referred to as the Passchendaele campaign, or the 1917 Flanders offensive. While its importance was no greater than several others, it did possess, as we shall see, certain unique features which have set it somewhat apart in drama and interest. My aim has been to examine this fearsome and controversial episode in general terms rather than from a military standpoint alone. I have tried to avoid saying that it unrolled with the inevitability of a Greek tragedy. It did; and the problem in writing of it was not to trace the familiar sequence of events but to throw light on them from an embarrassing richness of source material. Thus the book is an essay in interpretation, with whatever defects must flow therefrom. Its perspective is British (and I am not), and here again distortions may have arisen. Finally, I found almost all background sources more or less inclined against the military strategy that was adopted. These factors should be borne in mind in evaluating the narrative that follows, as well as my admission that I found it impossible to escape the point of view which probably colors much too plainly the telling of the story. Once I had hoped to relate it with such inhuman neutrality as would arouse the wonder and admiration of all shades of critical readership. I soon found that I could not believe what I was writing. The situation was most distressing, and I therefore decided to set down the facts and to comment upon them in the way which seemed to me inescapably logical. Yet I will never cease to suspect that I may be wrong, nor should the reader fail to do the same. All shades of opinion, however, are represented in the Bibliography which follows the narrative; and I have also consulted many periodicals of the day, especially the London *Times*, but since these are referred to by name throughout the book they are not listed here.

Other than these sources (and others used too meagerly or obliquely to require formal credit) I am in debt to my wife, who brought about changes in certain chapters, and to my publishers in New York and London, who uncovered many small blunders and who suggested ways of reorganizing and rephrasing portions of the manuscript. They did not concern themselves with my interpretations and attitudes; and the usual formality concerning the sole responsibility of the author is perhaps more meaningful in this case than most. The argument about Passchendaele continues with unabated bitterness. Haig and his campaign have been seized upon as ideal targets by those who abhor the military mind and its works, while their opponents defend their own way of life and thought with equal vigor. Thus the conflict now seems to be running deeper than its origin. I hope this book will contribute a trifle to the understanding at both levels.

—L. W.

1. The Deadlock

Somewhere in the limitless darkness a man coughed, a bird twittered an isolated phrase, a muffled voice spoke up. Many miles behind the front, thousands of lorries, wagons, gun limbers, horses, and men moving endlessly along the Belgian roads furnished a soft, pulsating background, like that of a kettledrum stirred by felt hammers while the orchestra rests and watches its score. Here in the advance zone of the dread salient around Ypres hardly a man moved, nor did many even know or care that the old year was dying.

The officer standing beside the field piece watched the glowing second-hand of his wristwatch. At the stroke of midnight he said, "Fire." The gun roared, and a shell was lobbed somewhere into the German positions. A few seconds later there was a single, distinct far-off explosion, after which a strained silence hung in the air. Then the enemy threw up anxious flares, ghastly green but of great beauty. These illuminated No Man's Land lingeringly, froze it briefly into the aspect of a charcoal sketch, and then faded away. The British battery fired nine rounds in erratic succession, paused, and then fired seven more. Thus the new year, 1917, was advertised by seventeen shells, to which the Germans did not respond; and the rest of the evening passed in relative peace there and elsewhere on the Western Front.

A cheerless morning dawned some hours later. In Belgium there were snow and sleet flurries beneath a steel-gray sky, in France temperatures below freezing and strong damp winds that chilled the men in their icy entrenchments; and only near the French-Swiss Alps did the sun appear elusively, though here the cold was even greater. Most of the front from Switzerland to the English Channel was a black snake writhing through white snow that covered the hills, plains, and woodlands of belligerent Europe.

As the skies lightened the great armies stirred. The big guns boomed their required number of rounds at registered targets in a lackluster way. Men filtered sleepily into the forward trenches and took up their arms, groaning and cursing in the way of early risers. To revive their spirits, snipers fired a few careless rounds at the enemy sandbags. Machine gunners cut loose and swept No Man's Land for a minute or two, to clear the area of spooks and enemy prowlers. The British troops yawned and stretched, were issued their daily half-pint of rum, replied with age-old complaints as to quantity and quality, and sipped meditatively. Through peepholes and periscopes they scanned the enemy parapets about a hundred yards away.

Blue smoke arose where the enemy was frying bacon. As the snipers watched through their tiny loopholes, blackish-brown heads and shoulders occasionally hurried past narrow gaps in his parapets. These blurred fragments were actual enemy soldiers, briefly visible against the misty sunlight and under the star shells that now blazed whitely. Still the countless wheels, hoofs, and boots rumbled like faraway thunder, and could clearly be heard between the pounding of machine guns, rifle fire, mortar explosions, and the roar of artillery.

For the first time the soldiers were no longer betting that the war would be over by next year. They had begun to whisper, "It might last a lifetime," and the ancient joke usually followed: "They say the first seven years will be the worst." Nobody sang "Tipperary" any more—that dashing, inspiring tune of earlier days. It had been replaced by "Take Me Back to Dear Old Blighty." And hopelessly, sardonically they hummed to the tune of "Auld Lang Syne":

> *We're here because we're here,*
> *Because we're here, because we're here;*
> *We're here because we're here,*
> *Because we're here, because we're here.*

The third New Year's Day of the First Great War had arrived on the Western Front.

The conflict which had exploded in 1914 was, it was felt at the time, fortunately going to be a short one. All the generals on both sides (as in the paradox of conflicting prayers) stated that they would prevail in short order; and even among the few pessimists there was a feeling that military operations of such magnitude had to end in a rapid decision one way or the other. The German and French General Staffs had been especially sanguine. The latter, under the influence of General Foch, felt that any morally righteous offensive had to triumph if pursued with sufficient zeal. Thus, the French were bound to triumph by merely undertaking their plainly righteous offensive with the zeal to triumph. That there might be a flaw in this gemlike reasoning escaped them. And the Germans were also caught in their own trap of rapid conquest. For, in the event, the unexpected power of the defensive (though it should not really have been so surprising in view of lessons taught in the American Civil War and the Franco-Prussian War) brusquely smashed the respective military schemes of the equally aggressive and confident Great Powers.

For the first two months, events had seemed to bear out the German warlords. They had counted on waging a speedy war of movement against the French through Belgium, while holding off the slow-moving Russian bear. Thus they expected to win before either

Britain or Russia could effectively join in the fray. At first all went well. Liége was captured; the German armies swept through Belgium; soon Paris itself was in sight. But then the German goose step was stopped at the Marne. Each side now tried to outflank the other to the west. Each easily parried the other's slow, courtly counter-motions, and the so-called "race to the sea" continued until the front rested on the Channel coast. For all practical purposes the war of movement was now dead, two months after birth. The Germans sensed the futility of attempting to revive it; it would be more than three years before they would again go over to the offensive.

The French were slower to learn. General Foch had insisted that "any improvement in firearms is bound to strengthen the offensive." Napoleon had stated that victory was certain to be won by the "big battalions," and the revered Clausewitz had told of the invincibility of great masses of troops. The French and Russians alone, not to mention the British troops gradually being fed into the fight, drastically outnumbered the Central Powers. The mobile, rapid-firing 75-mm. French field gun was the greatest of its type in the world, and the French had thousands of them. The French, having recovered from their initial shock, found the hated Germans deep inside their borders and determined to drive them out and go forward to inevitable victory, muttering Napoleon's plausible axiom, "The moral is to the physical as three to one."

How this would apply to pious, moralistic Mother

Russia was another story, short as she was of rifles, rail-roads, cannon, machine guns, foodstuffs, roads, motor transport, even uniforms. Only in men did the Czar possess an abundance of riches. With this flood of brave, blindly obedient manpower (plus her French and British allies) Russia too felt certain of winning, despite early setbacks.

As for Great Britain, though the home islands entered the conflict with a mere 160,000 expeditionary troops, these were the acknowledged cream of the world's striking forces on land. Her navy, of course, was unparalleled and in itself would certainly strangle the enemy coalition if the war lasted any great length of time. The trend of thought among British military planners was as bullish as that of their counterparts. Britain, like France, like Russia, like Germany, like Austria, expected successfully to solve by one surgical excision the political ills of the Western world. Never before had a war started with such grim confidence on the part of all concerned.

But after the opponents had met head-on like two mountain goats that first summer of the war, and were halted dazedly by each other, a rigid front was formed that defied all efforts of the French and British to break through. Under the command of "Papa" Joffre, dull battering-ram efforts took place that served only to demonstrate the incapacity of this general and of others whose mental processes were confounded by the deadlock and the impossibility of turning maneuvers. All they could think of was a policy of attrition and frontal attacks.

In 1916 Foch, under the continuing delusion that sheer will power could break through barbed wire and machine guns, further drained the life blood of France in vast, notorious battles, the worst of all (through 1916) being the one fought on the Somme. The disaster here sealed the fate of his army, and perhaps of France herself as a world power, forever.

By this time the British under Sir Douglas Haig were fighting in numbers equal to that of their ally; and at the Somme they were similarly cut down. They lost 60,000 men the first day alone; and when the offensive had dragged to its weary end in November 1916 only a few square miles of worthless tortured ground had been captured, while the losses of 538,000 troops on the part of the Central Powers compared to 794,000 of the Allied attackers. After this blood bath a plaintive cry went up: "No more Sommes!"

When the year ended a few weeks later, it was clear to all observers who still respected the meaning of human life—even soldiers' lives—that some kind of crossroads had been reached, and that this state of affairs could continue no longer.

From the northern border of Switzerland to the Belgian coastline near Ostend a scribbled line of entrenchments stretched southeast to northwest for 350 miles, dividing the French, Belgians, and British from the Germans and Austrians in opposition. This complex system of trenches and dugouts, behind which were more trenches and dugouts, existed in combination with dense sworls and loops of barbed wire, thousands of armored machine guns (that new and utterly frustrating "concentrated essence of infantry"), and various other new and old methods of defensive warfare.

Now there was little scope for the brilliant commander, for the Hannibal-like maneuver, for the cut and thrust of traditional warfare waged by artful foot soldiers and speedy cavalry. There was no flank to be turned, unless by some miracle the mountains and the sea could be mastered by forces of decisive size. With no way to go around, with no way of crashing through, with no generals or statesmen sufficiently subtle to find another key that might turn, both sides settled down in despair and frustration to a mutual siege. Neither could enforce its will upon the other; and since the folklore of the times excluded any settlement other than military the war went on, in its fashion.

In and near the front several millions of men lived like moles, fearing even to show their steel helmets above the sandbagged parapets. Front-line trenches were the dominating features of the stalemate. In time, after they had been fought over a good deal, almost all sense and direction were lost to them and they became murderously confused, interconnected in haphazard new ways, astounding labyrinths in which the men moved warily and felt little security. Sometimes

British and German troops occupied what was in effect the same trench, separated from each other only by a bomb barrier and an unspoken agreement. Sandbags, boards, mud, and tree branches were used as supporting revetments, and the job of keeping the trenches deep and erect never ended. To prevent their being taken in enfilade, they were dug with sharp kinks every few yards, called traverses, in which swearing, squeezing traffic jams were chronic.

Perpendicular to the front lines were communication trenches—poor, shallow affairs, usually wet and crumbling, that weaved as much as five miles rearward to the reserve areas. It was through these, as a rule, and not "overland," that troops traveled to and from the front during daytime.

And finally in the intricate, molelike maze of the Western Front were the dugouts, in their most primitive form merely extra-large holes scooped into the side of a trench for the personal use of one man. But many caverns were minor marvels of crude engineering ingenuity that housed dozens of troops. Here in the fetid smell of unwashed bodies and dank earth the men lived when not on active duty, made coffee in brown pots, dried their stockings, played chess, warmed potatoes, dozed, argued, cleaned their rifles, wrote letters, waited for morning, or guard duty, or a bit of action, and shuddered peaceably under the pounding of enemy artillery exploding overhead with dull, harmless thuds. Candles flickered (far back in the dugout the air was so bad they often went out), the

rats prowled, but there was no peril even from the direct hit of a 15-inch railway shell. The sound of war
was muffled almost to extinction and the men enjoyed
some of the comforts of home. They were going nowhere; they were there to stay; and this they did as
best they could. They sang:

> *I love the ladies,*
> *I love to be among the girls* . . .

and on the slimy walls they hung mirrors, clocks, even
electric bulbs, pin-up pictures that showed daringly
trim ankles and saucy smiles. Life was almost comfort-
ably lazy. There were toothbrushes, magazines, sometimes even straw floors, and stoves that heated the
clammy interiors sporadically, if not well. In the midst
of desultory bedlam the men smoked their pipes, came
down with boils, shored up the sides of their trenches
and dugouts, munched bully-beef in tins and Belgian
cheese, and waited to be put back into reserve.

On both sides were the card players—German, English, French, Austrian, Canadian, Welsh, Australian;
the mania cut across all national lines. Not even the
war could interrupt their gambling and never did they
seem to sleep. Day and night the card players, a race
apart, continued their relentless games.

Between the lines was No Man's Land, above which
nightly hung the star shells thrown up to probe the
stripped, blasted wasteland with a nightmarish glare.
Machine guns in set patterns raked the desolate

ground, searching for enemy patrols. The snipers aimed at gaps in the sandbags, the communication-trench entries, the mess areas farther back; and every man knew the whiplash crack of a rifle bullet near the direct line of fire, and the melancholy whine of a ricochet.

As for men, they were seldom to be seen. For this was the peculiarity of the Western Front: the uproar seldom ceased and the number of men involved was countless, but the terrain seemed deserted. Nothing moved in the lethal zone where the great armies brushed against each other. Nobody appeared to be fighting. Here and there somebody stared through a loophole. Occasionally a man actually fired a gun of some size, seemingly at random. It seemed impossible that anyone could be hit by it. Yet the casualties went on—about seven thousand each day, except when serious fighting occurred.

The enemy was remote. It was difficult to hate him. All the usual procedures were reversed, and the hero of last century, charging forward with a shout, his rifle at the "engage," was no longer brave but a fool. Religion and chaplains were tolerated sourly, even by men of real faith, and patriotism was something of a joke. After years of stalemate there had been heavy losses not only in men but in normal standards of belief and behavior. Militarily, morale was neither good nor bad. In a war where the individual counted even less than in any other war before or since, the men merely stuck it out and did their best, up to a point.

The solemn axiom was, "Never obey orders—they're already canceled."

No decisive warfare was attempted along the Western Front during the long intervals between vast, convulsive campaigns. Mostly there were mere trench raids with the object of capturing the trench or dugout directly in front, or to kill some of the enemy, or to take prisoners. From a company point of view, in fact, the entire war sometimes seemed to be nothing but a series of trench raids—hysterical melees in which hundreds of opposing troops often occupied the invaded trench along with the original inhabitants. What with clumsy Smith-Wesson revolvers, armored machine guns, Lugers, Lewis guns, rifle fire, Mills grenades, bayonets, flame-throwers—all at close range—the casualties were enormous by the standards of later wars. By 1917 thousands of these routine, unknown, forgotten trench raids had taken place, and many had cost more lives than famous battles of a later generation. When they were over, the trenches were left piled with dead and wounded; and, if it became necessary for the visitors to leave hurriedly, they could scarcely be blamed for trampling friend and foe underfoot with their hobnailed boots.

And during the lulls the wounded called and groaned in No Man's Land, lingered for as much as a week, and usually died there, and sometimes screamed in their incoherent agony; while above them sounded the joyous songs of the birds. The thrushes, especially, twittered wildly each morning, for they were used to the guns. During the height of battle the wounded begged their friends to save them, but the latter, rushing from shell hole to shell hole, were usually too distracted to be of service. A German poem ran:

> *I can't give you a hand;*
> *You're for the Promised Land,*
> *My Comrade, good and true.*

Except during trench raids the stagnation of siege warfare gave the illusion of peace. For weeks and months on end nothing happened of any importance, and the daily communiqués reported, "On the Western Front small-scale infantry actions took place west of Lens" and *"Im Westen nichts neues,"* leaving the usual collection of grayish corpses between the lines. After a day or two their features became swollen, and there was no expression in them. They lay in the dirt not in gallant positions, but stiffly, like store-window mannequins. Their bodies were horribly plump; they were in truth swelling out of their clothes. Nor did the stretcher bearers who collected them have an enviable task, for there were many on both sides who took a malicious pleasure in sniping at them.

Only the artillery never entirely ceased any day or night. Every shell had a personality of its own and could be identified with fair accuracy by old-timers. Most cannon were light horse-drawn field pieces which fired small shells, usually shrapnel, about three miles. The British 18-pounder, the famed French 75, and the German "whiz-bang" 77 were all in this category. They were not too difficult to detect en route and gave the men several seconds to dive into cover. On the other hand, high-velocity pieces were hated because their projectile was thrown at terriffic speed in a nearly straight line and gave almost no warning. And except for the great railway guns the howitzers were the largest of all: gaping monsters that tossed their fat shells almost straight up and down. The men called them "crumps."

The German 5.9 was also polite and gave the recipient some small time for acquiring shelter. The last part of its passage was a deep roar; one was safe if the roar lasted, but if one was in its path it descended fast and the best that could be hoped for was an extreme case of shell shock. These were called "coal boxes."

The sounds of the projectiles created a bizarre symphony. Field-gun shells buzzed in a crescendo and burst with a clattery bang. The heavies flung their black bodies like great loaves of bread (they could be seen in flight) across vast reaches of the infinite sky and approached with the roar of an oncoming express train. Over valleys they all echoed distractingly and defied prediction. Those that fell in hollows burst with terrible suddenness and a double crash. Fabulous indeed was the blast of the 30.5 Australian trench-mortar. And there were shells that screamed, shells that hissed, gas shells that exploded with a simpering pop, shells that whistled, and shells that wobbled across heaven rattling like a snare drum. Finally there was drumfire, reserved for special occasions, when all the instruments blended into one homogeneous mass of sound of such intensity as cannot be described, all bursting into jagged fragments of hot metal that slammed into the bodies of men and mules with familiar results.

The troops hated artillery more than machine guns, more than snipers, or bayonets, or even gas; for there was no fighting it, nor could much really be done to elude it.

And above it all flew the airmen in their rickety little machines—Albatross, Spad, Nieuport, Fokker, and Sopwith fighters, DeHavilland bombers, RE-8 observers—fighting, bombing, strafing, and watching the motionless scene beneath them. Yet the men in the trenches had no great hatred for the fliers who thus plagued them, but looked up to them with mingled fear and admiration. For the moles felt a certain inferiority, weighed down as they were by a score of impediments, wedded to the earth in shell holes, mine galleries, trenches, and underground pits where man was never intended to exist, except in death.

But for these feeble biplanes and triplanes that droned and flickered aloft, there was no longer any military motion of consequence along the Western Front. Sandbagged trenches, in themselves, were splendid for defense. Tanks were almost unheard of. A single machine gun could stop five hundred men.

There was no real air power. Barbed wire often ten rows deep was staked out to trap and retard advancing foot soldiers. (A mordant comment when a man was missing from an informal roll call was, "Hanging on the barbed wire.") Concrete pillboxes peered sullenly through narrow slits of eyes from which protruded the swaying muzzles of machine guns and semi-automatic rifles. And there were booby traps, sharpshooters cunningly hidden in devious nests, contact mines underfoot, and armored short-range artillery ready to blast any small target that appeared— even a single sniper revealing his hideaway, or a guide chancing a short-cut to the latrine.

The use of gas also helped the defense, not only because it burned, blistered, and asphyxiated, but because it forced attacking troops to advance through the yellowish swirling fumes in cumbersome equipment. The clouded mica of the masks made accurate rifle-aiming impossible. Soldiers tired quickly, and moved slowly and vulnerably across the nerve-racking strip toward the opposing trenches.

After the Somme debacle two and a half million men had been killed on the Western Front out of the total of nearly seven million casualties there; and still the lines held. The titanic armies sat—squatted, as the armchair critics contemptuously put it—amid scenes of unique desolation. Everywhere near the battle zone where the trench system had finally congealed lay the debris of war—smashed, rusty rifles, empty haversacks, stricken and abandoned heavier equipment, here and there among the scrub a lonely grave adorned by a single wooden cross, as well as more formal cemeteries. Trees were nude stumps. Moon craters studded the landscape. Peasants' houses gaped in the middle of their patches of ground. Inside, one might still salvage scraps of clothing, broken crockery, and sundry rubbish. Always the roof was half off. Potatoes rotted in the cellars, cupboards were torn open, pictures blew in the breeze, old French and Flemish prayer books invariably lay tattered in a leeward corner. The people had long since left the advance zones of battle. For over two years the Allies and the Central Powers had contemplated each other balefully out of the ruins of the countryside and the wreckage of their respective war plans.

2. The Home Front

IN LONDON the tone of the New Year was set by Lord Curzon, president of the House of Lords, in a message to the Primrose League: "It is impossible to say as yet that the end is in sight. . . . It seems likely that well into another year, perhaps longer, must we continue the dreadful tragedy that is turning the world into hell. . . ." This was hardly news to the people of the home island, who by 1917 had relapsed into an apathetic silence that concerned their leaders almost as much as the enemy did. It was not that revolution was likely, but that a negotiated peace might become necessary some day unless matters took a turn for the better. The prospect, though as yet no larger than a cloud the size of a man's hand, definitely existed now and was ominous to contemplate. Nor were the Germans making matters easier. Their recent peace overtures, though scornfully rejected, had created much embarrassment. Even now, three weeks later, the London *Times* was still rejecting them; on New Year's Day, a Monday, their editorialist wrote, "To the illusory peace proposals of Germany the Allies with one accord have given a definite negative. . . . Germany's conduct demands penalties, reparations and guarantees. . . ."

And, as if to add emphasis, another peace meeting in Victoria Park was broken up—this one conducted by the notorious pacifist Miss Emmeline Pankhurst and four of her lady cohorts, all of whom had voiced the usual inflammatory sentiments concerning the nebulous Allied war aims, the motives of David Lloyd George in not exploring the German proposals, the logic of attempting to solve political problems by so-called organized murder, and so on. A sizable crowd had listened in silence, but the surrounding police had made no move until an opportunity presented itself: "During the speeches two little dogs rushed in and made an opening for active interference. Two old soldiers, waving the Union Jack and singing 'The Red, White and Blue,' made for the platform, and with the help of the crowd swept it away with all upon it," throwing the five ladies to the ground.

Nowhere in any newspaper that day was there a single item about New Year's Eve celebrating. No gay parties were reported, no drunken uproars out of the ordinary, none of the usual whimsies of the January 1 press. Instead, the columns were full of firm resolves, grim warnings, and dour expressions of determination

to carry on to ultimate victory regardless of cost. No
more cheerless fare could have greeted the average
Londoner over the morning tea.

Certainly there was little enough to celebrate. By
now nearly every family knew at first hand the meaning of death, capture, or injury at war. London was
a city of women, children, old men, and walking
wounded. The ingredients for merry-making were
missing. The glories had long passed, along with most
of the starry illusions of 1914. Those had been days
when the men had volunteered in overwhelming numbers (now they were conscripted), days of the exciting spy mania, when one child had pleaded about her
family's old German house servant, "Mummy, *must* we
kill poor Fraülein?", when bands had played daily in
the streets, when women had rushed by the millions
into any kind of war work, when flags had everywhere
fluttered. Then it was that excited girls thrust yellow
feathers at young men who failed to join up quickly,
and the newspapers had published that splendid re-
cruiting song, "Your King and Country Need You":

> *Oh, we don't want to lose you,*
> *But we think you ought to go;*
> *For your King and your Country*
> *Both need you so.*
> *We shall want you and miss you,*
> *But with all our might and main*
> *We will thank you, cheer you, kiss you,*
> *When you come back again.*

In sullen obstinacy people by 1917 had become resigned to the necessity for winning the war, hating it,
seeing no end to it, no longer able to understand it by
standards that had once seemed so brilliantly clear.
Now it was only necessary to get the thing over with,
to sweep it out of existence and to try, somehow, to restore life to normal. But beneath it all was a suspicion
that it really might never end. The people of Britain
were like a person in a bad dream—half awake, half
knowing it to be a bad dream, but a very long one
which somehow did not end, as other bad dreams
always did.

Especially disillusioned were the liberals. Before
the war they had been opposed to participation. When
Britain did declare war, they fell off the pacifist train
and became the most ardent warriors of all. Suddenly
electrified, they looked forward to a world cleansed
and socially advanced, once this last war of history was
won and Prussian militarism smashed. But now they
felt tricked. The war, it turned out, was just another
cynical and sordid affair. There was nothing to hope
for, nothing to do but win it. Their misery was the
greater, for they were ashamed of having been
trapped, and because they had flown so high before
falling so far.

Only among duller minds, by that January 1, was the
war still a splendid canvas without warts. One writer,
after a conversation with a worker of this mentality,
reported, "Like much general talk in war-time, it was

vague, jumpy and incoherent. The man's views reflected oft-repeated prejudices; he showed total failure
to grasp historic sequence of happenings. He displayed a loose kind of ignorance. You felt that he was
incapable of acting on reasoned grounds or steering
among the heap of prejudices that jostled one another
in his mind."

People seldom exclaimed, "How sad!" at news of
others' deaths or casualties but hurried on to tell of
their own misfortunes. Rumors flew thick as locusts:
Turkey was leaving the war, Austrian emissaries were
discussing peace terms in Switzerland, the German
Crown Prince was dead, the United States would declare war next week, a German regiment near Bullecourt had mutinied, and so on. But neither false
reports nor optimistic speeches could lift the general
depression for more than a moment. The French Minister of Munitions, M. Albert Thomas, had been dismayed during previous visits by the serene attitude of
the British toward the war. But now when interviewed
by the *Chronicle* he was struck by their proper grim-
ness: "The whole 'tonality' is different," he said, with
satisfaction.

Food was scarce, especially meats and fats. On
New Year's Day the Food Controller ordained only
"straight-run" flour for bread. "White Loaf in Excep-
tional Cases Only" was the *Times* heading. But still
there was no rationing (it might alarm the populace,
the government thought), and there were queues for

meats and margarine, and sometimes for sugar, potatoes, and even tea. Housewives tramped from shop to shop in hopeless quests for certain supplies. All imported foods were desperately short because of the German submarine blockade, now approaching its peak; and servicemen had first call on whatever did get through. The people did not understand all the reasons for foreign shortages (much data and facts having naval significance were withheld) and complained sourly that Britain was not fighting the United States and the Dominions. There were food meetings, food demonstrations of great size and organization, food complaints, and endless food conversation among the bedeviled citizenry. It was far and away the favorite routine vexation of the war, surpassing even that concerning the Zeppelin and airplane raids which by 1917 had killed or injured nearly three thousand British in London and various coastal cities.

Rivaling all this was the coal shortage, and many were the comments with regard to the private profiteering and hoarding of that commodity. By January 1, 1917, the coal queues were starting to equal the great food queues in size. There was much shivering and actual suffering that winter in Britain, and people who lived where gas or coke were burned enjoyed a great popularity.

Because there was no gasoline for owners of private cars, unless they were engaged in important war duties, the crush in trains, trams, and busses had become astonishing that winter. "Getting home during rush hours was a daily terror. . . . The crowds of office workers were vastly increased and the scramble to get into some of the longer distance trams and omnibuses constituted a bear fight out of which those of both sexes, who were worsted or driven off the overladen vehicles by the conductors, retreated to the pavement with hats bashed in, umbrellas broken, shins and ankles kicked and bruised, in a dazed and shaken condition. The darkened streets added to the confusion of people returning from work." And that Monday the *Times* told of "Dearer Travelling Today. Fewer and Slower Trains."

As for taxi drivers, surely they were the most hated of all human beings. Their independence, rudeness, and profiteering were positively infuriating. To travel alone in a taxi was unheard of, and it was usually necessary to bribe the driver in order to change his dourly premeditated route.

Inflation, that disreputable cousin of war, had been on the scene from the beginning. Women's stockings had risen from 1s. 8d. in 1914 to about 3s. 8d. in 1917, and the average price of a man's suit from 28s. 6d. to 60s. The food price index stood now at 187 compared to 1914. And, of course, the official figures told only part of the story, because in the absence of rationing and price control everything was sold for anything the seller could get. In the case of rabbits, cereals, most luxury items, or whatever else was really scarce at the moment, such prices became scandalous. And the people complained bitterly over the exorbitant profits made by business out of the misery of war. Wages had increased, but longer working hours, ugly working conditions, speed-up routines, and higher prices created much discontent. By 1917 strikes were commonplace, and these in the very depths of war.

John Bull, that frenetic scandal magazine of the day, had achieved an enormous circulation by pungently expressing the people's weariness and disillusionment. Its editor, Horatio Bottomley, roared out in stories headed by such captions as "Who Are the Liars?" "What a German Officer Told Me," "Still Taking Odds," "Why Haig Is Silent," "Murderers, Not Ministers," and, after the German peace overture, "No more Peace parleying with the enemy—no more damned nonsense about consulting the wishes of the niggers in the captured German colonies." The people loved it, and clamored for more.

That New Year's Day there were clearances everywhere, and the newspapers (pitiful, shrunken things because of governmental restrictions) were full of the ads. And elsewhere in the *Times* were other items heralding the glad new year. Sir Douglas Haig—that silent, humorless, gray-mustached, level-eyed Scot who had long considered himself the right-hand man of God in this holy struggle—commander on the Western Front, was named a field marshal. The King and Queen, Princess Mary, Prince Henry, Prince George,

and Princess Victoria all went to the intercession service that morning at Sandringham Church. An Am-
sterdam correspondent reported "Criminals for the
German Army" and enlarged glowingly on that vulnerable theme. *Samson and Delilah* was still hanging on
at the Oldwych Theatre. Gilt-edged stocks had closed
firm that morning, and bank shares rose in brisk trad-
ing. Madame Tussaud's Wax Exhibition advertised,
among other delights, a "Lifelike Portrait of the RIGHT
HON. DAVID LLOYD GEORGE."

The military reports were unusually dull. Russia
reported that scouts had captured nine men in a
trench west of Koniuchy. The French told of a *"coup
de main* against a small German post south of Chilly
[which] gave us a number of prisoners. Everywhere
else the night was calm." British GHQ in France
spoke of artillery fire southeast of Le Transloy, but
concluded that beyond this "there is nothing further
to report."

The only war items of the slightest interest were a
German communiqué to the effect that in Rumania
the Russians had been thrown back as far as the Braila
bridgehead (even the *Times* admitted that "the enemy are making ground"), and another concerning
the sinking of the French battleship *Gaulois* by a submarine in the Mediterranean.

And, despite the shortage of newsprint, a few items
of a more pungent nature were included in the six-
teen-page New Year's Day *Times*.

Under the heading "German Savagery at Sea" it

was told how the skipper of the U-18 had deliberately murdered a Danish captain and sailor by striking their lifeboat broadside with his submarine.

And in a related vein:

THE MURDER OF A RACE
How Armenians Were Exterminated
Moslem Evidence

Among the abominable cruelties and extensive massacres perpetrated by Germany and her Allies [etc.] . . .

Everywhere women had taken over the bulk of civilian duties. By the dawn of 1917 they were heavily engaged in munitions work; they were firemen, tram conductors, taxi drivers, window cleaners, chimney sweeps, horse and mule trainers, farmers, ambulance drivers, even mechanics. And, of course, they had enlisted by the hundreds of thousands in the Army, the Navy, and the Red Cross. While all this had at first been wonderfully new and thrilling, the bloom now had worn off and much cynicism had become rampant among the women as well as male workers and soldiers. Nowhere was this more evident than in the squalor and hopelessness of the East End, where poverty traditionally reigned, especially now that the heads of the families were gone to war. There had been a great movement of women and girls from this district into heavy labor and surreptitious prostitution. Soldiers' wives moved in with other men, and the civil authorities were deluged with morals complaints.

Liquor was served in restaurants and night clubs in unprecedented quantities. To evade the ten-o'clock ban, whisky was customarily poured in coffee cups, and champagne in lemonade glasses. Soho, "that square mile of vice," was in its heyday. Nearly two hundred disreputable night clubs, countless ladies of unfortunate repute, thugs, and confidence men thronged the area in wait for the soldiers and sailors who drifted there as though magnetized, almost begging to be set upon for their money in the age-old ways. Luridly Sir Arthur Conan Doyle appealed for the protection of these young men (whether they wanted to be protected is debatable) "preyed upon by harpies" in darkened London, and, along with many others, he asked for official state regulation of vice. By 1917 there was an average of four thousand monthly convictions for drunkenness alone in England, Scotland, and Wales.

In Germany everything was much the same that dismal New Year's Day. Prices had gone up even more. The sea blockade was total. The Crown Prince of Germany in his memoirs tells bitterly how

as early as the beginning of the year 1917 . . . weariness of the war was already very great. I also saw a great and menacing change in the streets of Berlin. Their characteristic feature had gone; the contented face of the middle-class man had vanished; the honest, hard-working bourgeoisie, the clerk and his wife and children, slunk through the streets, hollow-eyed, lantern-jawed, pale-faced and clad in threadbare clothing that had become much too wide for their shrunken limbs. Side by side with them jostled the puffed-up profiteer and all the other rogues. . . . Nevertheless, nothing was done to remove the evil . . . whoever wished to profiteer, profiteered—profiteered in state contracts, in essential victuals, in raw materials. . . .

And one German woman later wrote to an English friend:

One of the most terrible of our sufferings was having to sit in the dark. It became dark at four in winter. It was not light until eight. Even the children could not sleep all that time. One had to amuse them as best one could, fretful and pining as they were from underfeeding. And when they had gone to bed we were left shivering with the chill which comes from semi-starvation and which no additional clothing seems to alleviate, to sit thinking, thinking, thinking. . . .

By New Year's 1917, most British people of democratic views had become dismayed by the Defense of the Realm Acts, which had generally torpedoed civil liberties and had substituted courts martial for much civil law. Any "reports likely to cause disaffection or alarm" had become an offense. The police and military were given the power to search and inspect any premises at any time, to seize documents or "anything" else which the military had reason "to suspect" was being used, or might be used, for subversive purposes. Anyone could be arrested without a warrant. Suspects could be detained by the military police almost indefinitely, until they could be dealt with in the normal course of civil jurisdiction. Military boards could force anyone to live or not to live in a specified area. These and other regrettable regulations had reduced most citizens to a paranoid furtiveness. They tended to avoid strangers, to utter nothing critical, and to refrain from reading or listening to anything defeatist or anti-patriotic. In stereotyped phrases they backed the war effort.

Only a few courageous possessors of dissident views spoke, wrote, or acted in such manner as almost deliberately to invite intervention by the authorities; and primary among these were the conscientious objectors. One was the writer Lytton Strachey, who though he had been classified physically unfit preferred to go through the mill as an objector. At the military tribunal he inflated an air cushion to sit on, in protest against the hard benches, an opening gambit which did not endear him to his inquisitors. When the chairman stated the usual preliminary, "I understand, Mr. Strachey, that you have a conscientious objection to war," he replied in his curious falsetto, "Oh, no—not at all; only to this war." And to the triumphant stock question, "Tell me, Mr. Strachey, what would you do if you saw a German soldier trying to violate your sister?" he had replied with pious virtue, "I would try to get between them."

But the great masses of tired and depressed ordinary people merely got on with the war: not for them the calculated protest, the sardonic analysis, the deliberate affront to entrenched power. The ignorant saw no reason to doubt. The religious prayed. The poor worked. The liberals wrung their hands. Few surrendered to thought. The very rich called Sunday their "munitions day," when they replaced regular war workers, and survived the war coldly and determinedly, drinking hard at the better places, flirting and love-making, dancing, dressing to the fashion, and living as usual, but more so.

And while life variously went on in the cities and farmlands of Britain, death held sway on the Continent, where, on the Western and Eastern and other fronts, after the near-truce of New Year's, the gigantic armies turned again to the business of war. Said General Smuts, "We cannot contemplate without feelings of profoundest emotion this spirit of self-destruction which has come over our civilization." But when was it all to end, and in what fashion? By New Year's Day, 1917, the answers to these questions were as obscure as the early-morning fog that drifted over the Thames and locked in its gray arms the towers of the Houses of Parliament, the riverside wharves, and the rocky canyons of Piccadilly.

"We are going to lose this war," remarked David Lloyd George to a Cabinet official as 1916 drew to a close. It was, perhaps, an unduly pessimistic statement, especially for him, but after the cruel disappointments of 1916 few in the upper echelon expected any longer to win a clear-cut victory. It was a period of drift, uncertainty, irritability. Everybody pretended to have a pet solution, but at heart nobody knew just what to do. Hope was flagging in London and Berlin that dreary New Year's Day. Both sides were exhausted. People high and low had begun to forget what they were supposed to be fighting for. At the top there was much concern about protocol, personalities, politics, and gossip—always a sure sign that a dead end has been reached—and a vulgar search for scapegoats, both military and civilian. There were lightning shifts in command. Always officials were resigning, or threatening to resign, or meticulously pointing out conditions under which they positively would resign. But upon one matter everyone was agreed (with the exception of a very few who thought the war was coming along splendidly)—that the war was coming along miserably. The Rumanians were finished. Bulgaria had joined Germany. Russia was fading fast, and by the end of the year was heading for civil chaos and military ruin. The naval battle at Jutland had been a confused, indecisive disappointment. The German U-boat campaign was climbing toward its triumphant apogee. The Somme fiasco had just ended. The Americans were still maddeningly neutral.

And the Northcliffe press fanned the flames of despair; the *Times* and the *Daily Mail* castigated the politicians, of whom there were twenty-three in the War Cabinet. Placards reading "Wanted: Twenty-Three Ropes" were displayed on the streets to advertise a late edition.

Everybody blamed the leaders. Nobody blamed the Germans. The military blamed the politicians. The politicians blamed the military, or other party members in the Coalition Government. The masochistic conviction that England herself was at fault had sputtered slowly for two years and had exploded after the Somme, causing the fall of mild Mr. Asquith and his replacement by David Lloyd George, the violent Welsh politician, a passionate, imaginative, scheming man who knew well that his one and only mandate was to conduct the war more effectively.

His first problem was not the German General Ludendorff but the London War Office. For it was from this quarter, Mr. Lloyd George believed, that policies had emanated which had brought the Empire so near exhaustion. It was the War Office, so intent on holding the reins of military power, which Mr. Asquith had said "kept three sets of figures, one to mislead the public, another to mislead the Cabinet, and the third to mislead itself." It was the soldiers' War Office and its specious statistics that Lloyd George himself had once compared to desert sands: when the wind changed, the humps turned to hollows and the hollows to humps. And why these deceptions? To Mr.

Lloyd George they were plainly designed to insure an enormous flow of drafts and munitions to France and Belgium, and nowhere else.

For after the military paralysis had set in, two schools of strategic thought had arisen. On one side were those (mostly soldiers) who thought the war had to be fought on the Western Front against the main concentration of German strength. On the other were the so-called Easterners (mostly civilians) who considered it hopeless to attack the enemy where he was strongest and who recommended various other ways of outflanking, or dismembering, or blockading, or otherwise demoralizing and defeating him. The position of Lloyd George was stated in his own words: "I never believed in costly frontal attacks in war or politics, if there were a way around." He considered General Haig a clumsy, murderous fool. His own plan was to turn the Western Front into a holding operation, and by means of certain peripheral operations to leave Germany isolated, heavily outnumbered, and set up for the final kill.

Amateurish nonsense of this sort was resisted doggedly by Sir William Robertson, Chief of the Imperial General Staff, as well as Douglas Haig and other high British officers who felt that the only sure way to ultimate victory was to exert pressure continuously in France and Belgium.

Winston Churchill, at the moment merely Member of Parliament for Dundee, was in turn contemptuous of such strategy. All the agility and subtlety of his

Albert Thomas, Haig, Joffre, and David Lloyd George

mind revolted against generals whose idea of warfare was to throw vast amounts of men and guns head-on against a prepared enemy and then, when it was all over, to "count heads" and compute who had won the battle. His 1915 Dardanelles expedition designed to knock out Turkey, reinforce Russia, and slice through the soft underbelly of the Central Powers had been bungled by half-measures in London and by commanders on the spot, and Churchill had fallen into disfavor. For a time he had even served as a battalion commander at the front. When he returned to the Government he had vivid plans for the Balkans, the Mid-East, and the Baltic Sea. He had ideas regarding tanks and other revolutionary new weapons, and he envisioned diplomatic and naval maneuvers to stun the enemy. All this represented a philosophy designed to bypass further failures on the Western Front.

But the commander on that front would not willingly release a single man or gun for service elsewhere. Though the Somme campaign had depressed most observers, it had fairly satisfied Sir Douglas Haig. Inflexible, impassive, he stated his unchanged intention of fighting a war of attrition on the Western Front. There was no substitute for killing Germans: that principle seemed so obvious to him that any other one smacked of imbecility, at best, if not outright treason. Momentarily Haig in 1916 had been induced to toy with the idea of an amphibious landing on the Belgian coast behind the German lines. After discussing it with Admiral Reginald Bacon, commanding the Dover Patrol, he had learned of the need for special landing craft (which did not yet exist) and, in view of steel shortages, he had on sober second thought dropped the plan. Anyway, his heart was not in such shallow trickeries. War seemed simple to Haig. A former cavalry officer, he felt that battles were won by charging at the enemy and trouncing him in a straightforward fight. To do this, what else was really needed beyond superiority in men and matériel, an enemy that could not run away, a crucial sector, and sound planning? In November he had even suggested to Lloyd George that Italian troops and guns should be transferred to the Franco-Belgian front; and he recorded hopefully in his diary that the (then) Secretary of State for War "said that he was much struck by my suggestion."

After the Somme, Haig had written a paper for the Government summarizing his views. In keeping with his character and beliefs it was optimistic. "There was reason to believe" (a phrase of which he never tired) that German casualties were far greater than those of the British and French. The morale of the enemy had shown "marked signs" of deterioration, while the British Army was "confident in its proved superiority." Bad weather alone, he continued, had prevented total victory. The effect of the campaign on German civilians had been demoralizing. And, finally, if yet another similar campaign were to be waged soon there would be "full justification" for expecting decisive results. (A year later Haig was to issue another such appraisal.) This memorandum confirmed Lloyd

George's suspicion that the man was quite hopeless. The Somme was the nadir of the war, to date, and almost everybody else knew it. From this moment on, his marginal confidence in the European commander dwindled almost to zero.

But, in a sense, the Somme had cleared the air. Opinions solidified. The majority thought it had gained nothing but a few devastated miles at enormous cost. The minority believed that the German Army had suffered a great blow, was tottering, and would fall after one more of the same. In support of this view they referred to the German peace feelers late in 1916, circulated immediately after the German capture of Bucharest. (These overtures had led President Woodrow Wilson to call upon the various nations to state, once and for all, exactly what they were fighting for. "That ass President Wilson has barged in and asked all belligerents for their terms," noted Sir Henry Wilson irascibly in his diary on December 22, although he was sure there would be no negotiations; and in this he was correct.)

And of those who considered the Somme a failure there were two subdivisions—one, as already mentioned, which was now certain that the war could never be won militarily on the Western Front; and another which flatly recommended making peace. This latter view was spectacularly summarized by Lord Lansdowne, who circulated to the War Cabinet a reasoned and meticulous letter suggesting that a meaningful victory was no longer possible. "Can we afford to go on paying the same sort of price for the same sort of gains?" he asked, and pointedly suggested, "Let our naval, military and economic advisers tell us frankly whether they are satisfied that the knock-out blow can and will be delivered." A large uproar followed. Lloyd George called it "a terrible paper." Winston Churchill and Lord Balfour felt that Lansdowne's argument could not be brushed aside. Haig replied coolly that the prospects were "excellent" for 1917. And when also asked for an opinion, Robertson stated innocently to the Government, "Quite frankly, and at the same time respectfully, I can only say I am surprised that the question should be asked. The idea had not before entered my head that any member of His Majesty's Government had a doubt on the matter."

Even Lloyd George joined in rejecting Lansdowne's heretical views. As impending Prime Minister, the former knew that the Coalition Government in Parliament was there not to make peace but to contrive victory.

In this vein, by that New Year's Day, there was much talk by the Easterners of reinforcing the Bulgarian front, where, at Salonika, the Germans had bottled up hundreds of thousands of Allied troops. The French were even more inclined to transfer supporting troops there than the British, fearing that the front might otherwise collapse, though as it happened the

Germans had no intention of attacking what they had derisively labeled their "largest internment camp."

And there were operations in Turkey, Mesopotamia, and Palestine, having mainly to do with oil, where the Easterners saw further possibilities for outflanking the deadlock, or at least forcing the enemy to thin out his inventory of men and munitions. After all, the combined manpower of the Allies on all fronts was still far greater than that of the Central Powers.

To these schemes the Westerners objected. The interior lines of the enemy, they said, would make it easy for German reserves to be switched back to the Western Front in a pinch. Furthermore, the whole idea of knocking the props out from under Germany was a mistake. No success against Austria, for example, they said, could make the Germans give a single yard on the Western Front.

Not true, said the Easterners. Germany could not simply abandon her main ally, and thus expose herself to a gigantic enemy influx from the southeast.

But every Allied soldier transferred to "sideshow" operations, said the Westerners, increased the danger of a German breakthrough in France.

Demonstrably wrong, said the Easterners. The whole history of the war thus far has proved the impossibility of such a breakthrough on the Western Front.

But, insisted the Westerners, even if all the fringe campaigns in Italy, Turkey, Salonika, and elsewhere were to succeed, the Boche would be strategically unaffected; for even then the Allies could not muster enough strength north of the Brenner Pass to menace the south German frontier.

Whereupon the Easterners proved to their own satisfaction that this argument, too, was a deception designed merely to salvage the fading reputations of dull-witted warlords seeking vindication and personal glory. And the war of words went on, in bitterness and frustration.

Meanwhile the military leaders were proceeding with strategy as they saw fit. On November 15, Joffre, Haig, Robertson, and other Allied officers had assembled at Chantilly to decide what to do the following year, and obvious enough conclusions had been reached: The French and British (especially the British) would attack along the Western Front in February. Simultaneously the Russians, Rumanians and Serbians would attack on their respective fronts. And later in the spring the British alone would proceed to clear the Germans out of Belgium. This decision for the two major powers to continue, in effect, their Somme offensive did not meet with unanimous agreement. Most generals of every other country questioned the concept strongly and wanted basic operations to be switched to the Balkans for the coming year. However, the greater weight of Joffre and Haig had won out.

Meanwhile the despised politicians were also converging on Chantilly. They arrived the next day to find that the generals had outflanked them with a program which, remarked Lloyd George, would reiterate "the bloody stupidities of 1915 and 1916." Everybody —Britain's Lloyd George and Asquith, Russia's Izvolsky, France's Briand, and other civilians, plus all the military officers—sat down and tried to argue it out. The generals explained that the Germans were in trouble and that "wisdom demanded continuous hammering of the weakening vital spot." On November 16 there was much confused bickering. The conference ended indecisively. Nonetheless Haig and Joffre proceeded with their preparations.

Soon afterward everything fell through. In December, Joffre (patting his great head, no doubt, as he often did, and murmuring whimsically, *"Pauvre Joffre!"*) was removed as commander in chief and replaced by General Robert Georges Nivelle. The new French leader had a rather different concept, one which would change the complexion of the war in 1917, and which through a chain of unforeseen circumstances would soon bring in its wake a time of troubles for Field Marshal Haig and several hundred thousand lesser men.

3. The Overture

HARD BY THE WINDSWEPT curve of St. Andrews Bay lie the treacherous undulations
of Scotland's Old Course, most famous of
links, where Douglas Haig was so often
to golf in later years. He was born some
miles away at Cameronbridge on June
19, 1861, of a noted and wealthy family,
and there spent his entire childhood. Later at Oxford he failed to distinguish himself scholastically, and was looked upon
as "headstrong, bad-tempered, and in-
tractable"; and while he soon suppressed
the second characteristic and became the
most even-dispositioned of men, the
other two he would find more difficult to
master.

At college Haig had become, if nothing
else, an outstanding polo player. It was
a talent which was to have an effect on
his life, for after graduation he entered
the Royal Military College at Sandhurst,
and from there gravitated naturally into
a commission with the 7th Hussars. At

once he became a member of the finest polo team in the Army. Now in his middle twenties, aloof, handsome, with hardly a thought in his head but for polo, hunting, the social pleasantries, and more polo, he appeared a typically shallow career officer. But with maturity came the stirrings of ambition. He began, somewhat indiscriminately, to read military history and to study cavalry tactics. This was extremely unusual among young cavalry officers, a group not known for intellectual pursuits, in a branch of service the lackadaisical members of which were seldom distinguished by talent or diligence. Haig's superiors were surprised to find that they had a military scholar on their hands. Under the auspices of the Prince of Wales he began to advance, having already been placed in command of the 17th Lancers.

He became adjutant of his regiment in India, and attracted further attention by rewriting and finishing the *Cavalry Manual* started by Sir John French. In 1896 he was awarded a special nomination to the Staff College. And even here his individual ways persisted; he showed contempt for certain superior officers; he ignored studies in which he had no interest; he wrote letters of protest and criticism. Yet in two years as a captain he had become staff officer to the Cavalry commander, French, during the Sudan and South African campaigns.

He continued to write with extreme frankness—to his friend the Prince of Wales, to the Adjutant General. He berated his own commander in chief, Kitchener, as a planless leader who had invited disaster and was "truly fortunate" that the Dervish army was so inept as to rescue him from folly. His superiors, in short, were "old fossils." The future King Edward was amused but worried; such criticisms, he suggested, "may be correct, but it does not do." To this Haig referred in another letter, "What a stupid letter it would be if I did not express an opinion . . . but whether I am right or wrong . . . I consider our worthy authorities are old stupids, ignorant of the first principles of war."

But while his own work as chief staff officer to French was methodical, he had failed dismally to lay hands on the elusive Boer partisans while in command of a group of columns. Concerning this operation one Intelligence officer had in fact predicted:

> Haig will do nothing! He's quite all right, but he's too —cautious; he will be so fixed on not giving the Boers a chance he'll never give himself one. If I were to go to him one evening and offer to land him at daybreak next morning within galloping distance of 1,000 sleeping Boers, I know exactly what he'd do; he'd insist on sending out someone else to make sure the Boers were really there—to make sure no reinforcements were coming up to them, and to make so dead sure in fact, that when he did get there not a single d——d Boer would be within ten miles of him.

From a rather contemptuous, free-swinging youth Haig now veered toward orthodoxy, precision, and a hardening of the creative impulses. It was becoming increasingly difficult for anyone to change his mind. Silent in the past, he became more silent. The demands he made on his troops were exacting, his punishments severe. The appearance and precision of his command became famous. In 1904 he was named Inspector General of Cavalry in India with the rank of Major General. He began to be called "Lucky Haig."

His great favor with the King and with Lord Kitchener (whom he had criticized so severely in private correspondence) certainly had much to do with his appointment and future rise. By now he was spoken of by the King as "my best and most capable general." While a guest at Windsor Castle for the 1905 Ascot Races he was introduced to one of the Queen's maids of honor, Dorothy Vivian. Two days later he proposed and was accepted. The wedding took place in the chapel of Buckingham Palace, which had never before been used by anyone but members of the royal family.

His powerful connections, his dominating personality, the efficiency of his staff work, his fantastic rise, had made him an outstanding power among the military clique—if not with the politicians, whom he distrusted, and who generally disliked him in return. Only Haldane and Asquith, among the top-level civilians, had formerly admired and supported him. There was some talk about appointing him Chief of the Imperial General Staff; but this was going too fast, and an older officer received the assignment.

A disquieting event took place in 1912, when during

war games Haig commanded a corps and was seriously outmaneuvered. The official report referred significantly to the way he had pursued fixed aims without regard to new information. A conference was held
at Cambridge in which Haig tried to justify his actions. With the King himself presiding, Haig, according to a biographer, "became totally unintelligible and
unbearably dull. The University dignitaries soon fell
fast asleep. Haig's friends became more and more un-
comfortable; only he himself seemed totally uncon-
scious of his failure." Throughout his life Haig was to
be plagued by this inability to convey his military
thoughts in words.

What were his military thoughts? As a cavalry tactician he was devoted to broad concepts in the Napoleonic vein that were no longer appropriate. He wrote
that the "role of Cavalry on the battlefield will always
go on increasing." His one great axiom—that "mass
tactics" were the basis of this arm—had been abandoned long ago by even the most ardent cavalry officers. He believed that bullets had "little stopping
power against a horse." He conceived of cavalry as
the basic instrument of war, to which infantry and
artillery were secondary. He resisted innovations, and
in later years was to deprecate the airplane, the tank,
even the machine gun. He had come to epitomize
what a renowned French cavalry officer had once
said—that "the British cavalry officer seems to be impressed by the conviction that he can dash or ride
over anything; as if the art of war were precisely the

Field Marshal Sir Douglas Haig

same as that of fox-hunting." Sir John French wrote
of Haig that he would "show to greater advantage as
a superior Staff Officer than as a Commander."

When war came, all the qualities of Douglas Haig
—his underlying intelligence, almost inhuman grasp
of detail, coolness under stress, complete self-assurance—were matched by certain corresponding defects. In writing he advised His Majesty to sack Sir
John French as commander on the Western Front,
explaining that the field marshal "is quite unfit for his
command at a time of crisis in our nation's history."
And throughout 1915 he continued to pour scorn on
him in letters to the King and Kitchener, the impro-
priety of which never seems to have occurred to him.

But Haig himself had been strangely inactive as a
corps commander during the 1914 retreat. His troops
had retired (in an incorrect direction) while the adjacent corps under Smith-Dorrien stood and fought.
Though Haig was only partially to blame, the fact
remained that he had not met his first great test im-
pressively. Later, at Ypres, he conducted defensive
operations with skill. On the other hand, his attacks
against the hardening German trench system were
turned back with heavy losses. Twice he had momentarily lost his nerve—at Landrecies when retreating
from Mons in August, 1914, and again in the crisis at
Ypres, October 31 of the same year.

Yet when French was relieved of his command,
largely through Haig's insistence, there was, at any

rate, no one much better to take over the British Expeditionary Force in France and Belgium than Sir Douglas. He accepted—if his diary is any indicator—with no more exhilaration or surprise than if he had been handed a set of cuff links for his birthday. The date, obscure but fateful, was December 10, 1915.

Yet his appointment was not received everywhere with enthusiasm. Among his intimates he was respected for methodical planning and firmness of will, but most of them considered him something less than a brilliant general. Even the sympathetic official historian writes, "it appears true that Haig himself was not swift of thought." George Bernard Shaw visited the Western Front soon after Haig took over, and appraised him similarly:

> He was, I should say, a man of chivalrous and scrupulous character. He made me feel that the war would last thirty years, and that he would carry it on irreproachably until he was superannuated.

Haig had expected the assignment and he had done his part behind the scenes to stage it. He believed that God had chosen him as a man of destiny. At spiritualistic séances had he not been told "to do much good and benefit my country," and that the spirit of Napoleon was "always near me"? And respectfully he consulted the medium on matters of more specific import—whether a battalion or company organizational basis was more efficient, how the Territorial Army problem

should be solved, and so on. But primarily he consulted God. "I feel that every step in my plan has been
taken with the Divine help," he wrote in 1916, just before the Somme offensive unrolled, where he lost sixty
thousand men the very first day for no appreciable
gain in ground—a portent of further such developments in this campaign.

Winston Churchill recalls how Haig once referred
to a brigadier as an officer who "did not show a sincere
desire to engage the enemy." This remark, says
Churchill, was "the key to his whole military outlook,"
and he continues thus:

> He presents to me in those red years the same mental
> picture as a great surgeon before the days of anaes-
> thetics, versed in every detail of such science as was
> known to him; sure of himself, steady of poise, knife
> in hand, intent upon the operation; entirely removed
> in his professional capacity from the agony of the pa-
> tient, the anguish of relations, or the doctrines of rival
> schools, the devices of quacks, or the first-fruits of
> new learning. He would operate without excitement,
> or he would depart without being affronted; and if
> the patient died, he would not reproach himself.

By 1917 Field Marshal Haig had lost not a particle
of his optimism and self-esteem, though all his offensives to date had miscarried, the war was a stalemate,
British casualties exceeded a million, and his fitness
to command had become a known matter of debate in
Parliament and especially in the War Cabinet. If he

had doubts, he reinforced himself with prayer. No trace of a sense of humor could evoke in him wry reflections on his omniscience. Still in perfect health, an imposing figure of a man, gentle in outward manner, fanatically supported by his staff officers, totally confident of eventual victory by smashing open the front and releasing his beloved cavalry for the kill, convinced that the Germans fought for the Devil against him and God, he stood on the threshold of his greatest crisis with the calm certainty of a genius or a fool. Time alone would deliver a verdict of one or the other or something in between.

While David Lloyd George and Douglas Haig had always disliked each other, this had not mattered much until the former became head of the Government. Both wheels spinning in opposite directions then moved into contact, and the friction began to throw off sparks and heat. At Chantilly, where Lloyd George found himself faced by a *fait accompli* diametrically opposite to his views, he had argued to no avail his Eastern philosophy of war. Bitterly he refers to the generals' plan as "mildewed . . . a legacy of inevitable disaster." Not yet being in power he was unable to head it off. But as Prime Minister he *sotto voce* began expressing doubts concerning the decisions reached by Haig and Joffre, and to call for a new conference in January, at Rome, to decide once and for all how to fight the war in 1917.

It appeared that Sir Douglas did not consider these

coming conversations much of a threat to his established plans, nor did he even plan to participate in them. On January 3 he met at Rollincourt with his Army commanders—Rawlinson of the Fourth Army, Plumer of the Second, Gough of the Fifth—and laid down the theme for coming operations in terms more or less similar to those suggested at Chantilly. "Rawly" was told that he would be sent up north to kick off the main offensive in the Ypres salient, following a preliminary French attack. Thus Haig chose to ignore Lloyd George and to imply disapproval of any plans to the contrary developed at Rome. His main regret, which he stated freely, was that he was forced to deal at all with politicians of this stripe, and that in theory he might actually be bound by their inept military thinking.

Some degree of conflict between the two men would have been inevitable in any event, even aside from their strategic differences.

Haig was bound to suspect the glittering, dangerously clever Mr. Lloyd George, that "mass man"—the new phenomenon of democracy—who differed from old-style aristocrats and warriors in his modes of thought as though he were an organism from another planet. But there were few indeed who truly fathomed David Lloyd George, and Haig was far from alone in despising and suspecting him. As a hard-bitten politician he had never been reluctant to throw overboard anybody who rocked his boat. He had entered public life as an accomplished Liberal orator and writer at the age of seventeen. Avid for power, he campaigned in a harsh, radical fashion for Parliament only ten years later, and won. That was in 1890; he was to represent Wales from the Caernarvon Boroughs for fifty-five more years. In Parliament he flung himself precociously into affairs, and almost at once was in conflict with the veteran Gladstone, who admonished him icily: "I ask my honourable friend not to interpose unnecessarily, not to search with something of a feverish heat for arguments of all kinds. . . ." The appeal had no affect on the barrel-chested young man with the hard blue eyes.

As Prime Minister he had not mellowed, and was still capable of transitory hatreds, especially for mental nonentities. To this day he had few devout friends in the world, though he was acquainted with thousands of people, had a thousand enemies, and sat on the shoulders of a thousand faceless lackeys. But—cohort, foe, or slave—he would use any of them on Friday and cut them dead after the week end. The only man with whom he had something resembling a true kinship was Winston Churchill—and even this forty-two-year-old upstart, could be (and sometimes was) shriveled by the fiery tongue of the master.

Possibly Lloyd George was the most accomplished orator of modern times in the melodramatic mode. His repertoire included hoarse screams of fury, ingratiating smiles, ghastly whispers, ominous scowls and mutters. With all this were intermingled the gaunt finger of shame, silky sneers, irony that could slash like a razor, and pure wit of high or low sophistication. Or he could move audiences to tears with pathos, with the Welsh-accented poetry of his words. All these were the traditional marks of the charlatan. But his friends and enemies knew him better, and realized that behind his theatrical façade existed a complex brain and a fair amount of principle. He had been a Liberal almost from birth, and his hatred of war and championship of the underdog were not entirely a pose designed to snare votes, though it was seldom that he had allowed conscience to block his way to fame and power.

He was completely lacking in military training or sympathies. But like other semi-amateurs—such as Caesar, Napoleon, and Cromwell—he seemed to possess an unorthodox low cunning in war. The generals hated him for his encroachments on their terrain, and the debate over his military talents will never end; for the approach he advocated was never tried. Yet he was passionately, stubbornly wrong at times. Often he was devious. Culturally he was lopsided. Intellectually he ranged from the sublimely penetrating to the blindly prejudiced.

This is the man against whom that silent, seemingly simple Scot, Field Marshal Sir Douglas Haig, fought the battle of wills which was to mean so much to so many.

Lloyd George had been Prime Minister of Great Britain for one month when the Rome Conference convened. His position then was far from secure. The Empire's military and naval leaders opposed him almost to a man. The Conservative members of Parliament tolerated him apprehensively and only for the moment. Many of his own Liberals suspected his personality and past tactics. The very way in which he had acquired office (a rather disreputable imbroglio had taken place, not entirely behind the scenes, in which Prime Minister Asquith had been shunted to a siding) had not inspired confidence in the serenity and character of his forthcoming leadership. The press had made these vulgar political maneuvers known to the people. So even in the most important sector—that of the general public—Lloyd George's reputation was weak. That January he was holding on by a thread, and it was touch and go whether he would last out the spring. To do so would require not only leadership far more resourceful than that of his predecessor, but a good deal of tact and compromise, at least in the beginning. As yet he did not feel strong enough to fight his powerful opponents to a finish at Rome.

At this sprawling conference of Allied military and civil leaders Lloyd George led off in a way that appears to have confirmed the suspicions of Sir William ("Wully") Robertson that the man really was a menace and a cad—a "cur," in Haig's melodramatic word. It was not because Lloyd George circulated a long speculation ("an amazing document," Robertson coldly termed it) on what he believed to be the military situation. Nor was it because this civilian recommended again his stale plan for an Eastern operation. The unkindest cut was that the formula had been sprung on the assemblage without the knowledge of a single British general. Robertson, Chief of the Imperial General Staff, had crossed the channel with Lloyd George and accompanied him on the train to Rome; and all this time not a word had been said about scuttling the Chantilly arrangements. The General was furious, and except for a few sullen expressions of dissent said little for two days. He left Rome in advance of the break-up of the conference, presumably confident that Lloyd George's suggestion would wither on the vine.

This turned out to be the case. The Italian general, Luigi Cadorna, had at first been delighted with the idea of shifting the center of Allied gravity to his poor front, but had learned all too soon that neither Haig nor Robertson knew anything about their chief's surprise package, nor did they have any intention of buying it. In deference to these awesome personages he reluctantly backed off.

As for Aristide Briand, the French Prime Minister, he gives the impression of having entered the conference in a state of indecision. He knew all about the plans jelling around his new French commander, General Nivelle, to conduct an assault near the old Somme battleground. He could not very well undercut his own man. Yet he agreed with Lloyd George that it would be futile in 1917 "for each general to continue punching on his own front." Though wedded as a matter of political principle to operations on the Western Front, emotionally he distrusted slaughterhouse

Somme-type offensives. He sympathized mildly with the plan to smash Austria, especially since large numbers of French (and British) troops would not be called into action there; Lloyd George asked only for an Italian offensive backed up by a terrific concentration of French and British artillery. He was aware of the deposed Joffre's warning that the French were so weak that their war effort was almost done, and that they were good for only one more grand offensive. If this assumption was true, and Briand accepted it, it seemed a pity to attack so soon after the last Somme debacle, and in the same bloody locale. Yet Briand was afraid to join the isolated British Prime Minister and feared to weaken his own front by transferring any of his forces or matériel elsewhere. In the end, after soulful deliberation, he too opposed the Italian adventure.

And the British generals in attendance, headed by Sir Henry Wilson (he referred always to politicians as frocks, an abbreviation of Frock Coats and boasted in his diary that "we never touched on Lloyd George's paper all day") and the dour, heavily handsome Robertson, openly blocked their own Prime Minister right down the line.

Lloyd George had plunged into all this with typical enthusiasm. He loved conferences. In front of large audiences all his talents of speech, personality, and mental gymnastics came through in fine style. Yet by January 7 his first big entree on the world's stage had turned out a humiliating failure. If Chantilly had been indecisive, Rome settled matters. For the moment at least the fluid military scheme for 1917 had frozen into solid and massive shape: the Westerners had won; the battle of the Somme would be fought all over again. Lloyd George was thrown a dry bone: his Italian scheme would be studied by the various staffs, so it was soothingly said.

Baffled and in a murderous frame of mind, Lloyd George left Rome for Paris. Huddled in his overcoat while the train jolted along, he improvised moodily regarding the military policy of his commanders, who knew only the British sector of the Western Front and nothing of their allies. "We must strike again against a soft front," he insisted to Robertson, Kiggell, and the French representatives. "The country would not stand much more of that sort of thing," he warned, speaking of the Somme type of offensive. Scowling and in a rage he shouted that he would not drive thousands to slaughter like cattle. Men who are needed on the farms and in factories are not going to be used for cannon fodder, he said. For three years we have been promised certain victory in France and Belgium. What is there to show for this ceaseless battering? And now another of the same! Lieutenant General Launcelot Kiggell, Haig's chief of staff, a Westerner and anti-French zealot, worsened matters by arguing with the

Prime Minister. That evening he wrote Haig that Lloyd George had

> poured out a lot of heretical, amateur strategy of the most dangerous and misleading kind and was far from complimentary to what had been done by our armies here. He ruffled me so thoroughly that I argued vehemently with him and I fear without displaying the respect due to his high office. . . . Robertson threw in a contribution now and then backing me up, but said little. Afterwards he told me privately that he had to meet this sort of stuff all day and every day, and was doing his best against it. . . . Robertson's line I gather is to delay the commission of serious mistakes and try to fill us up with all we want before the P.M. succeeds in sending things elsewhere.

Nobody's mind was changed in the course of this querulous dialogue, the only result of which was that Kiggell was henceforth labeled an insulting boor in the Prime Minister's book. And as the day dragged on, the talking dwindled accordingly.

When the train jolted to a stop near Paris, General Robert Nivelle was found to be awaiting them. He saluted Lloyd George and introduced himself. Lloyd George had heard from him in writing directly after the succession of Marshal Joffre. He knew that the Frenchman had a scheme for resuming the Somme offensive; in fact, he had received a memorandum about it on Christmas Day. This he had surveyed with total lack of interest. Its only redeeming feature was that it was to be mainly a French effort. Nivelle had asked Haig to take over twenty-five extra miles of front so that the French would be free to exert maximum force in the chosen sector near Champagne. Lloyd George had passed the request on to Haig passively and washed his hands of it. It was suggested again by Briand at the Rome conference; this time Lloyd George condescended to scorn it. Another Somme! Would these ridiculous generals never learn?

But now in the crowded, smoke-filled railway car Lloyd George began to size up the Frenchman and his scheme with more respect. Certainly the man's reputation could not be laughed off. A clever, suave tactician, he had been in field command at Verdun, had stemmed the tide there and had been the hero of the recapture of world-famous Fort Douaumont, in which operation certain new artillery methods had been used with surprising success. Lloyd George was surprised to find that this general could speak English without an accent and with captivating phraseology. Here was actually a French war leader he could understand —a man of subtlety and fresh ideas. His mother had been English. He was a Protestant. His way of thinking came closer to Lloyd George's than any other Western Front commander's. It turned out that Nivelle was not by any means advocating another Somme. His blow would be a two-handed affair on both sides of the wrecked woodlands where the previous offensive had failed. It would not be a campaign of attrition. It would be a "rupture of the front." It would be an audacious plunge, "a single stroke." It would involve new, fool-proof methods. For better or for worse the issue would be resolved "in twenty-four or forty-eight hours." It would be a "decisive battle" and its aim would be nothing less than "the destruction of the principal mass of the enemy."

The Prime Minister surveyed the trimly mustached, slit-eyed little general, calm to the point of arrogance, yet with hat in hand. Perhaps his puzzling new formula would work. Anything was better than nibbling on granite. Of course all generals were always confident. Lloyd George decided, at any rate, to invite him to London on January 15 to explain his plan before the British War Cabinet.

Nivelle arrived on that date and charmed everybody. Lloyd George began to entertain a positive enthusiasm for the proposed offensive. It was settled that operations would commence no later than April 1. Haig would take over part of the French front-line positions as far as St. Quentin with six new divisions from England. The Frenchman described the offensive with his usual lucidity: The British and French would attack in such fashion as to attract and magnetize the enemy's reserves. Then the French would strike on the Aisne River front, using special tactics made famous at Fort Douaumont. If successful, and success was "certain," the attack would be broadened and intensified to the last ounce of men and matériel, and the drive would be pressed all the way to the Belgian coastline. If not, theoretically speaking, it would be instantly abandoned, and Haig's long-cherished scheme of a third campaign in the Ypres salient—toward the

General Robert Nivelle

same objectives—would go into effect as soon as possible, spearheaded by the British Expeditionary Force.

Haig agreed to all this resentfully. He himself had hoped to attack in February, but now he would have to wait on the French. Furthermore, he mistrusted Nivelle's plan. Referring to a French memorandum on troop dispositions, he called it "a most misleading document. . . . I felt it was disgraceful that the French Staff should have put forward such an untrue statement of facts at such a time as this." And after the decision to back Nivelle was settled he confided in his diary, "I must say that these conclusions were hastily considered by the War Committee." Robertson, who was professionally loyal to Haig and almost never knowingly disagreed with him, also thought the program had "many fallacies." Even the French demigods, Foch and Joffre, felt that the attack would fail. Nonetheless, it was now policy, and, like a derelict locomotive running downgrade, could no longer be stopped by the hand of man.

But, at the moment, peace talk was overpowering the sound of the guns and the bickering of the warlords. It emanated from across the Atlantic where President Wilson was hoping to keep the United States out of war by ending it before the actions of Germany made his country's entry inevitable. He had tried (perhaps condecendingly) several times in the past without success to bring about negotiations among the belligerents, but this plea was by far his most dramatic.

On January 22 before the Senate he made a last desperate attempt to bring the warring nations to the conference table. He introduced the idea of a postwar league of nations to enforce "peace without victory"—one which would humiliate and deplete no nation, would guarantee freedom of the seas, and would see to it that all rulers would govern their nations with the consent of the governed. The reaction of most statesmen and soldiers to this proposal is perhaps typified by the entry in Sir Henry Wilson's diary:

> . . . an amazing speech about peace without victory —all countries to have access to the sea, and much other dangerous nonsense. Doumergue and Castelnau, and all Frenchmen, are furious.

British newspapers cast scorn on the President. The various diplomats tried to phrase a tactful no-thank-you. Their embarrassment was relieved quickly. On February 1, the Germans delivered one of several thunderbolts which were to make the first four months of 1917 among the most dynamic in modern history—they announced unrestricted submarine warfare. Neutrals were told that all waters around Great Britain, France, and Italy would henceforth be barred, and that any merchantmen therein would be liable to sinking without notice. This policy nullified assurances given Wilson by the Germans nine months previously, and two days later the President broke off diplomatic relations with Germany. But to the dismay of the European Allies there was not a word in his Congressional speech about declaring war. February dwindled, and still the two countries remained at peace with each other. The stunning thought began to be voiced that this weird state of affairs might continue indefinitely. The puzzle, the riddle, of America's continued neutrality might face them sphinxlike for the duration of hostilities. Was it really possible?

The hard-headed men of war paid little heed to these speculations. Neither Lloyd George nor Haig in his published memoirs refers to President Wilson's peace formula or Germany's reversal of naval policy. Wilson's proposal seems to have struck both men as beneath contempt. Naval matters were usually ignored by Haig as a matter of professional policy; to meddle in them unduly, he felt, would be most presumptuous. As for the Prime Minister, for once his spacious outlook failed him; he seems to have underestimated the reluctant decision of Ludendorff to give the admirals a free rein. That February intense Allied plans were under way for gigantic military blows which were intended to win the war. Nothing else mattered. Shortly there was to be still another conference. It would be held in Calais on the 26th and, for a change, would not be another of those tumultuous, argumentative affairs, but would concern itself decorously with the chronic congestion of the Nord railway, which for many months had impeded British operations in France and might even wreck the forthcoming spring offensive unless improvements were worked out.

Saturday before the Calais talks the War Cabinet held a secret meeting. Robertson was phoned by its secretary and told that he need not attend unless he had special questions to bring up. That seemed strange, but the chief of staff drew the necessary conclusions and stayed away; and in the course of the long Monday trip to Calais an interminable conversation between him and the Prime Minister divulged nothing about the Cabinet meeting, nor did the civilian drop any hints about the forthcoming agenda.

In France Lloyd George quickly brushed the transport problem into the hands of a technical committee. Then the bomb burst: Haig and his armies were to be placed under the supreme command of Nivelle. "The enemy has but a single army," the Prime Minister explained. "We should secure for ourselves the same advantage. If we do not we cannot hope for success."

Robertson hit the ceiling. "Get 'aig!" he roared.

The idea that all British units would be considered a group of armies in the French line of command, that Haig, as he notes helplessly in his diary, "would apparently only administer the discipline and look after reinforcements," and that Nivelle's orders would be transmitted to the British commander in chief via an intermediary, struck the British military chiefs like a slap in the face. They "agreed we would rather be tried by Court Martial than betray the Army by agreeing to its being placed under the French." Robertson suggested that they all resign en masse. Haig that night confided to his diary, "And so we went to bed, thoroughly disgusted with our Government and the Politicians."

In the end it was compromised; Haig would be technically subordinated to Nivelle only for the duration of the latter's private offensive, but would have the right to appeal. Henry Wilson (whom Haig despised) would be the liaison officer. But the incident left Haig barren of any further respect for the Prime Minister, if, indeed, anything of the sort had remained. To his wife he wrote:

> Why I cannot think but I am told that L. G. finds himself slipping down the hill in popular favour, and is looking about to find something to increase his reputation as the "man of the hour" and the saviour of England. However, I am doing my best and have a clear conscience. If they have someone else who can command this great Army better than I am doing, I shall be glad to hand over to him, and will be *so happy* to come back to my darling wife and play golf and bring up the children.

Feeling that the arch-devil Lloyd George was at the bottom of the scheme Robertson wrote Haig, "I can't believe that a man such as he can remain for long head of any Government. Surely *some* honesty and truth are required."

And Sir Douglas, who had secretly told all and offered his resignation to the King, entered in his diary, "All would be so easy if I only had to deal with Germans." And finally he wrote to Nivelle in a more friendly way, ". . . I feel confident that 'unity of effort' will be assured with absolute certainty if you and I are allowed to settle our affairs together without interference from London or Paris."

There has been a suspicion that the incident was engineered to bring about the resignation of Haig and Robertson. Certainly Haig was not oblivious to the possibility. It was at about this time that he was visited at GHQ by General Gough, one of the rising young stars. Haig for once was worried, and remarked, "Of course, if they don't approve of me, they had better appoint someone else." Then he looked at Gough suspiciously and added, "Is it going to be you?" Though Gough protested that such a thought could have crossed nobody's mind, much less his own, both men were quite aware of the crude affront delivered to Haig at Calais, that his status in the eyes of the Prime Minister was close to nil, and that his replacement was now a definite possibility.

To rub salt into the wound, Nivelle now began ordering Haig about in communications so peremptory that the latter quietly exploded and called upon his Government for a further clarification of the distribution of power. Referring to one of Nivelle's orders, he wrote Robertson, "Briefly it is a type of letter which no gentleman could have drafted. . . . I intend to send a copy of the letter with my reply to the War Committee with a request to be told whether it is their wishes that the Commander-in-Chief of this British Army should be subjected to such treatment by a junior *foreign* commander." In later years this communication was to

plague the Scottish marshal. Nivelle *was* plainly a for-
eigner. And, since France had a different grading system, technically he *did* hold a lesser rank, though he
was Haig's senior in service. As one historian has suggested, the phrasing is nonetheless of interest "if one
is to understand the subconscious working of the military mind." But these regrettable piques subsided in
time, and Nivelle was left in peace with his own difficulties with his own politicians, who were, if possible,
even more obstructive than Haig's.

So it went early in 1917. Two generations later these
fitful quarrels and portentous conferences were to
fade, all but forgotten, down the dim corridors of time.
But at the moment nothing seemed more important to
their participants. Even Lloyd George was far more
alert to his own political fences, to impending French
plans on the Western Front, to the immediate problems of troops, matériel, food, and submarines than he
was to remote international developments. But now
came events of overpowering magnitude.

The Russian revolution detonated in March, with
the Army and Navy in effect following George Bernard Shaw's bland advice "that if the soldiers had any
sense they would go home and attend to their own affairs." This exodus from the Eastern Front began upon
the abdication of the Czar, who had made "every possible mistake" and in autocratic blindness had denied
his country even the rudimentary glimmerings of democracy. A moderate provisional government took

over. Now the Russian soldier-peasantry, who had been butchered since 1914 in numbers far more (both relatively and absolutely) than even the French—ragged, underfed, half of them still without rifles—began to clamor for release from a war which had even less meaning for them than for the soldiers of the other Allies. The first provisional government, like the one to follow, tried to walk a tight-rope between war and peace. From the beginning it encountered foreseeable difficulties. Colonel Charles A'Court Repington, military writer for the Northcliffe press, began to refer to serious concern among the warlords in France and England, and called attention to allegations that the new Government did not seem to be capable of pressing the war effort. General Robertson stated glumly to Repington in an interview "that the Russian position is rotten," and confided that Russia was about finished because the people behind the Army were good for nothing "except music and dancing and tommy-rot love stories." The Germans well knew what a ripe plum had fallen into their laps; it was the greatest stroke of luck they had enjoyed thus far in the war.

Strangely enough there were those in Britain who thought the revolution would benefit their side. These were the liberals, who heretofore had been so bravely despondent. Suddenly they were revitalized. The once naughty member of their coalition—despotic Russia—had finally seen the light and was turning toward democracy. At last the war had a shred of meaning. Revival day came and voices were raised in hosannas.

On March 17 the leading liberal paper, the *Daily News*, contained an ecstatic article on "The Twilight of the Gods." It was "the greatest victory that had yet fallen to the Allies."

Until then there had been little enough to celebrate or even hope for, except desperately to pray for the entry of the United States into the conflict. Rumors to that effect had not ceased in three years. After German-American diplomatic relations ended, the speculations and yearnings swelled. The *Daily News'* Washington correspondent reported, "It may be safely said that the country [America] is nearer war." But this was an old, tired phrase. Was there really any truth in it? By now everybody was in a state of exasperation over the dilatory tactics of the overseas giant. It was always a "puzzle" or a "riddle" when any neutral, especially America, failed to "come in" quickly. And after Wilson's "peace without victory" speech there were many who despaired, because it further seemed to imply nonintervention.

Until the Russian revolution it had been a dreary winter, mostly marked by soothing speeches and optimistic predictions. For example, Haig had limned "The Coming Break-Through": "We shall break the German front completely—we shall strike without respite and terribly. . . ." The *Daily News* spoke cheerily of the "Splendid Success of the War Loan." And there was Lloyd George's "Inspiring Message to

France" in which he promised what would happen "when John Bull gets his teeth in . . ." and so on. But these hypodermics could not forever stimulate the idealists or the people at large.

Then at last on April 6: "America In With All Her Resources." Near-hysteria followed. The liberals professed to see wonders in Woodrow Wilson's war message to Congress even greater than guns and dollars and troops, and the *Daily News* intoned:

> In this great utterance we seem to hear at last the authentic voice of humanity stating the issue and pronouncing the judgment, awakening the conscience of the world to the mighty things at stake. Never in history have there been such declarations as those made in the past few days in Russia and in Washington. Deep has answered to deep, and across the sundering ocean the democracy of America clasps the hand of the democracy of Russia, freed at last from the gyves of centuries. In the light of this prodigious union we see the issue of the war emerge with a grave simplicity of outline.

By Easter the paean had far from subsided. In the *Daily News* one journalist wrote a hymn for the occasion:

> *I hear a noise of breaking chains,*
> *I hear a sound of opening doors;*
> *It comes from Transatlantic plains,*
> *Across the green Atlantic floors.*

She sings the old redeeming songs
That Lincoln taught her lips to sing;
The death songs of a thousand wrongs,
The birth songs of a thousand springs. . . .

And so on and on until the ghastly finale:

And Britain with her sea-knit brood,
Locked fast in world-wide conflict grim,
Hears the high call of her own blood
In Woodrow Wilson's Battle Hymn.

At a Savoy celebration one overwrought reporter wrote:

Gathered for lunch between the twined flags of America and Britain, we seemed to have recaught the glad, early spirit of the war. Youth was everywhere . . . an incubus of doubt was lifted. Even through the tobacco smoke, America's clear young eyes shone with that utter faith in a just cause which is the assurance of victory.

And Lloyd George, who was present, spoke more playfully about the "bunkers" Britain had been in during the past three years; but now, he said, "We have got a good niblick and have struck right on to the course."

These glad tidings, one must conclude, failed to thrill Sir Douglas Haig to the fever pitch felt by other people. There is not a word in his published diary concerning the Russian revolution or America's entry. For a year he had been looking forward to his offensive at

Ypres, one which he felt would be successful in breaking the German front, in reaching the Channel, thus dislocating the enemy communications and perhaps nearly ending the war. All this he intended to accomplish almost solely with British troops. He had little interest in the cooperation, then or eventually, of French or American forces. The Third Battle of Ypres was to be Britain's day of glory, and his plans for the conduct of this offensive were already complete.

Meanwhile he was forced to await the outcome of Nivelle's experiment. It was bound to fail, he knew; that was why the delay was so intolerable. As for Nivelle, he was an arrogant straw boss, a junior officer improperly promoted over the heads of other Frenchmen far more senior and experienced. Haig silently fumed. Worst of all, Nivelle was behind schedule. Why had his wretched battle not yet commenced? April 1 and 5 and 10 and 15 came and went, and still the French squatted. At this rate, the British offensive would not get under way till doomsday. Haig realized that the British should strike early in the summer, for later rains would make the Flanders plain difficult to operate on. The French would have to fight, fail, and retire quickly. But bad weather and supply difficulties continued to delay them. Two weeks after the deadline the French had still not moved, and now it was becoming really questionable whether Haig's Flanders offensive would get under way in time to force a decision before the rain, the snow, and the paralyzing cold stopped the British Army dead in its tracks.

4. L'Affaire Nivelle

BUT SURELY nobody could have been more eager to attack on schedule than General Robert Nivelle. His appointment as commander in chief over the heads of such figures as Foch, Pétain, and Castelnau, not to mention the exalted Joffre himself, had occurred, Nivelle knew, because it was hoped that he had something new to offer—a magical artillery formula, a scheme that would at last produce a breakthrough, an "unlimited offensive" that aimed at total victory. Such, at least, were the anxious dreams of the French Ministers who had dumped "Papa" Joffre because he had proved incapable of so delivering. And unlike his rival Pétain, the new commander knew how to deal with his politicians. Though secretly despising them (he referred to all of them as "foreigners" in a talk with Robertson) he was anxious to fulfill their desires and to vault from relative obscurity onto the center of the world stage. His nomination to the supreme command went to his head; his normal good sense was unhinged by the premature position (his highest command heretofore had been a single army, which he had led for only five months) in which he now found himself. Drunk with the wine of history, he hoped to capitalize on his stroke of luck by attacking quickly and winning spectacularly. But many things had begun to go wrong almost at once.

First of all, his mentors, Briand and Lyautey, fell from power. Ribot, an octogenarian, became Premier and named M. Paul Painlevé as Minister of War. In the past Painlevé had been so bitterly opposed to Nivelle that he had refused to serve in the French Cabinet while that general continued in command. The war ministry, however, was too tempting a plum to refuse. Primarily a mathematician, an outstanding theoretical intellectual, a left-wing socialist, Painlevé had often insisted that Nivelle's plan to seek a decision on the Western Front was the equivalent of mass manslaughter. There was no secret about his conviction that the proper general to command at this juncture was Pétain, who in turn had stated his opinion that the exhausted French armies must rest and go over to the defensive for at least a year. Instead Painlevé was now saddled by a man advocating, of all things, a grandiose scheme of attack. But instead of replacing him at once, as he had planned to do before the event, the War Minister stalled. Soon he was in so deep, Nivelle's preparations had advanced so far, the deadline was so

near, that Painlevé submitted in despair and hoped
only for the best.

He assumed office on March 19. The following day
he learned—"I might say by public voice," he wrote
plaintively—that the offensive would begin on April 8
and that the British would attack near Arras on the
4th.

At this point it appears that conscience made him
pause. Could he really sanction this madness? On the
22nd he summoned Nivelle to the first of a pedantic
series of lectures designed to stop him. Nivelle remained adamant and a situation developed which
Winston Churchill describes:

> So Nivelle and Painlevé, these two men whose high-
> est ambitions had been newly and almost simultane-
> ously gratified, found themselves in the most unhappy
> positions which disillusioned mortals can occupy: the
> Commander having to dare the utmost risks with an
> utterly skeptical Chief behind him; the Minister hav-
> ing to become responsible for a frightful slaughter at
> the bidding of a General in whose capacity he did not
> believe, and upon a military policy the folly of which
> he was justly convinced. Such is the pomp of power!

But this was only the beginning of Neville's avalanche of problems. The weather turned wet, and day
after day the already late attack was further post-
poned. The notoriously inept French hospital facilities
resisted all last-minute attempts at improvement. Under the load of gigantic preparations the efficiency of
the railroad system went from bad to worse. The Ger-

mans knew in a broad way what was coming, and as time passed French Intelligence in turn became alarmingly aware that the Germans knew. And the various means by which the enemy came to fathom Nivelle's intentions in detail are remarkable indeed.

First of all, the French newspapers proceeded to advertise the whole plan in its general outline. Nivelle himself had been surprisingly careless. He had told at a luncheon in London attended (in the icy phrase of Sir William Robertson) by "several persons of both sexes." Furthermore, the written plan sent by Nivelle to the British Foreign Office had been retyped and copies sent to at least ten individuals in England.

Next Nivelle had circulated innumerable copies of the detailed Order of Battle to front-line officers as low as company level. The sequel might have been predicted. On March 3 a French sergeant was captured by Germans in a trench raid and found to have one of these interesting documents on his person. The exultant reaction of Crown Prince Rupprecht is discernible in his words:

> This memorandum contained matters of extraordinary value . . . as to the particular nature of the surprise which the attacker had in view. . . . Graf Von Schulenburg at once formulated the logical reply for the defense.

All during March German officers intently watched the immense preparations proceeding under their noses. Aerial observation and other means of inference

Crown Prince Rupprecht of Bavaria

were also helpful. On April 6 another surprise raid cap-
tured another Frenchman and another document—the
Order of Attack of the French Fifth Army. The Crown
Prince continues:

> In it the French attacking units were mentioned by
> name. . . . Fresh information upon the anticipated
> French method of attack was given. The last veil con-
> cealing the intentions of the French offensive was torn
> aside.

By now the enemy knew Nivelle's plan with total accuracy and was preparing accordingly. A stream of reinforcements had already begun to flow toward the
threatened sector. The nine divisions stationed there
were increased to forty. Within a few weeks a vast new
system of barbed wire, machine guns, trenches, concrete strong points, and mountains of ammunition appeared as if by magic. Hundreds of batteries were
placed into additional positions, and special methods
of tactical defense were established.

Meanwhile (and this was, or should have been, the
last straw) the Boche simply proceeded to withdraw
from the exposed salient upon which Nivelle's offensive was supposed to fall. Even before the birth of the
Nivelle affair Ludendorff had long been wary of his
potential weakness there and for months had been preparing a new defensive chord from Arras to Royon—
the so-called Hindenburg line. As far back as February
the British under General Gough had been astounded
to discover that the Germans were bombarding their

own front-line trenches. Cautious patrols were sent forward. They found the German positions deserted. In one dugout only a black cat leaped out to greet Australian scouts. For several days local commanders continued to report the disappearance of the enemy. Eventually it dawned on everybody that the Germans were really conducting a mass disengagement from the front—in some zones as far back as fifty miles. The process posed an embarrassing question: Where was the Somme morsel now? What remained to bite off, when from Arras to Soissons the Germans had fallen back? For when they had finished the British Fifth Army was "in the air" and three of Nivelle's five armies were also separated from the enemy.

As the Germans retreated from occupied France they laid waste the villages and the countryside. Key towns such as Peronne were utterly devasted. Every house in the abandoned area was blown up. Wells were poisoned. Trees were cut down and laid across the roads. Orchards were devastated. At road inter-sections huge craters were exploded. Thousands of booby traps were laid everywhere, some of which were extremely ingenious. A new shovel lying among old ones would be wired to a bomb, a duckboard out of place awaited a neat-minded Englishman, an inno-cently open door, a closed door, fountain pens on a desk—these and other such devices inflicted many casualties on the Allies proceeding northward with glacier-like persistence. Delayed-action bombs were planted; the Town Hall of Bapaume was demolished by an explosion several days after the British moved in. The devastation was nearly total. Even the furniture in the houses was chopped apart, and the livestock carried away or slaughtered.

Of this operation, aptly designated by the German code word *Alberich* (the malicious dwarf of the Nibelung saga), Ludendorff admitted, "The decision to retreat was not reached without a painful struggle. It implied a confession of weakness. . . . But as it was necessary for military reasons we had no choice. . . . The retirement proved in a high degree remunerative."

Yet it was not easy fo the Germans to destroy the homes and orchards of the people with whom they had billeted for two and a half years. "He wept when he told me that the village was to be destroyed," one native said. And as the German tide receded it laid bare the hidden backwash of war. Seldom in history has an area been found so demolished, its inhabitants so improverished. One correspondent who entered the area was first struck by the young French mothers with flaxen-haired babies of German fathers. Was this too the result of atrocities? And the answer was, " 'They had no need to use violence in their way of love-making. There were many volunteers.' They rubbed their thumbs and fingers together as though touching money and said, 'You understand?' "

But as to the matter of Nivelle's attack, even he had to admit that affairs had somewhat altered. "The retirement of the enemy on the front of the Fifth British

Army constitutes a new fact," he announced in a directive to Haig rather less than brilliant in scope. But he was not alarmed. "On the contrary, the so-called Hindenburg position is so disposed that the directions of our principal attacks . . . will outflank it and take it in reverse. In this respect the German retirement may be entirely to our advantage." Therefore he decided "not to modify in any fundamental way the general plan of operations already settled." The more matters changed, it seems, the more they remained the same. Was it possible that in the face of these new facts Nivelle could still be right?

Yet the situation as it now stood was at least disconcerting. It would take two months even to bring up railroads, roads, supplies, and men through the ruined area. Even then, Nivelle would only be in a position to move against the strongest fortified defensive system on the Western Front. On the other hand, the only other sectors where an attack could be mounted without delay were on the flanks of the abandoned area. Thus there would have to be two disconnected assaults. This was not at all what Nivelle or anyone else had envisioned. On March 12 the massive German retirement began in earnest. Machine gunners stayed behind to slow the gingerly advance of Allied troops. A handful of picked men with rifles, flares, and mortars rushed up and down the deserted trenches to give the impression of substantial forces still in position. And, for better or for worse, the Allied follow-up was so slow that the methodical enemy retreat was consummated by the end of the month with the most trifling of losses.

Nivelle's reaction to this basic dislocation of his plan was an intensified show of bravado. He began by stating that "if he had whispered orders to Hindenburg, the latter could not have better executed what he desired." Though he was now faced with attacking a nearly impregnable line with a mere collection of three armies, he briskly predicted "Laon in twenty-four hours and then the pursuit." When told about a third line of German trenches behind the other two in Champagne he retorted, "Don't be anxious, you won't find a German in those trenches, they only want to be off!" He would break through with "insignificant loss." When his top general (Micheler) suggested caution, Nivelle refused even to discuss the point beyond commenting, "You won't find any Germans in front of you." Across the years these loom as the sentiments of a person divorced from reality.

The incredulity of Pétain, Haig, Robertson, Painlevé, and even his own generals only spurred Nivelle on to a greater frenzy of optimism and activity. On April 1 he told Micheler:

The character of violence, of brutality and of rapidity must be maintained. It is in the speed and surprise caused by the rapid and sudden eruption of our infantry upon the third and fourth positions that the success of the rupture will be found. No consideration should intervene of a nature to weaken the élan of the attack.

Yet, as caustically suggested by Churchill, in war a commander though absorbed in his own plans must at times take the enemy into consideration. Painlevé tried to reason with his man. Let bygones be bygones, he begged, and pointed out, "A new situation ought to be considered with a new eye." Don't consider it a sign of weakness to reconsider; bear in mind, he said in effect, not only the German retreat but the imminent American entry, the Russian revolution, the threatening state of affairs on the Italian front.

The general would not yield. The German retirement played into his hands, he said. Concerning the Plateau of Craonne, "he had it in his pocket" and only feared that the Germans would run away before being demolished. And if they tried to reinforce their troops they would only lose that many more. After three days and about eighteen miles of pursuit the French might pause for breath on the Serre River, but "it would be difficult to hold the troops back once they got started."

Meanwhile high French officers were secretly transmitting to the new Minister of War their professional opinions that the impending operation was no longer practical. The commanding generals of his three army groups—Pétain being one—openly stated that the concept of a breakthrough then and there was out of the question. Painlevé was now distraught. He decided to try once more to stop Nivelle, and for this purpose summoned a conference at the War Ministry April 3 which included himself, the commander in chief, and several Cabinet members. There, laboriously and meticulously, Painlevé spelled out all the objections to Nivelle's offensive.

The latter replied in character. He would not abandon the attack, though the politicians were invited to abandon him instead, if they preferred. "Under no pretext will I recommend a Somme battle," he insisted. Everything would be over successfully (or otherwise, theoretically speaking) within two days.

Was he not aware that to capture the third and fourth positions he first had to capture the first and second?

Naturally; and he smiled. Did they think him a child?

What about leaks of information to the enemy?

Exaggerated. The Germans knew nothing of importance regarding his intentions. Surprise would be achieved. The front would be ruptured—brusquely, inevitably, and in great depth.

Confronted by such confidence, the politicians morosely surrendered. The meeting appears to have been sulphurous. General Sir Henry Wilson, gossip-monger and go-between, discusses it at length in his diary:

> I hear that the Government, aided by Pétain, wanted to force Nivelle to abandon his great offensive and have a small one instead. Nivelle stood firm and won. What time of day for such a proposal, and Haig not consulted. . . . Nivelle listened for some time and then weighed in by remarking that there were so many C. in C.s that he was confused, but as C. in C. he would not tolerate the present state of affairs, and

would do as he pleased or resign . . . but I am quite
clear that, if our coming offensive does not succeed or
is only moderately successful, the politicians will un-
load Nivelle. What a scurvy crowd. I then discussed
Foch having been sent to Italy on Thursday. . . .
The whole thing is a mess.

As of April 3, the Nivelle assault became a final certainty. Yet in truth the plan was far from unique. Substantially it was a reincarnation of Joffre and the
Somme, conceived on the model of the local battle for
Fort Douaumont in the naïve hope that what had
worked on a small scale could be duplicated in a grand
offensive. Furthermore, Nivelle planned to extend the
front of the assault to include certain sectors so formidable that even Joffre had taken care to avoid them in
his plans for 1917. Thus, in the words of Winston
Churchill, "the effect of the Nivelle alterations upon
the Joffre plan was to make it larger, more violent,
more critical, and much later." The Germans could not
be touched at all for the seventy miles between the
south of Arras and Soissons. This left only the marvel-
ously fortified neighborhood astride Arras itself and
around Champagne. And, as we know, the element of
surprise was even less than before the Somme offensive
had been kicked off. This Nivelle must have known,
for he had been told a dozen times exactly how his detailed plans had fallen into enemy hands.

The obstinacy with which he persisted was to some
extent induced by two subordinate officers. Primarily

there was a certain Colonel d'Alenson, his chief of staff, who had Nivelle's ear just as Brigadier General John Charteris had Haig's. Unfortunately d'Alenson was in the last stages of consumption, had very little time to live, and wished to be the architect of a supreme gamble for victory before he died.

This tall, sullen sliver of a man had determined to risk his reputation and country on a last throw of the dice. Ceaselessly and autocratically he spurred on his chief and other French professionals. To a divisional general he frigidly stated, pointing to a map, "We shall advance there, there, and there, and then there we are!"

"And if we fail, what then?"

"Well, if we fail, we will throw our hands in."

Then there was General Charles Mangin, Nivelle's sharpest sword and most dangerous fighting commander, swarthy and flamboyant—the Hero to some, the Butcher to others. Reckless, defiant, teeth white and eyes flashing, the true unsung hero of Verdun as a mere brigadier, the epitome of the offensive, he would command the vital Sixth French Army. Nivelle seems to have feared and reversed this brutal, competent man who dragged him willingly into battle.

Thus the trio Nivelle-d'Alenson-Mangin, not one of whom was a balanced individual at the moment, drove forward to the fray against the warnings of every competent civil and military leader in the Allied camp. Now events began to unfold in a grim pattern.

The British moved first. In a gale of sleet on April 9, Easter Monday, the Third Army under Allenby attacked at Arras with the aim of distracting the German reserves from Champagne. Behind a curtain of artillery and gas shells which smothered the enemy batteries, Canadian and Highland troops quickly captured the entire Vimy Ridge. Then the advance began to slow down against hardening resistance; also a traffic jam developed in the British rear which snarled the movement of men, guns, and supplies, and furnished a vulnerable target for heavy German guns. Though Allenby kept the pressure on for weeks, nothing more could be gained, and the casualties kept mounting. Yet by the standards of the Western Front at that time, the battle of Arras was successful. The Germans had been kept busy for the moment. They had lost three to six miles in depth, 14,000 prisoners, and 180 guns; and the English press was as enthusiastic as though a major triumph had been achieved.

On April 11 the edge was blunted by the failure (also a success in the newspapers) of General Gough's Fifth Army at Bullecourt, an operation conducted by Australians and concerning which the Australian *Official History* says:

> Everyone was aware that the 4th Australian Division had been employed in an experiment of extreme rashness, persisted in by the army commander after repeated warnings, and that the experiment had failed with shocking loss. . . . The gross blunders of the

general plan . . . have, indeed, never found a defender. . . . It was indeed employed by British in-
structors afterwards as an example of how an attack
should not be undertaken.

In this small enterprise the artillery failed, the tanks
got lost, the division lost 3000 men, gained no ground,
and inflicted minimum losses upon the enemy. From
this day on it became traditional among Australians to
hate General Gough. It was not the first time the staff
work of the Fifth Army had collapsed in a welter of
airy inefficiency, nor would it be the last. When Haig
was told by a friend "of the opinions concerning
Gough that were widespread in the army, he curtly in-
timated that he wished to hear nothing on that subject." The course of this battle and the statement
quoted have a bearing, as will be seen, on future events
of greater significance.

On Monday, April 16, General Nivelle finally had
his day. It began to rain just before zero hour. Cold
showers slashed against the crouched Frenchmen in
their trenches and the colored Senegalese, "France's
colonial children," who waited apathetically beside
the whites for the signal to go over the top. If there had
been the slightest question of surprise up to now, it
existed no longer; a protracted artillery bombardment
had alerted the Germans once and for all so that again
the French infantrymen were faced with the bleak
prospect of walking forward almost helplessly against

thousands of intact German field and machine guns.

The first sour taste of things to come occurred soon: the Senegalese broke and ran, even boarding hospital trains to speed their departure. In general the offensive proved immediately to be a fiasco. By dusk, along the main front, six hundred yards had been gained. Nivelle had predicted six miles. The essential advance of Mangin's Sixth Army was stopped cold. Other French armies, plus the British Third and Fifth, made small headway.

That evening French communiqués were studiously vague. They stressed enemy resistance and inexcusably bad terrain. Such phrasing was always a portent that things were going badly and would probably get worse. Sir Douglas Haig inferred as much, and before going to bed noted in his diary that "the much talked of victory has not been gained by the French to date. It is a pity that Nivelle was so very optimistic as regards breaking the enemy's line."

The Germans had been ready except in one flank sector where the decision to attack had been made at the last moment, and where a tangible gain had been achieved. German machine guns had been the primary instrument in cutting the French attack to shreds. Several counterattack divisions had been positioned through a fifteen-mile depth, and had gone into operation on a time-table basis. Light batteries—and this was the crucial maneuver—had been temporarily drawn back out of the range of the French counter-batteries, and were rapidly wheeled into position when the perfect moment came. And, finally, the German troops, in superb morale and fighting trim, had proved that the assumption to the contrary had been a delusion.

Sir Henry Wilson, liaison officer between the French and British, wrote Haig that the French

will look about them for some excuse, one of them will be that the whole German Army is facing them, and that we have not succeeded in easing their load! This would be pure French, *i.e.*, the woman's side of their nature, wounded vanity, jealousy and disappointment at their own failure and our success. I don't think luckily that the French losses are very heavy.

Wilson was wrong. By Tuesday Nivelle had lost almost 120,000 men. His maximum penetration was two miles. Over 20,000 German prisoners were taken, and the enemy had suffered only about twice that number in other casualties. Overnight Nivelle changed his tune and tried to convert the operation into one with more modest aims. But it was not humanly possible to forget his previous boasts. General Wilson wrote in his diary (in that war everybody seemed to keep a diary) that

Nivelle will fall and that we will certainly have Pétain here. Painlevé will certainly aim toward that. At 4 o'clock I went to see Foch who had just come back from Italy. We had a long talk. Foch was clear that Nivelle was done, owing chiefly to the failure of the Sixth Army. Foch said that he knew that the positions

which this army was told to attack were impossible—
and after what I saw yesterday I agree. He thinks
. . . Pétain [will be] put in his place, who will play
a waiting game. . . .

For once a prediction of Wilson's came true, and
sooner than even he might have expected. Lightning
rumors flashed everywhere in France that Nivelle's
casualties had been twice the real number. The troops
felt that they had been betrayed by callous generals,
that the preparations had been slipshod, that they had
been sent forward on a gamble to almost certain doom.
They learned that nearly everyone else in authority
had known that Nivelle's scheme was hopeless, and
yet had allowed him to proceed with it. Surely this was
too much to swallow. The reaction was swift and was
directed not only against the generals but against the
Government and the war itself.

Trouble began on May 3 when the 21st Division of
Colonial Infantry refused duty. The ringleaders were
arrested. Two days later the division went back into
action (Nivelle was still attacking) and was almost
wiped out. It was the first thunderclap in a stormy sky.
The 120th Infantry Regiment rebelled next. Attempts
to arrest the leaders of the insubordination failed this
time. To the entreaty of their frantic colonel the reply
was, "We'll never enter the trenches again." Within a
week mutinies had spread to sixteen army corps. Regiments began to unfurl red flags and to present written
lists of conditions which would have to be met before

they would fight again, including amnesty clauses for the instigators. The Government and the military command refused to negotiate. In general the mutinies took place only when the troops were ordered back into the front lines. Their views were expressed in such statements as "We'll defend the trenches, but we won't attack," and "We are not so stupid as to march against undamaged machine guns!"

The fighting units elected councils to speak for them. Entire regiments left for Paris en masse, singing and firing off their weapons, to demand a negotiated peace and to voice other demands. Secret Service reports to French headquarters concerning the state of affairs at the front became panicky in tone.

One regiment being led to the front went docilely enough, but persisted in baa-ing like sheep to indicate that they were lambs being driven to slaughter. When reprimanded by their commanding officer, the mutineers simply returned to the rest billets from which they had come. An artillery regiment tried to blow up the Schneider-Creusot munitions works. One general was severely beaten. Unit after unit refused duty, and 21,174 Frenchmen deserted outright. Officers who tried to use force on the recalcitrant men were killed or beaten. Trains were derailed. Strikes and riots broke out in the domestic interior. A total of fifty-four divisions—at least three-quarters of a million fighting men —were involved.

Meanwhile fact-finding committees of Deputies

gathered like vultures at the front. The affair was converted by opposition spokesmen into a political football, and the scandal in most of its details began to filter back to Paris. Painlevé (he was at his wit's end) estimated that out of the sixteen divisions on the Champagne front only two remained loyal. Some trenches were hardly manned at all.

Of all this the Germans remained generally ignorant, so closely was the secret kept from them. They heard rumors but discounted them, and when complete facts reached them later via Switzerland it was too late for them to act. In his memoirs Painlevé wrote:

> Resentment among the troops against the staff, and particularly against G.H.Q., became pronounced. . . . There were daily quarrels between the infantry, the artillery and the airmen, the former reproaching the latter for having massacred them or left them to be massacred. The French Army has never passed through so formidable a crisis.

A French official report claims that sixty per cent of the men engaged in revolutionary acts of "indiscipline" were drunk. One is entitled to doubt this interpretation. Some of the finest units in the French Regular Army took part, and it is clear from the calculated, rational color of the demonstrations that far more than wine had produced the debacle.

Whatever the reasons, it was plain that France was finished for the moment as a fighting force and possibly even incapable of defending herself against a major attack. It was also obvious that General Robert Nivelle's brief candle of glory had flickered out. Within thirty-six hours after the attack had started, Haig had already received a worried note from Lloyd George. What should be done, he asked, if the French War Cabinet advised Nivelle to cease fighting? Haig replied that he himself would continue the pressure insofar as this was possible, provided that the French could cooperate at least to some extent. Painlevé himself even went so far as surreptitiously to ask the recommendations of Sir Douglas concerning Nivelle's future and his possible successor. Haig refused to commit himself, though the French War Minister tried to coax him into suggesting Pétain.

Premier Alexandre Ribot also visited Haig that hectic day—April 26—"a tall, old man of eighty years of age," Haig scribbled in his diary, "a dear old thing, but I should think too old to deal with those tricky French politicians." He too inquired casually about Pétain's merits, but again Haig hedged. The assets of Pétain were, of course, common knowledge and the civilians were seeking moral support rather than confirmation of their views. Pétain too, had made his reputation at Verdun as a methodical planner. He was a cold man, sardonic, logical, contemptuous of democratic devices, but genuinely sympathetic toward the sufferings of the French ground forces. As to offensive spirit, this he had only when he thought the occasion warranted it, which was seldom. It was a foregone conclusion that Pétain would take over. He was the perfect man for the job. Painlevé named him chief of the general staff on April 28. Shortly Nivelle was asked to resign as commander in chief.

A disreputable and tragic scene followed at French GHQ. What had happened was all the fault of Generals Mangin and Micheler, protested Nivelle. Let *them* resign. In bitterness and fury they berated Nivelle in turn. The shouting could be heard by everyone through the closed doors; they accused him of moral cowardice; they poured scorn on him; they screamed at him. Nivelle nearly fainted. Without a further word in defense he tottered out. On May 15 Pétain succeeded him.

Next month Colonel d'Alenson died, arrogant gambler to the last—"a Napoleon devoid of genius."

Meanwhile the new commander was taking prudent steps to end the French decay. Twenty-three mutineers were officially shot. Two hundred and fifty were marched to a quiet sector and annihilated by their artillery. Over a hundred ringleaders were banished to various French colonies. Especially mutinous units were sent to the most dangerous fronts. Pétain himself undertook laborious personal measures. For months on end he visited the front lines by automobile and talked to the men, promised better conditions of service, and especially of leave, and in the rest camps, and assured both officers and privates that there would be

no more bloodletting of the type which had characterized French generalship in the past. When he was
done he had visited a hundred divisions and the
French Army was back on the road toward self-respect
and fighting spirit. For the first time, the average poilu
felt that in this stern patriarch he had a leader inter-
ested not only in victory but in the lives of his countrymen at the front. Incessantly Pétain said, "We must
wait for the Americans and the tanks." The French
troops took heart, went on leave in huge numbers (to
the disgust of Haig and Robertson), rested, and were
replenished by a flow of younger classes. But it would
be many a month before the armies of France would
again participate in a grand offensive in the grand old
way—perhaps many a year, perhaps never.

Haig's reaction to all this was anything but poignant. He remarks in his diary that as to Nivelle "some
suitable post, probably Russia, will be found for him."
He advised Ribot (perhaps too gracefully) that he
"had no knowledge of what Nivelle was supposed to
have failed in" and, he might doubtless have added,
very little interest. His main concern, of which he
writes Robertson, is that "pressure on the German
Army must not be relaxed in the meantime. This seems
to me of first importance for the success of *our* plan."
Therefore, he wrote the War Cabinet on May 1,
the French should take back those sections of the
front which the British had manned during Nivelle's
offensive.

The French had fought, failed, and fallen back, just as Haig had anticipated. Now it was the British turn—a little late, but was not late better than never? The question seemed to answer itself, but was it to prove quite that simple?

5. The Interlude

ARLY 1917 would have been a splendid time to stop the war. Both sides were exhausted. A military stalemate existed. The causes of the conflict were demonstrably trivial and implausible; one is reminded of Orwell's *1984*, in which the people no longer remembered why they were fighting but only knew that they had to continue. Certainly the war which had begun in 1914 had little enough to do with the welfare of the ordinary people of Europe, who could scarcely hope to benefit through victory in riches, security, culture, pleasure, social advancement, or in any other way. Those called upon to fight and die, to work, to be maimed, to be made homeless and bereaved were instructed to do so (in effect) with no clear explanation of the need for such sacrifices. From the purely nationalistic interest of each belligerent nation the war had to be won; but, since these interests turned on technical considerations of military prestige, economic power, and governing ideology, mostly other arguments of a more melo-dramatic nature were put forward. Thus the British and French and Russians were instructed concerning the mad Kaiser seeking world conquest, sadistic robot-like Junkers, bloodthirsty Bavarians whose sport it was to bayonet Belgian babies, and goose-stepping Huns ready to march in and take over London, Moscow, Paris, and the inhabitants thereof. Correspondingly, the common citizens of the Central Powers were stimu-lated by fables concerning revenge-crazy French politicians, bloodthirsty Sikhs, the demented monk Rasputin, savage black Moroccans seeking blond Teutonic Fräuleins, the British King plotting to dis-member Germany so that the Empire could continue to gorge itself on profits, and so on.

The propaganda was in the vein of the Old Testa-ment. People were warned by their rulers with stories of sundry fates worse than death unless the enemy were crushed. There was remarkably little promise of happiness or even loot upon the achievement of vic-tory; only its negative rewards were stressed. Yet all the people of Europe had embarked on the struggle three years previously more or less willingly, fairly convinced that they were the victims of aggression, that their lives would be miserable if their country was defeated, and that the motives of their rulers were pure. Even the intellectuals and international social-ists, by and large, were convinced—often more fanati-cally so than ordinary patriots.

By mid-1917 all this had worn terribly thin. Fortunately for the sanity of the military commanders, a caste anything but schizoid in nature, their duty was one-sidedly clear. It was Haig's job, for example, simply to fight the war on the Western Front and if possible to win it there. To do this he needed an aggressive plan promising decisive results, and this he was certain that he had.

Long before Nivelle's failure, before the Chantilly conference, before the Somme campaign, and even before Verdun, Douglas Haig had determined to attack the Germans in the Belgian province of Flanders in an offensive mounted primarily by British arms and centering around the salient at Ypres, some thirty miles from the Channel coast. Since late 1914 the eyes of many other Allied planners had been fixed upon northwest Belgium as a focus of operations, primarily to clear the twenty-eight-mile strip of Belgian coastline held by the enemy. If this could be accomplished two large advantages would be gained. The ports of Ostend, Zeebrugge, and Blankenberghe would be wrested from the German Navy—its submarine facilities in particular. In addition, if an Allied army could be based on the coast in a position to move east, the main German mass would find itself between the two arms of a giant nutcracker, the other being the existing Western Front. As early as December 1914, Winston Churchill had suggested a combined naval-military operation along these lines; but at the time the French were too busy defending Paris, and the British could not handle it alone.

A year later a similar plan was again suggested by the Admiralty, and now it was that Haig seriously turned his attention to it for the first time. It struck him immediately that the potential there was far more interesting than in the ponderous Franco-British campaign on the Somme then being considered. Unfortunately there were drawbacks. The Belgians had flooded the lower Yser shortly after the war had begun, and this entire area was still under water. Between the flood and the Channel lay only two miles of sand dunes. That was too narrow a frontage, Haig considered, for a blow of the magnitude that would be needed. Although Belgian experts replied that the Yser area could be drained off, they admitted that a month of dry weather would have to ensue before troops could operate on it. In turn this meant that the Germans would have a month of clear warning that an attack was coming at exactly that point.

The British field marshal therefore decided to drop that approach. Why not, he suggested, first attack from the Ypres salient and capture the vital ridges that surrounded it? After that the British would turn west, the French and Belgians on the coast would advance, and the amphibious maneuver would be launched.

This variation of the plan seemed an improvement, and it also possessed the bonus, if successful, of delivering the British from their death trap in the salient, where they were half surrounded and taking 7000 casualties per week for not the slightest purpose or advantage. Haig set the wheels in motion in a directive dated January 7, 1916, and throughout the balance of that year various Army commanders and Navy officers toiled dutifully at the detailed planning. Meanwhile the giant battles of Verdun and the Somme were fought, and throughout 1916 the Flanders offensive smoldered only in the brain of the British commander and his subordinates, awaiting the proper time to flare into action. Again it saw the light of day at the Chantilly conference in November, and again it was brushed aside while Nivelle tried his experiment. By the time Nivelle had failed, the Flanders scheme had developed into something of an obsession with the British commander. It was a year and a half since his tenacious mind had adopted it, and now there was to be no stopping its execution.

As time went on, the need for clearing the Germans out of Belgium had indeed become chronic. There was the aforementioned matter of the North Sea coastline. It was most embarrassing for the Germans to be holding even a small part of it. In doing so, despite the British Navy, they were able to menace coastal shipping not only with destroyers but with aircraft based near there, with great land-based guns, and with their smaller submarines. (An all-time record of 800,000 tons of British shipping had been sunk by U-boats in April.) Psychologically, to deliver the Belgians from under the heel of their conqueror was natural and almost instinctive. And what if the Germans should manage to advance even farther along the coast at some future time—perhaps as far as Callais, just opposite Dover? That prospect in particular was worrisome to the British mind.

Thus, in proposing operations along the coast, Haig or any other Allied chief was certain to get a sympathetic hearing from the British War Cabinet Committee.

Haig had other motives. Alone among the British, except for a few liaison officers, he thoroughly knew of the nearly complete collapse of French morale, and feared a serious breakthrough if the Germans were to attack Pétain's line. He was determined not to give them that chance. His summary is best described in his diary, May 1:

> Success seems reasonably possible. It will give valuable results on land and sea. If full measure of success is not gained, we shall be attacking the enemy on a front where he cannot refuse to fight, and our purpose of wearing him down will be given effect to. We shall be directly covering our own most important communications, and even a partial success will considerably improve our defensive positions in the Ypres salient. This is necessary in order to reduce the heavy wastage which must occur there next winter as in the past, if our troops hold the same positions.

The idea of simply withdrawing from the salient had been under discussion for two years; it was repugnant to Haig and almost everyone else on political and psychological grounds.

It is also beyond question that subjective factors existed. Since 1914 Haig had seen Foch, Joffre, and Nivelle successively fail to win the war in grand offensives under their personal banners. Now it was his turn to try. Intensely religious, he felt that God would favor his design. It had been said, too, that with Haig optimism was not merely a state of mind but a matter of policy. Supernatural aid aside, he was confident of victory. And behind a grim façade, this silent Lowland Scot dreamed, as any man would, of the glory that would accrue to him if he could win where his predecessors had lost. Finally there was Haig's patriotism; for he hoped to break through with British troops for the glory of the Empire before the Americans arrived.

In all these not unreasonable ambitions Haig had the backing of the Chief of the Imperial General Staff, Sir William Robertson. Together this powerful combination moved toward their objective, sometimes subtly with the moral support of the King (who disliked Lloyd George), sometimes blatantly with the propaganda of the Northcliffe press, sometimes directly by means of head-on verbal offensives against the politicians, and on occasion by less normal devices.

The trouble was that the plan had imperceptibly shifted. A coastal attack was one thing, but when it was abandoned, in effect, for yet another onslaught against the main German defenses on the Western Front, that was something else. The new concept did look suspiciously like another Somme. True, there would be amphibious and coastal operations later, but these were conditional upon victory farther south. And could success really be achieved at Ypres? Certain generals were already dubious. Primarily they feared the terrain. Years ago it had been a veritable swamp; through centuries of toil its inhabitants had converted it into farm land by a complex system of ditches, drains, and canals. This delicate maze might be ruined by a prolonged artillery bombardment, nor was it conceivable that troops could advance without such an advance barrage. Matters could be worsened by the heavy, invariable summer rains. It was evident to Haig and Robertson that their politicians would require some convincing, for the offensive would require the sanction of the British War Cabinet. Yet where else could Haig attack? Assuming that the Western Front would be the main theater of operations in 1917, what alternative existed? The case for Haig was summarized methodically by Henry Wilson:

1. Somme—i.e. wearing down the Boches.
2. Verdun—i.e. whirlwind attack.
3. Pétain—i.e. do nothing.

We have tried 2 (Verdun), which has been a complete failure. There remains Somme and Pétain. To my mind the Pétain plan is one to be avoided, and a Somme, with intelligence, is our only chance.

But where? Certainly not on the Somme again, for a dozen sundry reasons, including the assumption of employing British troops in the main onslaught. On the Arras-Vimy front? That would not be worth while, because the French could not cooperate properly; furthermore (as of the moment) Allenby had just been stopped there. The Lens sector? Haig's staff ruled that out; the entire neighborhood was so broken up by houses and little towns that the defense would have an unfair advantage. In the center, along the Aubers ridge? But British troops in that narrow position were too limited in scope to make the theater attractive for a major operation. So Haig and his supporters decided, somewhat lamely, that it would have to be the salient at Ypres "by a process of exclusion."

In truth, the theoretical possibilities there were exhilarating. If they could get to the Holland coast, their communications would be shortened, and without any great prolongation of the British line the entire German position might easily be turned. Then the key would be the Liége gap, that narrow route between the Ardennes and south Holland through which ran a great railroad; from this, in turn, fanned out all the smaller lines which supplied the German armies from the Aisne to the Channel. With these rails captured, a grand German retreat was inevitable. Primarily it all rested on the advance from the salient to Ostend— "only" thirty miles, as the adverb of Haig's planners had it. Was such a gain possible in 1917? To Robertson and Haig it seemed well worth the gamble.

Just before Lloyd George replaced Asquith as Prime Minister the latter had sent a memorandum to William Robertson which contained this sentence:

The War Committee were absolutely unanimous on the very great desirability, if it is practicable, of some military action designed either to occupy Ostend and Zeebrugge, or at least to render those ports useless as bases for destroyers and submarines.

Dated November 21, 1916, the message was interpreted by the General as something resembling official approval. However, it must be observed that the draft was unfinished and unsigned, and intended only for the information of the chief of staff. It merely asked him to "report" to Asquith "at an early date what action you consider feasible." Plainly these were not formal instructions. As it happened, no report followed, and Mr. Asquith left office two weeks later. And the reference, finally, was to a coastal maneuver— not to an attack at Ypres.

Sensing that the document was not enough to commit Asquith's successor, Robertson made haste to nail down matters more firmly. On December 1 he wrote Joffre:

> . . . my Government desire that the occupation of Ostend and Zeebrugge should form one of the objectives of the campaign next year. I am accordingly instructing Sir Douglas Haig to place himself in communication with you with a view to this operation being given a place in the general plans of operations for next year, and the necessary preparations being made to carry it out.

General Herbert Plumer, commander of the British Second Army at Ypres, had always wanted to relieve his vulnerable position there by winning the Messines-Wytschaete ridge dominating the salient to the south-east.This he envisioned as a purely limited operation, complete in itself. When he was told of the new grand plan, he balked. The ground was unsatisfactory, he pointed out, and the offensive might bog down with heavy losses. In reply, Lieutenant General Kiggell, Haig's chief of staff, deprecated Plumer's thinking, insisted that surprise and mobile operations were possible, and ordered him to recast his scheme by January 31 along broader lines. Two weeks later these instructions to Plumer were repeated and elaborated upon. None of these documents was shown to Lloyd George or other members of the War Committee. Throughout that winter and early spring great military preparations went forward in Flanders; and while the politicians knew of them vaguely they were not aware of their exact significance. Thus events proceeded through the Nivelle affair; and now followed a spate of conferences and conversations. Let us consider the sequence. . . .

First the War Cabinet met May 1 in an air of gloom brought about by the failure of the French at Champagne, and by disquieting news that Russian soldiers were already fraternizing with the Germans. Some Cabinet members even talked of making peace, but Lloyd George squelched these views and insisted that the pressure would continue. For the moment he was willing to approve methodical operations on the Western Front in order to keep the enemy off balance.

On May 4 a meeting took place in Paris including Ribot, Painlevé, Nivelle (for momentary decorative purposes), Pétain, Haig, Robertson, Admiral Lord Jellicoe, and Lloyd George. At the outset it was decided that defensive operations would not be considered but that attacks would be made "relentlessly" and "with all available forces." Lloyd George accepted this. But, he said, the French must cooperate on a large scale—not with only a few divisions. Would they pledge to do so? They would, assured Painlevé. As for Lloyd George, he did not pretend to be a military strategist, he said piously, but he felt that the enemy must not be given a moment's rest. "We must go on hitting and hitting with all our strength until the German ended as he always did, by cracking." He would not try to dictate the military scheme, nor (for the sake of secrecy) did he even wish to know its details, but he whole-heartedly accepted the thesis that "it is no longer a question of aiming at breaking through the enemy's front and aiming at distant objectives. It is now a question of wearing down and exhausting the enemy's resistance. . . ." Painlevé readily agreed. He too believed in a continuing offensive, he remarked, provided that it would not be a bloody, futile affair like those of the past.

The talks that day were friendly, and everybody agreed about everything; yet there was an undercurrent of doubt about the French. While only they and Haig knew the whole truth about the state of the

French Army at the moment, Lloyd George inferred that something was wrong. Why were they so reticent about explaining the sudden end of their offensive? he wondered. He found Pétain silent and mysterious. In the corridor later, Pétain came to him and said playfully, "I suppose you think I can't fight."

"No, General," the Prime Minister replied, "with your record I could not make this mistake, but I am certain that for some reason or other you won't fight." Pétain turned away with a smile and said nothing.

Yet it seemed that the conference had cleared the air and that the two Allies were in agreement. While the French never intended to attack on a mass scale, they did agree to the idea of limited offensives for small gains, at a minimum cost in lives, provided that sufficient artillery could be collected at the points in question practically to guarantee such gains. But Haig's private Flanders plan was not that at all; it envisioned a breakthrough on a grand scale—one in which great masses of cavalry would pour through the gaps and reach the Channel coast. Privately Robertson did not share in this expectation, nor was he as uninterested as Haig in the probability (known to both of them) that the French would not cooperate in strength. Nevertheless Haig assumed that the conference gave him sufficient authority to attack in a big way at Ypres. Immediately he advised Pétain that he would continue heavy pressure along the Arras-Vimy front, and that he would move against the Messines ridge early next month with sixteen divisions. And that same day he sent Sir Henry Wilson a plan of operations to transmit to the French. Here, for the first time, he stated to that officer that he would begin his campaign to take Ostend and Zeebrugge in July.

Later in the week Haig held talks at Doullens with his army commanders and divulged the entire Flanders scheme. To the intense disappointment of General Rawlinson (Fourth Army), Haig announced that Gough (Fifth Army) would conduct the main attack, though he had originally told the former that the job was his. Plumer would run the Messines operation; meanwhile Rawlinson was to go into reserve near the coast and prepare to assist the amphibious operation. Also, Haig told them in strict confidence, the French were finished for quite some time to come.

On May 11, Wilson wrote in his diary, "Went to see Pétain. . . . He is opposed to Haig's plans of attacks . . . to big attacks, and favours small fronts and great depths."

The following week Robertson advised Haig that the French, in a written résumé of the May 4 conference, had omitted any reference to their own offensive. This, he warned, "might signify that the French Government, on reflection, had decided not to bind themselves to that resolution."

To clarify the point, Haig consented to arrange a private conference with Pétain for the 18th. The moment they met, the Frenchman took issue with Haig on the scale of the Flanders operation. It was, he said, entirely too grandiose in its aims and went far beyond the previous area of agreement. However, he added, it was vital for the British to keep on attacking; and exactly how and where they did so was not his business. At any rate, he would try to cooperate, and promised to deliver four small attacks starting in June. Haig was satisfied. He found Pétain "businesslike, knowledgeable, and brief of speech. The latter is, I find, a rare quality in Frenchmen!"

Wilson visited Pétain the very next day and was told that "in his opinion, Haig's attack toward Ostend was certain to fail, and that his effort to disengage Ostend and Zeebrugge was a hopeless one."

May 21 Lieutenant Colonel Repington, the military writer, had an informal talk with Robertson at the York House. "I gave him a warning," he writes, "to keep out of Low Country fighting and said that I had warned Foch when he disclosed ideas to me in this sense. I said that you can fight in mountains and deserts, but no one can fight in mud and when the water is let out against you, and, at the best, you are restricted to the narrow fronts on the higher ground, which are very unfavourable with modern weapons." Robertson does not seem to have argued the point, but Repington noted how closely he listened and began to suspect "that some operation in this sense may be in the wind."

On May 23 Henry Wilson wrote in his diary, concerning a letter from Pétain to Haig regarding their talk the previous week, "I object strongly to this answer, both to its tone and to its substance. . . . It absolutely ignores Haig's suggestions as to dates for French offensives. . . . Then he comes to a dead stop, never mentioning any further operations during the autumn. . . . Of course, all this is quite hopeless. There is no sign of combined operations at all." This appears to have been especially annoying to Sir Henry, for, since he was liaison officer between the two Allies, such a non-meeting of minds might be traceable to his own lack of statesmanship. So again he interviewed Pétain and pressed him for more concrete assurances. Why, he asked, had Pétain's commitments seemed to end in July? Without elaborating, Pétain stated that he could promise nothing more.

"Very well, then say so," Wilson replied irritably. Fuming, he left for Paris. There he saw General Foch, and on June 2 recorded the following in his diary:

He wanted to know who it was who wanted Haig to go on "a duck's march through the inundations to Ostend and Zeebrugge." He thinks the whole thing futile, fantastic, and dangerous, and I confess I agree, and always have. Haig always seems to think that when he has got to Roulers and Thourout he has solved the question. So Foch is entirely opposed to this enterprise, Jellicoe not withstanding.

And on June 4 this entry:

I saw this morning the notes made at the conference the day before yesterday. . . . They are disquieting.

The French attack for June 10 is cancelled. . . . The Marshal must understand that no infantry attacks would take place anywhere for at least a month. Gun and aeroplane attacks, yes; but infantry attacks, no. This endorses and underlines all that I have been saying for the last month or more, and I think, and hope, that it will finally dispose of Haig's idea of taking Ostend and Zeebrugge.

None of these objections to Haig's offensive was conveyed to the British War Cabinet Committee. The lack of French cooperation was concealed or minimized. And even Wilson, who had just been strongly prevailed upon by Haig, made light of the French mutinies in his report; they were "not yet serious." Thus Lloyd George and his colleagues at the moment had no reason for qualms over the impending military conduct of the war on the Western Front, nor had they yet been enlightened about the specific offensive Haig was readying in the salient. They knew only that Plumer was about to attack the Messines ridge that overlooked the British position from the south and southeast, and that this "life-saving operation" was expected to begin at any moment.

And on the other side of the front the enemy also waited. Major General Max Hoffmann wrote in his diary:

I am very curious to know what is going to happen in the West. I cannot suppose that the English are going to give up their great offensive without a word or an effort. I think they are going to collect their forces again somewhere else, perhaps in conjunction with a landing. The West is strong enough in reserves to face such an event with equanimity—thanks to the Russian Revolution.

As for Ludendorff and Crown Prince Rupprecht, they were fairly certain of what Hoffmann seems only to have suspected—that the next big blow would be delivered by the British, and that it would be some-where in Flanders. But even by the end of the first week in June, they were not fully aware that the exact locale would be the infamous salient at Ypres.

The fields of Flanders are mostly flat, flatter than the plains of Kansas, flatter than the lowlands of Hungary. On such terrain a ten-foot rise was erroneously consid-ered a military prize worth fighting for. This was once a land of grassy, tree-filled, primeval swamps. Even after three years of war its scrubby desolation still gave the impression of a forest clearing. The plain is part of the one that runs from the Pyrenees to Russia, the only gateway into France which bypasses formid-able mountains and plateaus.

Flanders at any time is a monotonous countryside. There are no landmarks except houses and the gentlest of ridges. Single hills are rare. One of the few is Mount Kemmel, the loftiest peak in all the land, three hun-dred fifty feet high. Rivers and canals wind their way at random, merge into one another, separate, flow toward the ocean, then away from it; for the slope of the ground is too slight to create a normal pattern.

During the rainy seasons the rivers cannot discharge their waters because of the faintness of the gradient. Most of them flood once or more yearly. When they do, they spread their waters far and wide. Many of them have been straightened and canalized. Dikes and drainage watercourses are everywhere and marshes have been generally reclaimed, but still the waters overflow to some extent yearly, especially in the late summer and fall. And in the words of Sir Douglas Haig's Chief of Intelligence,

> Careful investigation of the records of more than 80 years showed that in Flanders the weather broke early each August with the regularity of the Indian monsoon.

The one major exception to the flatness is the famous ridge, an arc of feeble hills and highlands running from some miles north of Passchendaele southward to Messines and then west toward Hazebrouck. Its average elevation is about one hundred fifty feet. Yet the German holders of these modest heights enjoyed a great military advantage not only in observation but in the placement of guns and defensive fortifications.

Since earliest times military offensives have failed in this mild-seeming land because of a physical obstacle not apparent to the glance; for in Flanders the ground is almost pure fine-grained clay, sometimes with a crust of sand on top or a thin coating of loam. In certain places there is no topsoil at all; these clay fields, called clyttes, exist at their worst north of Ypres in the vicinity of the Houthulst Forest. Because of the impervious clay, the rain cannot escape and tends to stagnate over large areas. Unable to soak through, it forms swamps and ponds, and sluggishly spreads toward one of the already swollen rivers or canals. The ground remains perpetually saturated. Water is reached at an average depth of eighteen inches and only the shallowest of puddly trenches can be dug by the troops, reinforced by sandbag parapets. When the topsoil dries during fair weather, it cracks open. The next rain floods the fissures. Then the clay blocks slide upon themselves, causing little landslides.

The problem of terrain has bedeviled military commanders in Flanders throughout history. In the early 1700s Marlborough told how "our armies swore terribly in Flanders." By a curious transposition of numerals, in 1197 Philip Augustus was trapped with his army in the morass southwest of Ypres, and similar frustrations occurred during the days of the Roman conquest. For clay plus water equals mud—not the chalky mud of the Somme battlefield to the south, but gluey, intolerable mud. The British War Office Archives are full of reports in this vein:

"Part of company bogged in communications trench south of St. Eloi; two men smothered."

"Three men suffocated in mud near Voormezeele."

Men had to lie "flat and distribute their weight evenly in order to prevent sinking into the mire."

"The trenches are very wet, and the water is up to the men's knees in most places."

"Trenches full of liquid mud 2 to 3 feet deep."

Men "in pitiable condition coming out of trenches; wet through, caked with stinking mud from head to foot . . ."

When one officer was instructed to consolidate his advance position, he wrote back, "It is impossible to consolidate porridge."

"Trenches full of liquid mud. Smelt horribly. Full of dead Frenchmen too bad to touch. Men quite nauseated."

Everywhere by 1917 the water was contaminated, and the delivery of fresh water was a major operation. The filthy surface wash was locked in by the clay. Rivers and canals were polluted by refuse from the flooded land, and even the artesian wells had become poisoned. The decay and refuse of millions of men, alive and dead, sank into the soil and were carried by the blackened waters throughout the inland plain. These conditions were most severe on the maritime strip west of the Yser, where the land is lower than sea level at high tide. If not for the drains and dikes some sections would be ten feet under water, and, in fact, this had become the precise situation after the Belgians inundated the area in 1914.

In October of that year the salient was formed, after two great offensives hurled at each other simultaneously and ending in stalemate. Next year the Germans won the entire ridge, though not Ypres itself, which now lay in a protruding pocket held stubbornly by the British, who did not realize that in time it would become a suicide trap half surrounded by Germans on the heights above them. For over two years the lines had remained stationary. But the fighting never ended, and innumerable were the tiny battles waged henceforth, mainly for meager topographical advantages. By the spring of 1917 the salient that curved roughly from the Wytschaete-Messines portion of the ridge to Boisinghe was as rigid in its contours as a portrait in stone, feared and hated like death itself by soldiers of the Empire everywhere in the world. Already a fourth of all the British killed on land or sea since the beginning of the war had died here.

In this landscape nothing existed but a measureless bog of military rubble, shattered houses, and tree stumps. It was pitted with shall craters containing fetid water. Overhead hung low clouds of smoke and fog. The very ground was soured by poison gas. Not one building was intact. Only mounds overrun with scrub grass, interspersed with old brick and fragments of wood, showed where many houses had formerly stood.

In the center of this incarnation of ruin lay the dead city of Ypres—"Wipers" it was always called—obliterated, crushed like a pile of discarded baby's toys left out in the rain. Yet this mournful corpse, like a skeleton in a nightmare, seemed to live; for though it no longer possessed a normal spirit it was a turmoil of military activity. The traffic on the roads and in the shattered market place was enormous and without end, though the town was shelled day and night, and since 1914 had been bombed more than any other target on the Western Front, Major General John Monash, commander of the 3rd Australian Division, in a war letter to his wife described the scene thus:

> . . . streams of men, vehicles, motor lorries, horses, mules, and motors of every description, moving ponderously forward, at a snail's pace, in either direction hour after hour, all day and all night, day after day, week after week, in a never halting, never ending stream . . . ploughing its way slowly and painfully through the mud . . . a reek of petrol and smoke everywhere.
>
> Here comes a body of fighting troops, tin-hatted and fully equipped, marching in file into the battle area, to carry out a relief of some front-line division. There follows a string of perhaps one hundred motor lorries, all fully loaded with supplies; a limousine motor-car with some division staff-officer; a string of regimental horse- and mule-drawn vehicles going up to a forward transport park; some motor-ambulance wagons . . . a long string of remount horses, marching in twos . . . a great 12-inch howitzer, dragged by two steam-traction engines, returning from the workshops after repair of injuries received; more infantry, thousands of them; more ambulances, more motor lorries; a long stream of Chinese coolies, smart and of magnificent stature . . . dispatch riders on motor bikes threading their way skilfully between the gaps; a battery of artillery all fully horsed and clattering and jingling; motor lorries again, heavily

loaded with artillery ammunition . . . wagons bringing forward broken stone and road-making materials
. . . a mounted police detachment . . . an "Archie"
(anti-aircraft gun), steam-motor drawn, going to take
up a more forward position . . . a Royal Flying
Corps car carrying parts of aeroplanes to forward
hangars; more ambulances; and so on and on and on
in a never-ending stream.

In the center of the town only two buildings could,
with difficulty, be recognized from out of the past: the
enormous Cloth Hall, epitome of the power of the
ancient merchant guilds of the fourteenth century,
when Ypres was the center of a hand-weaving industry; and the adjacent gothic Cathedral. Their interiors
were open to the sun and the rain. Dense weeds and
grasses waved, field mice scurried, birds built hundreds of nests within the scribbly bombed-out walls.

Ypres was completely surrounded by the remains of
its medieval walls and moat. On the south were the
infantry barracks, on the west the prison, the reservoir,
and the water tower. In and under all these ancient
structures lay a honeycomb of nine hundred dugouts
that housed troops and headquarters.

From the eastern ramparts there issued the Menin
road, past the wrecked Menin Gate and onward to the
front lines. Full of water holes, weeds, and mud, this
was a nightmare path, swept by shrapnel, strafed by
airplanes. By the spring of 1917 hundreds of thousands who still lived could recall it with a pang: its
mess, its muddle, its ceaseless traffic of apathetic men,

sleepy and stumbling, marching in the fine rain that always seemed to characterize the salient. To the north the Dixmude Gate was used for traffic to and from the Poelcapelle and St. Julien areas. The primary artery for transport farther back was the road from Poperinghe ("Pop") to Ypres through Vlamertinghe. Years ago it had passed through long lines of trim little houses and elm trees. Meadows and fields of flax, corn, and hops had blossomed on both sides. Now all this was gone.The houses moldered under the clay, the trees were blackened stumps, the meadows were mud and reeking water. Only the road still existed, for the army had macadamized it and kept it in operation. Now it was lined by thousands of rotting vehicles, guns, equipment, and dead horses.

Other than that pertaining to war, all civilization had long ago left the salient. The last inhabitants had departed early in 1915. Only some stray dogs and cats stayed behind, wild and terrified, still roaming the land where their masters had once lived and played with them in quiet farms and cottages.

Flanders lies at fifty-one degrees north latitude, about a hundred miles relatively north of the United States-Canadian border. Its average mean temperature is about forty-nine degrees. Rain falls on an average of every other day through the year. Fogs drift inland from the coast. Even during peace the climate is not inspiring. This was the countryside where the First and Second Battles of Ypres had been fought to a standstill, and where the Third Battle of Ypres

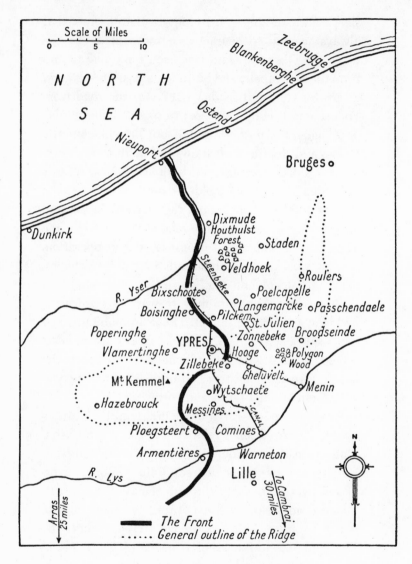

The Flanders Front, June 6, 1917

would soon explode under the calm but relentless guidance of Sir Douglas Haig.

When German cartoonists drew the salient during the war years they usually likened it to the mouth of a skull, the teeth of which were biting down on Ypres. For the British to push farther into the open mouth would leave them in danger of being swallowed up altogether. Plainly it was necessary first to capture the Messines-Wytschaete lower jawbone, and then to proceed up the molars through Broodseinde, Passchendaele, and Westroosebeke. After that would occur the coastal operation under the Navy and Rawlinson's Fourth Army. By June 1917 plans for the attack at Messines were completely and meticulously in readiness; and so was General Sir Herbert Plumer and his Second Army.

6. Triumph at Messines

SIR HERBERT PLUMER's hair had turned white during his two thankless years as warden of the Salient. A heavy responsibility had been his, with no chance for glory, for there was hardly a point within the loop of ground held by his Second Army which German guns could not enfilade or fire into from behind—a state of affairs hardly calculated to improve the nerves of this commander or his troops. Nonetheless he had made of the salient a nut so hard to crack that the enemy had not tried to do so since 1915. An ideal officer to hold any position in bulldog fashion, Plumer was a prim little old man with a pink face, fierce white mustache, blue eyes, a little pot-belly mounted on tiny legs. As he walked, he panted and puffed. Only the dour cast to his mouth hinted at the essential stubbornness of his nature. Yet he liked to give lifts to women and children in his staff car as he toured the Belgian roads behind the front; and he

took childlike delight when troops of his own kind—
Lancaster or London—accomplished anything useful
in battle.

He was fortunate in possessing an efficient chief
of staff, the cultured and wise Major General Sir
Charles ("Tim") Harington—also a cautious planner,
but with, perhaps, an extra dash of imagination and
verve. He was tall and thin, nervous, had a card-index
mind and a sense of humor. The combination of the
two men had proved outstanding in the war to date;
and now they hoped to prove that they could storm an
objective as well as hold one. Surely they had been
allotted more than enough time to get ready. During
the long, lean years while they had hung on, improv-
ing their defenses, not looking for trouble, they had
studied their terrain with microscopic thoroughness.
Of Plumer it was said that "he knew every puddle
in the salient." Plans for capturing the Messines-
Wytschaete ("White Sheet") flank of the ridge had
been endlessly cast and recast in conference after
conference, order after order. By spring 1917 the operation had been worked out with an intensity un-
matched in the war thus far.

Plumer's trump card was a system of enormous land
mines burrowed beneath the German front. This work
had begun in 1915 with the construction of shallow
galleries and small charges about fifteen feet underground. Next year the idea of concentrating on a deep
mining offensive, with tunnels and charges nearly one
hundred feet below the surface, was contemplated.

But to penetrate secretly with galleries of substantial size the saturated, semi-liquid layer that made up the Flanders subsoil was on the face of it quite impossible. Might there be another way?

The problem was studied by Lieutenant Colonel T. Edgeworth David, chief geologist of the BEF, and the engineer in chief, Brigadier General G. H. Fowke, who analyzed sand and clay layers and the variations of water in each. Perhaps, they thought, the layer of heavy blue clay lying even farther down—between eighty and one hundred twenty feet—might be a practical medium for their purpose. At that depth the tunnels and charges could not be blown up, accidentally or otherwise, by mortar fire or shallow counter-mines; and the sound of digging would be so muffled that secrecy might be possible. Under the harried conditions of war, with the time element so important, and specialized heavy equipment so scarce, was it possible to construct such shafts, to lay gigantic charges accurately under the key German front-line positions, within a reasonable time, and without being detected? Though the odds were not good, it was decided to try.

By January 1916 six tunnels had been started (the signs above them read "Deep Wells"); and during the next year twenty of the largest mines in the annals of warfare were in place or in process of being placed. Twenty underground communities came into being. From the sandbagged openings wooden stairs led down to sleeping quarters. Below these, planked passages slanted to headquarters posts and thence to the actual three-by-six galleries. In these bowels of the earth, the molelike character of the war was fantastically intensified. The hum of pumping engines never ceased. The thousands of men who worked here with picks and shovels, coughing in the dampness, white of skin, shoved their tunnels a pitiful ten or fifteen feet forward each day under the glare of electric lamps; and as each gallery was completed a mine was laid in place (sometimes two) containing charges of ammonal up to ninety-five thousand pounds. Some tunnels were almost half a mile in length. By June 7 the total had come to a million pounds of explosive and amost five miles of gallery.

Meanwhile the Germans were also mining toward the British lines, but in a smaller way and much more shallowly, for they had neither the equipment nor the plan for deep works possessed by their enemy. Yet in places they did venture to considerable depths—sometimes nearly sixty feet down—and many was the time when the British, listening with microphones at the forward, boarded-up faces of their galleries, heard with dismay a German tunnel approaching their own. Early in 1917 the enemy had dug within eighteen inches of the British at the northern corner of the ridge.

A colonel came to Harington with the news and recommended that the mine be blown. Harington thought for a moment, walked to Plumer's door, knocked, and entered.

" 'Mines' says we must blow the Hill Sixty mines today."

"I won't have them blown," snapped the general. "Good night."

Work stopped, the British evacuated the tunnel, and by chance the Germans veered away.

The enemy knew that the ridge would soon be attacked. Preparations above ground were obvious, and they had captured many prisoners who had talked. One specifically told them on May 29 that the assault would begin June 7 after eight days of bombardment. But what about the mines, the only element of real surprise? The Boches had their suspicions. While they did not greatly fear the small, shallow charges they had become apprehensive concerning deep mining. They sent out many raiding parties primarily to bring back not prisoners but samples of the soil thrown up by diggings. On April 9 one of these parties returned with blue clay. While this was a sure sign that the British were constructing at least one mine at great depth, the Germans reacted inconsequentially, assuming evidently that the shaft was only an isolated one (if it existed at all), and that, since the attack was so imminent, little further mining could be accomplished by the British in the brief time remaining.

To the British it seemed doubtful that their opponents could not know of the twenty deep mines. Certainly, they thought, some prisoners had disclosed them by now. (Not one had done so.) Surely the Germans had been able to hear the work going on, despite many soundproofing measures. (They had not, due to the inferiority of their microphones.) For once even Sir Douglas Haig seems to have been troubled by nervousness. His greatest fear was that the enemy might abandon his front lines just before the attack, a suggestion in fact made by Lieutenant General von Kuhl, Crown Prince Rupprecht's chief of staff, early in May. But this projected withdrawal, which would have dislocated Haig's plan even worse than the one which upset Nivelle, was rejected by Rupprecht. The blow to morale would be too great, he estimated, if such an outstanding defensive sector were to be discarded without a fight. It could and would be held. As for British mining, the Germans had rather decided by May that it had ended, except for small efforts of no importance. Only at Hill 60 was it definitely known that the British were still digging in earnest, and here, according to the German officer in charge, their work had been hopelessly damaged by countermining. Thus misled by faulty Intelligence, the Crown Prince could not see how the clear and aboveboard preparations of the enemy could possibly succeed.

Accordingly on June 1 he caused the XIX Army Corps to issue an order concerning Wytchaete and Messines:

> These strong-points must not fall even temporarily into the enemy's hands. . . . They must be held to the last man even if the enemy has cut them off on both sides, and threatens them from the rear.

Furthermore, the German troops were told that they need have no fear of a breakthrough. Reserves were already in place and would move in swiftly to seal off any gaps that might occur. In these orders and reassurances the opposing high command clearly showed the value they placed on the east and south ridges of their precious encirclement.

So Haig's one great worry was baseless; the Germans would stay put and make their stand. Not knowing this, he recommended in a conference on May 30 that all mines be exploded before zero day; next the troops would occupy the ground; and later they would try to cross over the crest of the ridge. He also suggested moving the target date forward a day or two. Plumer begged to reject these last-minute changes, and Haig agreed to let matters go forward on schedule.

The trepidation of the British is understandable. The greatest series of simultaneous explosions in history was about to take place (it would triple the former record set in New York during subway construction late in the 1800s). Hundreds of thousands of men had been working toward this one day for over two years. The immensity, the importance of the operation was incalculable. And it all hung on the feeblest of threads. One British private soldier taken prisoner could have nullified it. German detection devices could have been alert to the entire plan for months. Airplane observation might have detected any number of blue-clay diggings, despite efforts to camouflage them as they were hauled to the rear. How much did the Germans know? From Haig on down, the British would have sold their souls for an answer.

The very fact that German countermining continued was noteworthy, even though most of these efforts were at shallow levels. In one place the Germans were known to be digging along a line that was bound to intersect the British gallery. Again this was near (or rather under) Hill 60, where the most spectacular mining, countermining, and mine fighting took place. The state of affairs was later described:

> . . . on May 9th the enemy was so near that work was stopped, and the branch gallery was loaded with 1600 lb. of ammonal. The Germans had evidently completed their shaft and were driving a gallery past the end of the branch gallery. As, however, there was only a month to go, and the *camouflet* (a small defensive charge which ruins the enemy tunnel but does not open the surface of the ground) might detonate the great mine, or at least cause the Germans to probe vigorously, it was decided that the safest course was to accept the risk involved in letting the enemy work on, and not to fire the mine unless he touched the actual timbers of the branch gallery. . . . The Germans could now be heard putting in timber, working a truck, walking, and even talking. On May 25th in some other workings they fired a mine whose position was "dangerously correct" directly above the Hill 60 gallery. It crushed in the junction of the galleries and entombed two listeners. One, Sapper Earl, in the Hill 60 gallery, coolly went on listening and heard a German walk down an enemy gallery apparently directly

over the great mine. . . . The listeners had to be withdrawn, and from then onwards the staff could only trust that the enemy would not reach the British workings before the mine was fired.

At Petit Douve, near Messines, one mine, already laid and electrically charged, was discovered by the Germans. They blew a *camouflet*, wrecked the main British gallery, and the mine had to be abandoned. This left nineteen. It was a race against time at Spanbroekmolen, where the major in charge of the tunneling company scribbled in pencil a note to division headquarters on June 6 that it was "almost" definite that his mine would explode the following morning of the attack.

It had indeed been a tense two years of underground digging and fighting, and the records of the period recall the strangeness of it all, and the peril:

Captain Woodward and Lieutenant Clinton . . . heard the enemy "hard at work" and earth falling within twenty feet of them. The gallery commander . . . ordered the nearest part of the gallery to be at once silently loaded. While the charge—2500 lb. of ammonal—was being put in, the Germans could easily be heard "with the naked ear." So close were they working that the vibration kept shaking down flakes of clay on to the tin containers of the ammonal, which had therefore to be covered with sandbags. Woodward reported the situation "critical," and . . . when the Germans were probably ten feet away, the charge was fired.

Sapper Sneddon, having clearly heard the Germans boring and then charging the bore-hole, temporarily withdrew his men. As no "blow" followed, Major Henry suggested that means might be devised of simulating work while the gallery was empty, so that the enemy might fire his charge uselessly. Before this was done, however, early on April 7th the Germans fired their mine, crushing the ricketty gallery and killing Sapper Sneddon, who was listening there.

. . . he had been working underground for nearly two years in the dark saps pierced under the German lines, and running very close to German saps nosing their way, and sometimes breaking through, to ours, so that the men clawed at each other's throats in these tunnels and beat each other to death with picks and shovels.

So the digging went on, and the never-ending pumping out of water; and seldom it was that men could last in this work for even a few months without a breakdown of nerve and health. "Listeners all a bit windy," one Captain Avery reported. Replacements flowed into the diggings, and as time went on the fighting infantry were relieved by labor batallions. Every tunnel had a name—the Newcastle shaft, the Snout, the Sydney, the Perth, the Hobart, the great Brisbane. One started from over two hundred yards behind the British lines, descended to ninety feet, and, the men said solemnly, would in time lead to Berlin. It was called the Berlin Sap. By late evening, June 6, these nineteen mines were in place and charged, their shafts were tamped down, and the only remaining question was how many of them—especially the old ones that had been laid down as long as six months ago —would actually explode next morning.

The mines were to be only a curtain-raiser. Because they were an unknown factor to large degree—nobody really knew how many would go off, whether each lay in exactly the right position, and how much damage they would do to men, trenches, and guns many yards above—the greatest artillery mass of the war had been arrayed against enemy lines between Ploegsteert ("Plug Street") Wood and Observatory ridge, about a mile northeast of Hill 60. Over 2400 guns and howitzers were to participate, fully a third of which were heavy pieces: one gun to every seven yards of front.

Other than the mines, as we have seen, there would be no surprise at all (except possibly for the precise moment of zero hour itself, and this was not officially told to the troops until the 5th); and the artillery preparations were unusually brazen. In single file the heavies were hauled directly to the frontal area from the rear towns and assembly points. Behind them jostled the little field guns, galloping up without the slightest caution, a wild noisy collection followed closely by their ammunition wagons. They were emplaced wheel to wheel, with no attempt to hide them. From May 18 to 30 the guns rumbled forward, and on the latter day they began shelling in earnest the enemy's wire entanglements, his roads, camp areas, supply dumps, and in particular the routes and points where it was known that water and food were being delivered to troops up front.

In the final days gas shells were thrown in vast numbers to force the enemy to don masks and lose sleep. And, further to confuse him, the bombardment was twice increased to pre-attack intensity, and twice the Germans reacted spasmodically to false alarms. By the morning of the 7th the British gunners were thoroughly rehearsed, every gun was registered on its target, and the Germans were weary and on edge. All that remained was the final performance, the efficiency of which was a near certainty from an artillery standpoint.

Tanks, too, were in readiness—seventy-two Mark IVs that assembled a few miles southwest of Ypres and waited under camouflaged shelters for the signal to proceed toward the front. The night of the 6th they emerged, throbbing and clattering, and approached their starting points under the cover of airplanes which flew back and forth to drown out their noise. It was the first appearance in battle of these new models. While their best speed on battle terrain with a crew of eight was only about three miles per hour, their plating was impervious to German armor-piercing bullets, and it was hoped that they would be able to help the infantry overcome strong points.

Three hundred planes of the II Brigade Royal Flying Corps went into action late in May, mostly to assist the artillery by observation and photographs.

The attack itself was to be a straightforward operation along a ten-mile front toward a final objective two miles away at most, known as the Green Line, or Oosttaverne Line, running slightly to the east of that former village in a nearly straight line that formed a chord across the base of the German salient. Three corps (IX, X, and II Anzac) would participate with three divisions each, and each corps would have one division in reserve, ready to leapfrog through upon signal. About 80,000 infantry would go over the top at dawn, at which moment the mines would be detonated and the artillery barrage would commence with every operable gun along the Second Army Front.

During the long months of working, waiting, and suffering almost helplessly under the guns of their tormentors ringed around them on the slopes, the British troops had practiced their great freeing operation. Behind each of the three corps, training areas had been constructed. Roughly similar to the terrain that would be met June 7, they were marked with colored flags and tape lines designating ravines, woods, strong points, and other objectives. In full battle dress, infantrymen and artillerymen rehearsed their attack six times. A model of the entire ridge was laid out in a field about the size of a tennis court, and here all officers studied the slopes up and down which they would soon lead their men. Various of the twelve divisions, too, made clay tabletop replicas of their individual sectors.

As training progressed, and while the guns and

supplies moved in opposite the German ridge-salient, commanders from Plumer down visited the front daily and saw to it that the movements of troops as small as corporals' sections were understood by the men and coordinated with the larger plan. Patrols increased their activity, seeking new information. Major General Monash, leader of the 3rd Australian Division, distributed circulars among his men telling how Australian prisoners had been nearly starved by their captors in a dungeon after the battle of Bullecourt; whether this tactic fed the ferocity of his assault brigades is doubtful, though the tale was true.

The men waited, worked, and trained. For once, in World War I, they approached zero hour with a sense of optimism, though they understood what they faced. "The enemy will fight his hardest for the Messines ridge," said an officer. "He has stacks of guns against us."

And another, who knew the salient perhaps too well, peered at the German-held ridges, lofty and arrogant in the hazy distance, flaming with guns, webbed with row after row of sandbagged trenches, peppered with thousands of machine-gun emplacements, pillboxes, and sharpshooters' nests. He turned to a newspaper man and murmured, "It's a Gibraltar." The mines would have to do their job.

Major General Harington opened his advance press conference with these words: "Gentlemen, I don't know whether we are going to make history tomorrow, but at any rate we shall change geography."

Let us examine now the German side of the coin.

The Messines-Wytschaete portion of the ridge had been in the past manned by a total of four divisions. When in January 1917 Ludendorff became aware of the growing danger there, he placed two more in reserve. In February it was noticed that new British batteries were moving into position. On April 29 a spy advised the German high command that the British would attack the ridge two weeks after stopping their main effort on the Arras front—an estimate which was very nearly correct.

At about the same time, aerial observation disclosed that British movement on the roads and railways behind the salient was reaching alarming proportions, far greater than that which had preceded the assault farther south under Allenby a few weeks previously. After weighing these and other Intelligence reports Crown Prince Rupprecht decided that the Arras attack was merely a large-scale feint and that the Messines ridge was Haig's true objective. From this moment on, and for the next five weeks, the Germans reinforced their positions substantially opposite Plumer's army.

But five German weeks were not equal to five British months. In those five weeks the German air arm covering the salient was driven out of the sky, and the former's batteries were nearly crushed by counter-bombardment. A few figures tell the story, and in reading them one can sense the intensity of this greatest of all counter-battery operations, and the despair of the defenders who helplessly watched the shattering of their artillery shield. By early June almost half the German howitzers, light and heavy, were out of action. Hardly one captured Russian gun remained operable. The Third Bavarian Division faced the coming attack with the astonishing total of only nineteen field guns; the Second Division up north had lost fifteen of their eighteen medium and heavy howitzers.

Under such conditions, German infantry could expect only trivial support during the coming fight. Ominously, they had already been driven from at least one strong point even before June 7 and had been forced to take refuge out in open trenches. British gas shelling on an unprecedented scale had indeed accomplished its purpose of keeping the enemy awake for days, and the disruption of food supply had further demoralized him. The night before the attack a lucky British hit exploded a great ammunition dump near Menin, and gas quickly spread throughout the area. Many civilians who still inhabited the outskirts of this section of the rear zone were killed, as well as an undetermined number of corralled mules and horses. So shaken were the Germans by British shelling to which they could not effectively reply that five divisional replacements had to be consummated during the first week of June. One of these, as we shall see, was actually in progress during the morning of the 7th.

Too late it dawned on the Crown Prince that he was in trouble, and during the last few days he worked feverishly to save his position. More small bodies of

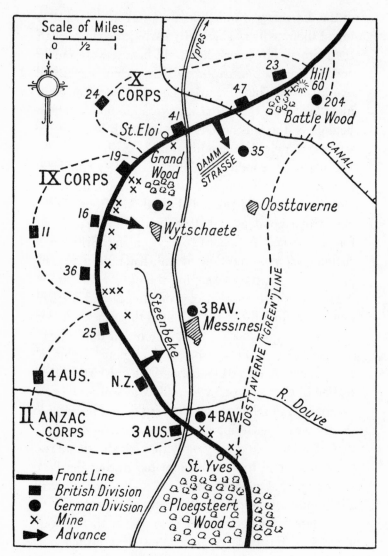

Messines, June 6, 1917

infantry were hustled into action. Artillery was added, especially on the flanks of the threatened sector; more planes, pioneers, and machine guns were thrown into the pre-attack fighting. On June 3 thirteen thousand gas shells were poured into the Australians around Ploegsteert Wood. On June 6, knowing that the attack was due next day or the day after, Rupprecht ordered an even heavier gas barrage, in an attempt to smother the enemy artillery and catch troops on their approach march to the jumping-off line.

These last-minute measures embarrassed the British but failed to hamper them to any large extent, except in the case of General Monash's 3rd Australians, five hundred of whom were gassed en route. For once, the forty-eight-year-old Bavarian Prince, field marshal of the northern armies on the Western Front, descendant of the Stuart kings of Britain, brother-in-law of the Belgian queen, world traveler, and gifted military commander, had been too late with too little, outwitted underground, outmanned and outgunned on the ground, and overpowered in the skies above. The battle of Messines was lost by the Germans before it began.

During the evening the men marched silently in columns of fours like groping tentacles toward the communication trenches, and thence to the front, where white jumping-off tapes lay on the soft wet ground of No Man's Land. They were troubled and wearied by the need for wearing their masks, for gas

shells were plopping all about them, laying low the un-
wary and careless as well as many pack animals gasp-
ing and heaving in the poisoned air. It was warm that
night. Fog lay on the salient like a heavy caress, and in
it not a breeze stirred. Overhead forked lightning
played, accompanied by the mutter of thunder. At
midnight a sharp thundershower broke. It lasted only
a few minutes, and after it passed, a three-quarter
moon floated regally in a nearly clear sky. Now brilliant flashes against the enemy slopes could be seen,
and the steady whamming of the big guns sounded
perceptibly louder as the blanket of fog melted away.

A half-hour before zero hour the British guns
stopped firing, and the night became so still that one
could hear nightingales singing in the nearby woods.
The men fixed bayonets and removed their gas masks.
Some of them dozed. Officers changed to enlisted
men's tunics and kept peering at their wrist watches.
Zero hour would be 3:10.

At 2:52 the Germans threw up yellow and green
flares, calling for artillery fire—a disconcerting sign.
How much did they know? At 2:57 heavy bursts of
shrapnel swept segments of the British front; but
quickly it ceased.

At 3:05 the first streaks of dawn filtered over the
Messines ridge. On Mount Kemmel the cocks began to
crow. Two green star-flares burst directly in front of
the New Zealand division at 3:06, then machine guns
and another flare. Had this unit been discovered?
(Some of their assembly trenches had been dug dan-

gerously forward in No Man's Land during the early evening.) But at 3:09 the German guns stopped chattering. For one minute absolute silence saturated the air, while at whispered orders the troops crawled over their parapets and lay flat in front of the tapes.

A few seconds befoe 3:10 some of the heavy guns rearward began to fire. Then each of the nineteen land mines exploded almost in unison. The earth quaked, tumbling and staggering the British soldiers as they rose in awe to see the rim of the hated ridge burst skyward in a dense black cloud, beneath which gushed nineteen pillars of flame that lit the salient with the red glare of hell. The pillars fused into greater mushrooms of fire that seemed to set flame to little clouds above. Then, a moment or two later, the long roar of nineteen explosions blended and reverberated into one long blast that stunned even the British troops, awakened the countryside, rolled through Flanders and northern France, hurtled the Channel, and was heard in London by Lloyd George, awake in his study at Number 10 Downing Street.

From the German positions yellow flares soared imploringly high into the sky, the pathetic prayers of doomed men crying for help. As the villages of Messines and Wytschaete disappeared into oblivion, the heaviest of all artillery barrages struck the German front, and the British assault brigades scrambled over the top.

Plumer and his staff had breakfasted at 2:30, after which everybody went to the top of Cassel Hill near

Second Army headquarters, a few miles deep in the salient, to see the mines go up—all but Plumer, who returned to his room and knelt at his bed in prayer. When the first news of the infantry advance came, he burst into tears. It was quite clear that his Second Army was winning as planned, and with greater ease than had been expected. So swift and thorough was the British success that subsequent fighting came as an anticlimax.

The enemy was in a state of near shock when the British fell upon them. They surrendered en masse, weeping, waving handkerchiefs, grasping the ankles of their captors. Thousands lay beneath the ground, to be forever entombed there. Some of the mine craters were three hundred feet across and seventy feet deep. The wreckage of their front left many Germans cringing in derelict shelters "like beaten animals" while the British walked along throwing Mills bombs at unresisting clusters of men too dazed to surrender. One Australian lieutenant reported how they "made many fruitless attempts to embrace us. I have never seen men so demoralized." Another distraught prisoner said that only two men in his section of the line had survived the blast. A captured officer reported that of his two-hundred-man company only thirty were alive when the British foot soldiers arrived. The 3rd Bavarian Division was relieving the 24th Saxons precisely when the explosions and the attack burst; both relieved and relievers were decimated, and most of the balance were made prisoners.

While the British dug in near the crest of the ridge, German defenses began to tighten. Machine guns took a heavy toll of these farthermost troops and of those moving up in support. By 11 o'clock appreciable enemy infantry reinforcements were seen to be approaching the eastern slopes. Soon afterward, sporadic counterattacks developed. Small bodies of Germans stubbornly holding out at isolated points throughout the area redoubled their fire. It was at this stage that hundreds of British were killed and wounded by their own batteries and fellow infantrymen; for as they descended the western slopes of the ridge after being relieved they were mistaken again and again for German counterattackers. At other sectors along the front of advance, errors in direction were committed; some companies got temporarily lost; others were held up by the great mine craters. Yet, all in all, the general sweep forward proceeded on schedule.

During the middle of the afternoon, following the first long pause, all three reserve divisions plunged forward with their tanks and brushed aside secondary German defenses. From a previous line running some six hundred yards west of the final goal the new assault lapped toward the little village of Oosttaverne, captured it within an hour, and reached the entire Green Line by dusk.

For the next few days advance posts were established by the victors, the new line was consolidated, the Germans continued to counterattack feebly; but in line with previous plans no attempt was made by the

British to exploit their success. The battle of Messines ridge was over, and would stand on its merits. The south flank of the great salient at Ypres no longer existed, and now British troops stood astride that portion of the ridge from which they had been murdered wholesale since early in the war. The front had been pushed back two miles at the farthest point. Seventy-three hundred prisoners were taken, and the Germans had suffered almost 20,000 other casualties. These figures apply to the period from June 1 to 10. During the same time British casualties came to something under twenty-four thousand. So, "counting heads," the difference between the losses in men on both sides was, after all, disturbingly small, though the achievement as a whole was (or seemed to be at the time) beyond question. Certainly the operation had been, in the words of one writer, a "siege-war masterpiece," one "in which the methods employed by the command completely fitted the facts of the situation," a triumph of engineers in what was essentially an engineers' war.

In his memoirs von Hindenburg admits:

> The moral effect of the explosions was simply staggering. . . . The 7th of June cost us dear, and, owing to the success of the enemy attack, the price we paid was very heavy. . . . It was many days before the front was again secure. The British army did not press its advantage; apparently it only intended to improve its position for the launching of the great Flanders offensive.

And in his dispatch dated June 12 Philip Gibbs wrote:

> From Messines and Wytschaete [the Germans] had absolute observation of a wide tract of country in which our men lived and died—how complete an observation I did not realize until after this battle, when standing in Wytschaete Wood and on the mound by St.-Eloi, and on the ground rising up to Messines, I looked back, and saw every detail of our old territory laid out like a relief map brightly colored ."My God," said an officer by my side, "it's a wonder they allowed us to live at all!"

Thus had Sir Douglas Haig cleared the first hurdle in his race against time and politicians.

7. The Signed Contract

I F SIR DOUGLAS, jubilant over Plumer's triumph at Messines, had assumed that it would end once and for all the objections to his larger plan, he was to be unpleasantly surprised; for the more Lloyd George thought about what was next on the military agenda the more apprehensive he became. One by one he began privately sounding out various members of the War Cabinet for their support in blocking Haig, and he let it be known that he was still as strong as ever for a serious offensive on the Italian front. The commander in chief first learned of this in a letter dated June 13 from Sir William Robertson, which read in part:

> There is trouble in the land just now.
> . . . The L.G. idea is to settle the war
> from Italy, and to-day the railway people have been asked for figures regarding the rapid transfer of 12 Divisions
> and 300 heavy guns to Italy! They will
> never go while I am C.I.G.S. but that

will come later. What I do wish to impress on you is this:—Don't argue that you can finish the war this year, or that the German is already beaten. Argue that your plan is the best plan—as it is—that no other would be *safe* let alone decisive, and then leave them to reject your advice and mine. They dare not do that.

Haig was appalled. What hurt most was that even Robertson, despite his strong written support, was wavering too. In the course of subsequent conversation "Wully" suggested that matters might become serious if Haig were to plunge into a long, bloody offensive without large-scale aid by the French. By fall Britain might be "without an army"! Was it not, after all, possible that Austria could be knocked out by one sharp blow? Perhaps it might be wise to send at least heavy guns to the Italians and, if only for the moment, to stand on the defensive in the West.

Haig could scarcely believe his ears. Never before had a British officer dared to contradict him on this issue of almost religious faith. His own staff was packed with yea-sayers of the most dutiful and orthodox type—especially his Intelligence chief, Brigadier General John Charteris, he of the feverish optimism and Western zeal. Coming from his most trusted cohort, Robertson's words were heretical and incredible. Haig replied stiffly that the Germans were practically at the end of their rope, barely hanging on, and ready for the *coup de grâce*.

While this view had been emanating from Charteris

for a year, few people other than Haig really believed it. Robertson brushed it aside. His own Central Intelligence chief at the War Office was saying exactly the opposite. Without the French, he feared, Haig would be walking into a political trap and perhaps a military dead end.

But the French *would* cooperate satisfactorily, Haig replied. Had not Pétain promised him only yesterday that nearly a hundred thousand troops under General François Anthoine were forthcoming, to be under Haig's orders? Pétain had said that he would be "most anxious to help in every way," and that the situation in the French Army was "now more satisfactory." As for the British assuming the defensive, Robertson could surely visualize its ineffable by-product: Lloyd George would, of course, seize the opportunity to snatch untold divisions from the West and squander them in Salonika or Palestine or Italy or heaven knows where else, or might even bring them back to England altogether, under some trumped-up excuse.

And Cadorna! Here both Haig and Robertson were in agreement. The Italian general plainly was incapable of handling a major offensive. Already his army had fought the Battle of the Isonzo River eleven times, and still it stood on the Isonzo.

Summing up, Haig felt that Robertson's opinion was, to say the least, unsound. He had, in fact, already formulated in his diary a capsule of his attitude; the only thing to do immediately was:

"1. Send to France every possible man.
2.   "   "   "   "   "   aeroplane.
3.   "   "   "   "   "   gun."

And Sunday, after church services attended by both men, Robertson had changed his mind. He was ready now to back Haig to the hilt, and suddenly "seemed to realise that the German Army was in reduced circumstances."

Yet it appears that the chief of staff sensed, as others did, that in spite of Messines things had not changed much. The Salient was still a salient—perhaps not as bad as before, but the Germans still had splendid positions and observation to the northeast; and as to the rest of the ridge everything was quite the same. From the Pilckem ridge southward the enemy was as powerfully placed defensively as ever, and a breakthrough was nearly as remote as before June 7. Perhaps it was even more remote, for many more pillboxes were being hastily constructed to meet the impending assault, and an avalanche of reinforcements was moving in from the Eastern Front. Luxuriously ensconced in their shell-proof dugouts that balmy June, the Germans fried their bacon, read Goethe, peered through their telescopes, laid down more barbed wire, trundled up more and more guns, played chess, oiled their machine guns, wrote letters, and with mingled apprehension and confidence awaited the Third Battle of Ypres under conditions that favored the defense more than ever before. And this time there would be no British mines.

Furthermore there was still the time element. Was there really enough time after the Nivelle and Plumer episodes to shift the center of gravity to Ypres and win a big victory before the rains came? On this basis alone, many thought, the new plan was no longer valid by midsummer and should be canceled.

And after Messines to achieve surprise was hopeless; visually and on the basis of Intelligence reports the Germans knew what was in store, just as throughout the war both sides always knew when and where a big attack was due. German Fourth Army headquarters and Rupprecht individually agreed that it was "certain" the next British offensive would be at Ypres. It was the same old story. To hide the immensity of the preparations was impossible, as always, and, in fact, the enemy was aware of most of the exact details. The Crown Prince, ever shrewd and pessimistic, had begun to strengthen his front by early June, believing that the attack at the salient would have the further aim of freeing the Belgian coast, along with an eventual landing from the Channel in cooperation with "limited" (his word) assistance by the French. All these assumptions, as we know, were quite correct. Thereupon he brought to the crucial sector many additional divisions for front-line duty, for reserve duty close behind the front, and for counterattack after the British had been stopped. And, as we have seen, he hurried the construction of hundreds more of the most forbidding obstacles of all—concrete pillboxes arranged checkerboard-fashion in depth all through his frontal area.

Later this month Canadian troops attacked at Lens. Still Rupprecht was not deceived. It was merely a feint, he announced; the British did not have the power to deliver two major blows at practically the same time, and the one that counted was coming soon enough at Ypres. On July 6 he reported that he was ready for an attack of any magnitude. By the 9th, German artillery was stronger than the British, and leisurely engaged in blowing up ammunition dumps; and by now Rupprecht's staff wondered among themselves why the British guns did not open up in reply, to herald the hopeless advance of the foot soldiers.

Early in July, to add insult to arrogance, the Germans attacked Rawlinson's Fourth Army by surprise and drove most of it across the Yser River, where it had been sitting in anticipation of its future coastal operation.

Not even Nivelle's plan had been so apparent to the enemy, nor had it been awaited more placidly by the Germans; and precisely as in the Nivelle affair careless words had done their deadly work. Again prisoners had talked. Again the politicians had squabbled openly. On July 7 Painlevé himself had delivered a speech in which unfortunate reference was made to the small amount of aid French troops would be able to render Haig. One Australian on leave in England wrote in his diary:

Everyone in England was talking of the coming British offensive. I heard more of it there than in France.
. . . The first thing X— asked me was: "Well, Z—,
when is the big offensive along the coast coming off?"
I pretended to know nothing. It simply shocked me to
hear the way people talked.

In mid-June the *Frankfurter Zeitung* published a
bland appraisal of British chances in the forthcoming
attack at Ypres. Lloyd George read it next day. That
settled matters, as far as he was concerned. Haig had
to be stopped—and not by the Germans.

Much of the story of Flanders, 1917, has to do with
conferences—at Chantilly, Rome, Calais, Paris, and
lesser ones elsewhere. Some reached sensible conclusions; most did not. Some only aggravated strained re-
lationships between mutually exclusive soldiers and
civilians. Many were dull and confused. A few were
of importance, if only in settling some dispute for the
worse, such as the final talk between Painlevé and
Nivelle. The minutes of all of them lie fading and
buried in the archives of the great states that fought
the war, of interest now only to the scholar of minutiae
and semantics. But the June deliberations in London
are of a class apart. During three days a pitched battle
was fought here between Haig and Lloyd George and
their supporters, from which three-quarters of a million men emerged dead or wounded five months later.
It was the showdown between Easterners and Westerners. Haig had the advantage, largely because his

opponents were divided among themselves, because neither he nor Robertson could be flatly removed without proving that the Allied cause was bankrupt, and because Lloyd George himself was not strong enough politically to sack them or override them unless they capitulated; and this they were not likely to do. The Prime Minister could only coax them to change their minds, and should this fail—as Painlevé failed versus Nivelle—he might be forced to let them have their way. The field marshal and the general were in the driver's seat; they knew it, and refused to step down or hand over the reins.

To reinforce his position Lloyd George formed a new Committee on War Policy. Headed by himself, it included Lord Curzon, Lord Milner, and General Smuts of South Africa. The job of this select group of four was to direct and coordinate the entire British war effort on land and sea, and, the Prime Minister hoped, to offer a united front capable of bending the Army high command to its wishes. We shall see whether the Policy Committee was indeed willing or able to accomplish this formidable task.

The Committee's first official act was to summon Haig and Robertson. Haig was at GHQ in northern France. He drove from there to Calais, took a destroyer to Dover and a train to Charing Cross. The chief of staff was already in London.

The deliberations that followed were grave and formal in tone. No direct recriminations were uttered. The name-calling by Lloyd George was so subtle, so polite, that the two generals were barely wounded at all. Superficially the talks proceeded on an unusually high level of objectiveness, though vast prejudices and preconceived notions lay submerged below, like an iceberg only a fraction of which shows above the surface of the icy, placid water in which it floats. Millions of words, spoken and written, made up the sum of the argument. Let us reduce them to simple terms.

The first meeting took place on June 19, in Lord Curzon's Privy Council Office, 10 Downing Street, and was dominated by Douglas Haig. Here, for the first time officially, he revealed his Flanders campaign to the civilians in all its breathtaking splendor, as based on a paper sent a week earlier to his army commanders.

He began by saying that the prospects for a successful attack were at the moment ideal. Russia was beginning a large offensive with "excellent results," and so heartening was this to the Russian people that more such fine efforts could be expected.

Lloyd George commented that both these premises were incorrect.

Impassively Haig continued to the effect that the Germans were demoralized by a suspicion that their submarine campaign was a failure.

The Prime Minister thought that Haig was trying to play it both ways. If the submarines were failing, the Germans were demoralized and susceptible to attack. If the submarines were not failing, the Germans should be attacked so as to deprive them of submarine bases. Since Haig scored a point either way, again something must be wrong with his premise.

The moment was ripe, Haig went on. He described in detail how the campaign would unfold. The scene has been sketched by Lloyd George:

> When Sir Douglas Haig explained the projects to the civilians, he spread on a table or desk a large map and made a dramatic use of both his hands to demonstrate how he proposed to sweep up the enemy—first the right hand brushing along the surface irresistibly, and then came the left, his outer finger ultimately touching the German frontier with the nail across.

Curzon and Smuts were impressed to a degree, but Lloyd George, Bonar Law (who now and frequently in the future attended meetings of the Policy Committee), and Milner remained skeptical. They began to question Haig and Robertson in detail, "tending to show," as Haig wrote in his diary that evening, "that each of them was more pessimistic than the other."

How could the French strike heavily, in view of their stunned military and psychological condition?

Haig replied that they could and would, and that Pétain had told him so.

Why had he said that the Germans were demoralized?

Because he had received unimpeachable reports to that effect. He quoted one emanating from an American committee: "They realize that they are beaten . . .

no longer present a smart appearance . . . ," and so on. Furthermore, their despair was accentuated by the recent setback at Messines.

But was it not true that according to the War Office the Germans were superior in artillery, especially heavy calibers?

Haig doubted this, and went on to say that, at any rate, German guns were quite inaccurate.

Here Sir William Robertson first spoke up at length. Previously he had ventured only his usual grunts, harrumphs, and muttered asides, for "Wully" was, if possible, even a poorer extemporaneous speaker than Haig. Now he felt impelled to state in his husky soldier's voice that he considered his own War Office estimates exaggerated, and that German artillery superiority on the Western Front was a myth.

Since this left the matter of artillery hanging helplessly in mid-air, the politicians changed the subject to casualties. Certainly they were bound to be enormous, were they not? And were the marshal and the general not aware of the Government's manpower difficulties?

There was nothing to fear, replied Robertson. Observe what had happened at Messines in one day. If the new assault were equally successful Passchendaele ridge would be seized in one day also, and with no greater losses.

Did he really expect to have enough guns, men, and ammunition to gain his objective?

More than enough; and he amplified this claim.

Speaking of objectives—in referring to the Passchendaele ridge did the generals consider it a final or a preliminary target?

Haig answered shortly that the operation would end
with the capture of the entire Flemish coast.

This statement was followed by a hush. Suddenly it
occurred to the politicians that he really meant what
he said. Heretofore nobody had inwardly felt that
such an advance was possible or seriously contemplated by the generals. Even the official historian admits that "the outline of the campaign may seem
super-optimistic and too far-reaching, even fantastic. . . ." Yet here was Haig stating it as almost an
accomplished fact. The self-assurance of the man was
disquieting, and the civilians other than Smuts, disturbed as always by a sense of inferiority in discussing
military matters with the leading military personages
of one of the world's greatest miltary powers, fell silent
and shuffled their notes and wondered uneasily who,
after all, was right. Lloyd George, least impressed of
all by "the aerial tower built . . . by the industry and
imagination of GHQ to view this thrilling prospect,"
suggested calling in Admiral Jellicoe for his opinion.
The melancholy and somewhat tarnished hero of Jutland appeared forthwith and intoned that unless the
Channel ports held by the Germans could be recaptured Britain would have to end the war in 1918
through lack of shipping.

Like a leopard the Prime Minister leaped forward

to denounce this bizarre opinion; but the First Sea Lord would not back down. The war was really lost unless Zeebrugge could be taken, he repeated. Haig and Robertson let the statement sink in. Yet, in the later words of Winston Churchill, Jellicoe's claim was "wholly fallacious." The Belgian ports housed only a few of the smaller U-boats and were by no means a worthy objective of a grand land offensive; and to deceive not only Haig and Robertson but the War Cabinet concerning their value to the German war effort made the Admiralty largely responsible for any decision that might follow.

It was now early afternoon. Soon Lloyd George would leave to attend the wedding of his daughter, and before doing so he delivered a few parting shots. To meet the voracious demands of the generals the Government was already "scraping men up from munition works, mines, and agriculture, and from among those formerly rejected on medical grounds." The population was growing resentful; and, while both he and the country wanted to back Haig, it would be regrettable if the Army drained the nation dry "on behalf of a failure." The French were wounded and quiescent, the Americans were a year away, the Russians were a forlorn hope, and only Britain was carrying the main load. He appreciated hearing Haig's views, but under the circumstances the Committee could not possibly go along with them. And on this defiant chord the meeting of June 19 adjourned.

That afternoon Lloyd George sent Haig and Robertson a written statement summarizing his outlook. Its key points ran as follows:

1. A failure might have "disastrous effects on public opinion."

2. The War Cabinet could not gamble with lives "merely because those who are directing the War can think of nothing better to do with the men under their command."

3. Before proceeding on an enterprise which might fail and result in "premature peace" the responsible parties had to feel "a reasonable chance of succeeding."

4. Even counting the French, the Allies would enjoy only a fifteen-per-cent superiority in men and mere equality in guns. In reserves the Germans had an advantage. To scrape the bottom of the barrel would lead to "the same unrest, disaffection, and labour troubles which have baffled all our other efforts to raise men."

5. The French Army was in no condition to fight effectively, and "it would be madness on our part to proceed on such an assumption." Yet the British high command proposes "that we should rush into the greatest battle of the War, against an enemy almost equal in number, quite equal in equipment, still the greatest army in Europe . . . with larger reserves than our own . . . holding formidable defensive positions which he has taken three years to strengthen and to perfect;

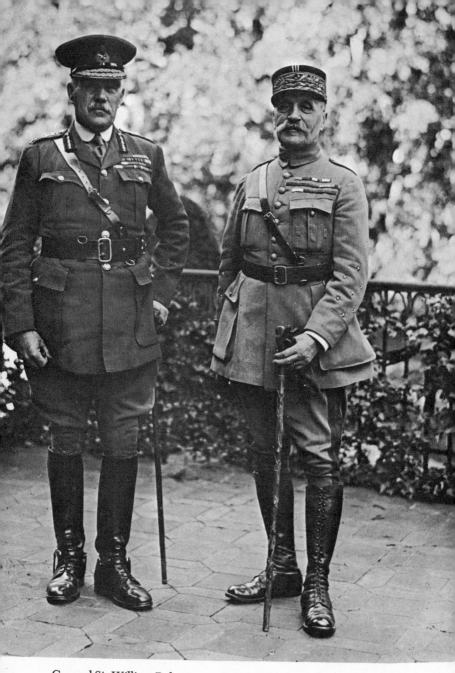

General Sir William Robertson and Field Marshal Ferdinand Foch

and we are to launch this attack with doubtful support from our most powerful and important ally. . . . If it pulls less than its full weight we shall be attacking the strongest army in the world with an actual inferiority of numbers. . . . Curious indeed must be the military conscience which could justify an attack under such conditions."

6. Could Robertson promise anything better than Vimy ridge and Messines, "brilliant preliminary successes, followed by weeks of desperate and sanguinary struggles, leading to nothing except perhaps the driving of the enemy back a few barren miles—beyond that nothing to show except a ghastly casualty list"?

He turned to his alternative. Allied strategy had never recognized that "the European battlefield is one and indivisible." Why pit strength against strength and weakness against weakness? Such a policy could only protract the stalemate. But Austria could be knocked out by a strong blow. The country was half beaten and had already made peace overtures. Transfer heavy guns secretly to the Italian front and let Cadorna attack. The latter was enthusiastic over the idea, and so was General Foch. Like a house of cards the Central Powers would topple. First Trieste would be captured; then would follow the collapse of Austria, the fall of Bulgaria, the defeat of Turkey. Now millions of Russians, French, British, and Italian troops could be switched to the Western Front, and breakthrough and victory would follow in 1918.

The argument came to five thousand impressive

words, and had it been sprung on Haig and Robertson the following morning their defense might have been ragged, for they were notoriously unskilled in verbal counterplay. As it was, they had several hours that evening in which to draft a heavy counteroffensive.

This they delivered starting at noon of the following day.

After admitting that the German Army was now ten divisions stronger than a year ago, Robertson rejected the notion that Austria could be easily knocked out. He doubted that heavy guns could be switched to the Italian front unknown to the enemy. In any event, it would take six weeks to get them there. If pressure were taken off the Germans in the west, they might attack there with success or even beat the Allies to the punch in Italy. Therefore, he reasoned, transfering weight to Italy might bring about results exactly the opposite of those predicted by the Prime Minister.

Amidst deathlike silence the chief of staff continued. Without being hard pressed in the west the Germans might even proceed farther down the coast and take Dunkirk; and he said, "I think we should follow the principle of the gambler who has the heaviest purse and force our adversary's hand and make him go on spending until he is a pauper." Conceding that Russia might be about finished, he warned against the dangers on the Western Front should it be weakened by the Allies and strengthened by Germany.

"I deprecate as strongly as anyone our incurring

heavy casualties without a corresponding return," he went on, "but the plan as outlined by the Field Marshal should secure us against this mistake . . . while at the same time it permits of our easing off if the situation so demands."

Here was the most telling stroke, the insurance policy, the protective clause which would be repeated many times in the future to the many prospects. For if the campaign truly would be stopped if it showed signs of approaching a dead end, nothing much would be lost by giving the generals their "good try." The question was whether they would really stop. Past history was not encouraging in this respect. Previous heavy offensives, such as at the Somme and Champagne, had ended only in utter exhaustion—not because Haig or Joffre or Nivelle had shut them down judiciously before tragedy set in. Could Haig and Robertson be trusted to use better judgment in Flanders? There could be no pat answer to this question.

While these thoughts flashed through the minds of the civilians Robertson was concluding. Germany, he thought, "may yet take a great deal of beating." On the other hand, she "may be much nearer exhaustion . . . than we imagine." Then followed an equally arguable sentiment—that "great mistakes have been made by endeavoring to find a fresh way around. . . ."

Sir Douglas Haig now arose. He began with a complex bookkeeping formula ("joyous arithmetic" Lloyd George later contemptuously termed it) which led to the conclusion "that the Allies will have a considerable superiority in infantry at the point of attack—probably not less than two to one." The assertion was received doubtfully. It contradicted estimates previously made, and evaded the likelihood of many German divisions' being moved down from Hoffmann's Eastern Front.

He too deprecated the hope of defeating Austria, and feared "very dangerous disappointment in France . . . a possibility of reverses on the Western Front" if the Flanders scheme were abandoned. Then he advanced Robertson's curious argument that if the Allies reinforced the Italians by weakening the west there would be "a possibility of still more serious reverses on the Italian Front," whereas sustained maximum pressure in France and Belgium might very well win the war before the end of the year.

When Haig sat down it was clear that nothing at all had changed. Imperceptibly a sense of hopelessness invaded the quiet brown-paneled room off Downing Street where seven men meditated around the large rectangular desk strewn with papers, ashtrays, and Haig's great colored map—Haig cool and erect, Robertson burly and sullen, Lloyd George staring pugnaciously at the commander in chief, the pompous roundfaced Curzon, saintly-seeming Smuts with his little white pointed beard, Milner narrow-eyed and balding, slim and handsome and tired Bonar Law. The two generals had not backed down, nor had their opponents. How was it to end? The war had to go on—

there was no dispute about that; armistice overtures were out of the question. They could attack in Italy or Flanders. They could "squat" and "pull faces at the Boches," as Sir Henry Wilson put it, and wait for the Americans and the tanks. Each general could keep punching away at his own little section of the various fronts, in a limited and hopeless fashion. But regardless of what it was to be, the decision that had to be made was as far away as ever.

After a pause, Lord Curzon asked Haig whether in referring to "a reasonable chance of success" he meant only the capturing of his first objectives. Haig replied that he meant the entire operation, from the salient to the North Sea.

Lloyd George remarked dismally that of course he was all for Haig's plan if it was really practical and likely to succeed.

General Smuts, the only member of the Policy Committee who strongly backed the Army chiefs, reported that Admiral Jellicoe had repeated his bombshell of the previous day to him in a private talk. It was decided to quiz the First Sea Lord again.

When he entered the council chamber Lord Curzon asked him to restate his views. This he did in even more pessimistic detail, ending with, "There is no good discussing plans for next spring—we cannot go on." The Prime Minister sardonically inquired whether he was basing his opinion on facts or whether, by implication, it followed merely from personal intuition. To ease the admiral's obvious discomfort it was decided to call for a proper investigation of the figures (nobody took this seriously), and morosely Jellicoe departed.

The meeting ended at about 1 p.m. After lunch the Committee members gathered to "count heads." General Smuts thought Haig and Robertson had presented a good case. Lord Curzon was not so sure. Lord Milner, Bonar Law, and Lloyd George were completely opposed; however, Law watered down his opinion by adding that he did not think they "were entitled to overrule the military and naval authorities on a question of strategy," a view which if carried to its bitter end should have dissolved the Policy Committee altogether, along with the very conferences now being conducted.

Milner and Lloyd George conceded that if they should ride roughshod over the military commanders they would probably receive no support from the War Cabinet as a whole. "It was therefore decided," in the Prime Minister's words, "that I should once more sum up the misgivings which most of us felt and leave the responsibility for decision to Sir William Robertson and Sir Douglas Haig, on the understanding that if the progress they made with the operation did not realize the expectations they had formed, it should be called off and effective help be rendered to the Italians to press their offensive."

The generals had conquered.

The deliberations next day took place more for the purpose of absolving Lloyd George and his followers from future blame than to kill the now inevitable campaign in Flanders. In later years Lloyd George was to state his opinion in language such as the following through more than a hundred pages of his memoirs:

> . . . inexhaustible vanity that will never admit a mistake . . . individuals who would rather the million perish than that they as leaders should own—even to themselves—that they were blunderers . . . the notoriety attained by a narrow and stubborn egotism, unsurpassed among the records of disaster wrought by human complacency . . . a bad scheme badly handled . . . impossible orders issued by Generals who had no idea what the execution of their commands really meant . . . this insane enterprise . . . this muddy and muddle-headed venture. . . .
>
> We were not informed that, so far from urging us on, the leading French Generals had done their best to dissuade us . . . thought it a foolish venture, which must fail.
>
> We were not told that the French plan was to wait for the Americans. . . . Headquarters . . . felt it would be undesirable to confuse and distract our innocent minds. . . .
>
> We were not informed that the new Commander-in-Chief of the French Army, and some of his leading generals, favoured a combined attack on the Italian Front. . . .
>
> We were told by the Commander-in-Chief that we should have a superiority of two to one in infantry—

it was untrue; that the enemy had no effective reserves—that was not in accordance with the facts; that
the German morale was so broken that they would
not put up anything like the resistance which they
had hitherto offered—that was misleading; that they
had inaccurate guns and inadequate ammunition we
found otherwise. . . .

Not a word was said about the meteorological
drawbacks and the peculiar conditions which rendered the terrain of the struggle specially disadvan-
tageous for a sustained attack.

But the most reprehensible . . . was withholding
from the Government of the fact that all the generals
called into consultation by Sir Douglas Haig had serious misgivings about the whole project and had expressed their doubts to him. . . .

We were invited to discuss Sir Douglas Haig's plan
not merely without full knowledge of the essential
elements, but with a definite suggestion that the decisive facts . . . were quite contrary. . . .

A prospectus issued with a view to inducing the
public to invest their capital in an enterprise must re-
veal all material facts. The Government were the
trustees of the public and were asked to invest in this
wild military speculation not only hundreds of millions of public money, but the lives of hundreds of
thousands of brave men. . . . They were invited to
risk the fate of Britain on what Sir William Robertson
later on called "a gamble," where the truth that mattered was wilfully and skilfully kept from their cogni-
sance.

In truth, Lloyd George was not nearly so unin-
formed as he later pretended to be. The record shows,

and this narrative has in part confirmed, that he was
more or less aware of French objections and counter-
intentions, of the doubts of at least some British officers, of the unsuitability of the terrain, of the contradictory estimates concerning manpower and German
capabilities. But at the conference on June 21 his
language and inferences were properly restrained. He
began by pointing out that the ultimate responsibility
for what might come lay strictly with the generals.
Their military decision would not be thwarted by the
Policy Committee; but he laid down one condition—
that they would break off the attack if it bogged down.
Then doggedly he proceeded to enumerate his objections, new and old.

First he referred to Robertson's sudden change of
mind. On May 4 and 5 the chief of staff had told him
that he was averse to heavy fighting unless the French
could cooperate seriously, and now Pétain was admitting his inability to do so.

He turned to the prospects of success, and pointed
out that the Germans already knew Haig's intentions.
What reason, he asked, "was there to believe that we
could first drive the enemy back fifteen miles and then
capture a place ten miles away?"—referring to objectives on the Channel coast.

The manpower superiority of the Allies on the
Western Front was, he insisted, only fifteen per cent,
even counting the exhausted French. Surely this was
insufficient for a modern-day offensive. Perhaps there

might be initial successes "but assaults on the German lines were like hitting India-rubber."

He pointed out that in three years he had never seen an offensive begun without positive predictions of victory. This time he was even more dubious. The Germans had plenty of ammunition for defensive purposes, especially since experience had shown that a five-to-one superiority was needed for the attackers.

He referred to German reinforcements available easily and in great number from the Russian front.

And what, after all, was so different between this proposed offensive and the Somme imbroglio, where the advance had been only an indentation of a few miles at enormous cost? Certainly there would be no greater factor of surprise.

Nobody on the Policy Committee, he said cruelly, whether they were willing to go along with Haig's plan or not, really expected it to work. Abandon it, he urged. Mark time with limited punches here and there, or augment an attack against Austria. For was it not futile continually to "aim our spear at the thickest part of the enemy's armour?"

He turned to Douglas Haig and asked him directly whether he thought victory could be achieved this year.

The chance was "very good," Haig replied. That very day he had been advised by the diligent Charteris that two-hundred-fifty-man German companies were down to about sixty men, that the 163rd German regi-

ment had refused to attack only last week, that some
men of the 1919 draft class were already at Rupprecht's front, and so on.

Lloyd George replied caustically that he welcomed
such "sanguine views, but did not personally attach
great importance to this sort of argument."

Lord Curzon interposed that the Italians had done
no good at all thus far in the war despite their large
superiority in numbers over the Austrians.

Of course not, Lloyd George retorted heatedly; they
had never owned enough heavy guns and ammunition
to support their infantry. He turned again to the two
generals, and in measured tones stated that he and
they "were at the parting of the ways."

Speaking for himself and Haig, Robertson replied
that he knew this was "the greatest decision of the
war," that neither of them resented the Prime Minister's opposition, and that their written replies would
follow. These were presented to the War Cabinet a
few days later, and in them the well-known views of
both generals were elaborated upon. The civilians decided to let Haig's military preparations in Flanders
continue. But still they refused to render an official
verdict, though by now it was informally understood
that the gamble was on, and that the die would be cast
across the soft Flemish plains as soon as the British and
French assault forces were ready. When would that
be? By late June, 1917, occasional delightful showers
were already dancing across the budding fields of

Flanders, hinting at more menacing weather soon to come.

Napoleon had once told his generals, "Gentlemen, ask me for anything but time," a sentiment with which Sir Douglas Haig must have agreed that Belgian summer. He knew that his long-cherished offensive was dangerously behind schedule and that he could expect only a few more weeks of ideal weather. At the very latest he hoped to send his infantry forward by July 25. This would give them perhaps two or three weeks of dry ground to fight on, which was still cutting things rather fine. He had once hoped to attack in the spring, but that was ancient history now; Nivelle had blunderingly intervened. Meanwhile Sir Douglas reflected that he was doing the best he could. Men, guns, ammunition, tanks, aircraft, food, gasoline, road equipment, horses and mules, hospital equipment, and a thousand other impedimenta of war were being funneled toward the salient in quantities that made the Somme preparations look almost primitive by comparison and reduced the Messines episode to a mere sideshow. The days scurried by at alarming speed; still the War Cabinet hesitated; and Haig began to wonder just when his Ypres contract would be signed, sealed, and delivered.

And while Haig waited and the British Expeditionary Force in Belgium swelled in size and muscle, other events proceeded apace during the fateful interval between the end of the talking in London and the start of the shooting at Ypres. . . .

June 27. The Germans began shelling Dunkirk with a 15-inch naval gun at Leugenboom, and people with compasses excitedly computed that Haig's General Headquarters lay within its range. Whenever the gun was fired, someone at the front phoned the city, whose inhabitants received ten or twenty seconds' warning in which to find shelter.

July 1. Kerenski finally got a Russian offensive going, with much Allied fanfare, until it quickly collapsed.

July 2. General Anthoine advised Haig that his six French divisions, which were to participate in Flanders, would not be ready on time.

July 6. Robertson wrote Haig that Lloyd George "is more keen than ever on the Italian plan. . . . Smuts wants to land 150,000 men at Alexandretta (I do not know where he proposes to get them or the ships from), Milner is rather inclined to think that the Balkans would be a good place, while Curzon sticks to our plan. It is pretty difficult doing business under these conditions."

July 7. General Gough, floundering with supply problems and worried about Anthoine, asked Haig for a five-day postponement. It was refused.

July 13. After a long talk with Gough the field marshal reluctantly authorized a delay to the 28th.

July 17. Bad visibility and maddening difficulties on the part of the French in getting their heavy guns into position obliged Haig to move zero day back still three more precious days, to July 31.

July 19. The German Reichstag passed a resolution, 214 to 116, expressing a desire for "a peace of conciliation." It was denounced violently by almost every military and civil leader in both camps.

July 19. Robertson wrote Haig that though the War Policy Committee had been talking incessantly among themselves for days "up to the present no official approval of your plans has been given. . . . I have twice reminded [Lloyd George] that time is running short." Haig boiled over and sent a strong letter in return. It was "somewhat startling to learn that the War Cabinet have not yet determined whether the attack is to be permitted to proceed."

But unknown to Sir Douglas this message crossed another heading his way from the civilians—a poor, half-hearted thing, breathing in doubts and exhaling reservations. Yes, he might proceed with his Flanders attack, but it would have to be stopped if the losses were too heavy for the gains achieved. In such case, the Italian scheme would take its place. Furthermore, Haig was to prepare at once for this alternate plan, should it become necessary to execute it. And finally they would like to know (for perhaps the fifth time) what his first Flanders objective really was, "so that," in the words of an official historian, "they might be able to judge whether the operation had, up to that stage, succeeded or not." Haig replied bitingly. He resented the insinuation of the War Cabinet that he was not to be trusted, and asked whether the members did or did not wish to render confidence and support to his plan of operations.

Four days passed, and one can well picture the earnest deliberations of the politicians during this astonishing delay. Here was their last chance to get off the hook. They decided, instead, to swallow it even if they gagged on it. On July 25 the War Cabinet wired the commander in chief their "wholehearted support." To say that it came in the nick of time would be an understatement, for three days earlier 3091 British guns around Ypres had already begun the greatest artillery bombardment in the history of land warfare.

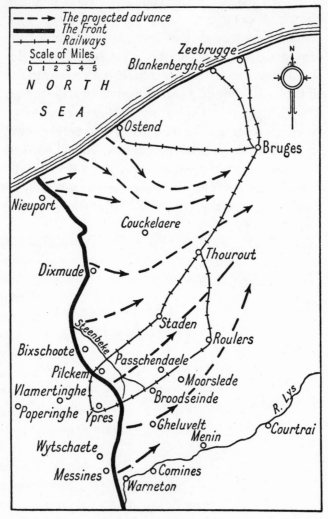

General plan, July, 1917

8. On the Brink

WHILE the great men pondered and argued in London and finally reached their uneasy agreement, events in far-off Galicia, of all places, were sharply raising the odds against Sir Douglas Haig's gamble in Flanders.

The Eastern Front had been generally silent all spring. Leon Trotsky in his history of the Russian revolution points out that a *de facto* armistice existed and that "the Germans availed themselves of it for a wholesale transfer of troops to the western front." This in itself was an extremely serious turn of events from the British point of view. Of course everyone knew that Russian troops had been deserting and fraternizing with the enemy in considerable numbers since March, and while defensively their front continued to be of value to the Allied cause Pétain had remarked with his usual insight into the ways of defeat and decay, "The Russian army is nothing but a façade; it will fall to pieces if it makes a move."

As we have seen, Kerenski forced it to make that move. In June with typical grandiloquence he told his commanding general, Brusilov, "I command you—forward!" and in desperation the Russian commander tried to get some kind of an offensive going. With no staff preparations, no time table, no coordination, no hope, local officers were simply told to start attacking whenever they could persuade or browbeat their more docile men into advancing. The absurd operation took place in piecemeal fashion, therefore, starting late in June—the major effort is said to have begun about July 1—at various disconnected sectors along the front. The main attack was against the Austrians in Galicia, and here, at first, some easy advances were made. Then came the counterattack, and on July 8 the Russian Eleventh Army reported "an overwhelming catastrophe." From this date on it might be said that the Eastern Front passed into virtual oblivion, and about thirty divisions of the Central Powers were now free to turn their attentions to France and Flanders.

The British high command, only anxious to plunge out of the salient at Ypres, paid surprisingly little attention to this ominous development. For in no other country—not even, any longer, in France—were the generals so indoctrinated with a spirit of the offensive, and by 1917 they were indeed a frustrated and embittered lot. In truth, they had not really won a victory of any consequence in Europe since the beginning of the war; and three years of deadlock had corroded their souls and driven them to an inchoate determination to smash through, to charge like a bull at the gate, to break out into open country, and there to continue attacking and attacking and attacking with infantry and cavalry, sweeping the enemy before them in the grand old way of traditional warfare.

And of all British generals with zest for the assault, the name of Sir Hubert Gough headed the list. In his hands Haig placed the spearhead of the campaign, though he and his army had never set foot in the salient before. Because he was only forty-seven, impetuous, and an ex-cavalryman like his chief, Haig considered him more likely to crash through than Plumer and Rawlinson, both of whom were older and (in the past) more sympathetic toward limited attacks for partial gains—precisely what Haig did not have in mind at the moment. But the field marshal could not possess the best of all possible worlds, and in appointing Gough for the main stroke he had also to accept a pair of attendant liabilities, like the man who in marrying the beauteous and rich widow also has to live with her two repellent children.

First, Sir Hubert knew almost nothing of the country in which he was asked to operate.

Second, he was saddled with a fairly incompetent staff, a bit too supercilious in its ways; and to these people Gough clung with an easy loyalty that did him no credit, though they had already compromised several operations conducted by the Fifth Army since its baptism in battle. Many combat officers resented the staff members; some were barely on speaking terms with them. Gough himself was a balding but boyish chap of high military quality, always half smiling, invariably courteous, witty, and personable. As an individual he was liked; yet the responsibility was indeed his for the frequent blunders of omission and commission emanating from his subordinates. All too often, in the past, Fifth Army supplies had arrived later or at the wrong place. Planning was far below the level for which Harington's group was famous. Tiresome, meticulous paper work to insure coordination between battalions and divisions was hardly a specialty of Fifth Army headquarters. Under such conditions Sir Hubert's reputation had been gravely damaged in the past—at Bullecourt, for example, to name an especially egregious instance. It would soon be ascertained whether affairs would be managed better starting July 31.

Nor was Gough's Fifth Army the keenest blade in Douglas Haig's arsenal. It had formerly been the Reserve Army, had received its new name only nine months ago, and possessed a rather bad reputation for always being pushed and pulled here and there and everywhere, thrown into the most dangerous fighting, suffering far and away the heaviest casualties of any British army in the war. It was, in fact, a vast sprawling collection of shock troops. Men hated and feared to be assigned to it. Furthermore, its components were always being internally shifted about. By the summer of 1917 it was an amazing hodgepodge of regulars, reservists, conscriptees, territorials, volunteers, and as-

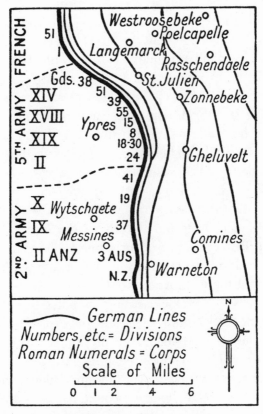

The attack on July 31, 1917

sorted units dropped into the caldron for lack of any better idea of what to do with them at the moment.

Officers were assigned, then reassigned; and the shifts in personnel were so frequent and seemingly capricious that few troops knew the names of their battalion commanders. All this was most disquieting, but by late July there was no use discussing it, much less trying to do anything about it.

It is a cardinal principle of so-called military science that an attack from within a salient must be directed against at least one of the sides and not against the apex of the angle, where any advance would only thrust the troops still deeper into their deadly noose. Thus Gough's main blow, upon which everything else depended—even Rawlinson's bound along the coast— would be almost due east toward the Gheluvelt Plateau, rather than north or northeast toward St. Julien and Passchendaele. Simultaneously the Second Army under Plumer was to stand almost stationary and merely capture strong points in the vicinity of Warneton. Next the Fifth Army would take Menin and the Pilckem ridge. Sir Douglas Haig computed that within eight days the entire loop of the Ypres-Roulers-Thourout railroad should be in Gough's hands—an advance of fifteen miles. Now, at last, Rawlinson's Fourth Army would move, the amphibious landing would take place, Plumer would move north and northwest and take over the defense of the entire captured ridge, Gough and Rawlinson would join hands, the grand sweep up the coast would begin, and the German western flank would be turned in and pressed toward Berlin. Meanwhile the cavalry would be released for the charge and the kill.

How much of all this Haig really believed is not certain, though there is evidence that he had been temporarily sobered by Lloyd George's gloomy lectures the previous month. While in theory the field marshal clung to his larger dream, he had evidently in practice come around to some degree, at least, of "step-by-step" thinking, until an episode took place which proved that he still had his eyes mainly fixed on a super-victory. Originally it had been planned to advance only a mile the first day to the German second defense line, which included the Gheluvelt Plateau and the Pilckem ridge, at which time and place there would be a two-day pause for establishing observation posts and bringing up artillery. Later Gough decided in a sudden, typical burst of enthusiasm to include the third German line in his first day's capture. And, he added, if his divisional commanders thought they could do so they might proceed without pause to the German fourth line running through Broodseinde— about three miles from the jump-off positions. Three days later the entire Passchendaele ridge would be occupied. It would, he suggested, "be wasteful not to reap all the advantages possible resulting from the first attack." To this Sir Douglas surprisingly agreed.

But immediately Gough was challenged by Haig's own Operations Branch headed by Brigadier General J. H. Davidson. What on earth had happened to

GHQ's original, laboriously conceived step-by-step plan? Gough's expectations were not practical, he predicted, and would not bring sustained results. For one thing, the fourth enemy line was even beyond the range of British field pieces. He urged the army commander to reconsider.

Gough responded that he still felt that his army should advance as far and as fast as it could. Now Haig was called in. He discussed the problem with Plumer. They decided to back Gough, provided that he would restrain his brigades farther north at least until his right flank was firmly secured around Gheluvelt. Strangely enough, the once cautious Sir Herbert Plumer had been the most vehement of all. As he pattered along with Davidson to the conference room, belly and mustache quivering, he burst out, "Do you think that after making the vast preparations for attack on this position . . . after sitting in the salient all this time, I am going to agree to limiting the progress and advance of my troops? I say definitely *no*, I would certainly not agree to any such limitation." So here the matter rested; and thus the step-by-step technique which Haig had promised in London was scrapped.

Although the politicians were not told of this interesting development, some of them, as we have seen, had long been wary. On July 22 Winston Churchill, for one, wrote Lloyd George confiding his regrets that Haig had been given a green light, and went on to say:

It is clear however that no human power exists which can stop the attempt being made. The essential thing now is to arrive at a definition of success and "great results" which will enable a new decision to be taken after the first or second phases of this offensive have been fought. Such a definition must, it seems to me, involve three conditions, viz., objectives taken; casualities sustained; and thirdly (very important) the time taken or required between any one thrust and the next. Thus it should be possible, by reference to these forecasts, to settle definitely after (say) six weeks of fighting whether there really is any prospect of obtaining "great results" before winter sets in. . . .

The point was not one of verbal phrasing or psychological attitudes. Either Haig anticipated a fast breakthrough, and prepared for it accordingly, or he planned to wear down the enemy step by step, and prepared for *that* accordingly. In his "mixture of motives lay grave disadvantages," an official historian later commented. In one case, surprise was vital. In the other, lack of surprise might be almost beneficial so as to lure more enemy troops into the mincing machine. In either event, vastly different staff preparations would be needed. Which did Haig really aim at? Forty years later we can answer this hazy question with some assurance: He was hoping for a breakthrough but willing to settle for more dead Germans than British—a victory of attrition.

Ignoring for the moment how the battle might end, let us first consider how it was to start.

It might first be noted that some officers mistrusted it on general principles. Among them was Gough's artillery adviser, Major General Uniacke, who feared that enemy guns on the ridge to the right would be able to dominate the Fifth Army the moment it jumped off. His argument worried Gough, who passed it on to Haig with the radical request that Plumer's Second Army be given as heavy a share in the attack as his own. This Haig refused to do.

As to cavalry, two divisions were brought up on the Fifth Army flanks, ready to charge toward the Pass-chendaele-Staden ridge. There was much talk and preparation for "putting the cavalry through the gap" and maps were issued to officers showing the terrain as far back as twenty miles behind the German lines.

About 180 aircraft were placed under Gough's immediate command. Intense observation work began during the middle of July. On the 29th, when air reports were most needed, the weather turned dreary and visibility from aloft became almost nil. On the 30th it was even worse; not one aerial combat was reported in Flanders that day and only a handful of planes got into the air at all. Buzzing along too fast and too low in the haze beneath a sullen ceiling of dense low clouds, they were unable to see much of anything.

Meanwhile Lord Rawlinson, Fourth Army Commander, had been instructed by Sir Douglas Haig "as and when the main attack to the east of Ypres made progress, to land with the assistance of Admiral Bacon's naval forces on the coast east of Nieuport, and eventually to advance, in conjunction with the main attack, upon Bruges. . . ." Although the Germans had embarrassed this army on July 10 by a lightning sortie and won commanding positions on the right bank of the Yser, thus complicating Rawlinson's problem greatly, his preparations continued in an aura of high enthusiasm. While Bacon and his marines trained in the Thames estuary for their amphibious operation, Rawlinson withdrew his 1st Division to the dunes southwest of Dunkirk. Here a secret training camp was built and surrounded by a wire fence. All leaves were suspended. Mail was censored. The landing force began practicing the scaling of the sea wall; tanks were constructed with special ramps to negotiate the steep slope and the artificial barrier behind the beach, and excited conferences without end took place between the Army and Navy officers involved.

The general line-up may be recapitulated briefly. Gough's main attack in the center would take place along a seven-mile front and would initially employ ten divisions grouped into the XIV, XVIII, XIX, and II Corps, running from north to south. Above them General Anthoine's First French Army would attack (primarily to guard Gough's left flank against German counterstrokes) with two divisions. Below to the south, acting somewhat as a holding operation in order to divert the enemy artillery, stood Plumer and his Second Army composed of three home divisions plus the New Zealand Division and the 3rd Australian

Division. This made about 100,000 troops actually assigned to the assault; and behind these seventeen divisions were seventeen more, ready to move upon signal. The entire offensive front—Anthoine, Gough, Plumer—measured fifteen miles.

Directly opposite lay the German Fourth Army under General Friedrich Sixt von Armin, whose chief of staff was Colonel von Lossberg, Germany's top defensive expert, who had been given a free hand to develop defenses that would smother Haig's drive. Von Lossberg was in his element and had plenty of time. He increased the German trench and pillbox system to six lines—five and a half, to be exact, since the second one stopped short of Plumer's front. In general, his dispositions emphasized strong points rather than rigid, densely packed frontal masses. Forward areas were held lightly. Several hundred new machine-gun posts were sprinkled throughout the forward slopes of the ridge, and the riflemen were mostly withdrawn to prepared defenses on the reverse slopes.

The crux of von Lossberg's formula, notwithstanding all the above, was counterattack. Bodies of troops for this purpose were staggered in depth throughout the rear, with the strongest ones farthest back. In this way, he hoped, his retaliatory blows would get successively more powerful, should the need arise.

In artillery opposite Gough's crucial front, the Germans emplaced 1556 light and heavy guns, compared to the Englishman's 2299. As for infantry, the Germans had arrayed three corps (groups) from Warneton to a

Ypres, October 27, 1917

point slightly south of Bixschoote. From south to north they were Group Wytschaete with five divisions, Group Ypres with three divisions, and Group Dixmude with one division. Close behind these front-line units were six reserve divisions. Behind these six were two more particularly mobile divisions. Behind these two were three more.

During the latter half of July it became depressingly clear to Allied officers near the front that the enemy was preparing for them in an unprecedented way. Shelling from the ridge increased every day until no point along the entire front of the salient could be considered safe. As at Messines the British field guns sat almost hub-cap to hub-cap directly out in the flat Flemish plain, with the heavies so close behind that the respective battery men could call back and forth to each other. Prior to Messines it had been the Germans who were in a salient, shelled and decimated from both sides; now the tables were precisely turned and the losses among British guns and gunners became tragically severe.

The enemy shelled selected areas without let-up, using everything from 8-inchers to "pipsqueaks," and at night he drenched the area with mustard gas. The incessant uproar, the aggravating donning and doffing of gas masks, the lack of sleep, the heavy casualties— all this had reduced Allied artillery personnel to edginess and exhaustion by the 31st. And the ordinarily pessimistic Crown Prince Rupprecht noted in his diary:

> My mind is quite at rest about the attack, as we have never disposed of such strong reserves, so well trained for their part, as on the front attacked.

Four of these divisions, by the way, had come from Max Hoffman's Eastern Front in May. Many more were now available and, in fact, were streaming toward the salient and other sectors of the Western Front. If Sir Douglas Haig was looking for Germans in vast numbers to kill, to exhaust, to bleed, and to capture in Flanders, he was about to find them.

The British Tank Corps in particular—all volunteers —was wild with excitement over its first test in battle on a large scale, but at the same time apprehensive about the ground and the weather. In the words of Colonel C. D. Baker-Carr, one of the brigade commanders:

> To anyone familiar with the terrain in Flanders it was almost inconceivable that this part of the line should have been selected. If a careful search had been made from the English Channel to Switzerland, no more unsuitable spot could have been discovered.

He went on to remark that Ypres had once been a seaport and was now an inland city only because of the man-made drainage system, that every farmer had been responsible at the risk of heavy fines for the state of repair of the ditches and dikes on his property, and that "To put it mildly, we were absolutely astounded at the decision to attack at this point."

The possibility of flooding worried the tank people more than the thousands of shell holes. Headquarters expected 216 Mark IVs to operate on the Fifth Army front regardless of circumstances and without excuses; nevertheless the Tank Corps staff began discreetly to acquire information from local inhabitants and the Belgian "Ponts et Chaussées." Their worst suspicions were confirmed: rain, plus a heavy bombardment which would wreck what remained of the watercourse system, was bound to convert the battlefield again into a swamp. Since this would leave no suitable ground for tanks to move on (not to mention men, guns, and vehicles) a warning memorandum was sent to the Fifth Army general staff. To this there was no reply.

Next the Tank Corps people forwarded charts which assumed the worst and indicated where the larger pools of water would collect. Now Gough's staff languidly bestirred itself and dispatched a curt note containing the following phrase: "Send us no more of these ridiculous maps."

If Fifth Army headquarters had few qualms, other persons, including Sir Douglas, were not so unconcerned. The field marshal dreaded the thought of rain and especially what it would do to the area in the northeast, "a tract of ground [in the words of one writer] which was difficult when dry but which became grotesque in its difficulties when it rained and the low-lying streams or 'beeks' which meandered through it spread out into broad marshy bottoms."

Colonel Repington sadly discussed the prospect with the commander in chief and said, "I hate the idea of thrusting an army into such a daedalus of mud and water."

Haig replied that if he only advanced "a bit, it was all to the good."

So the confused, nagging guessing game went on, and the forebodings of private soldiers at the front were echoed down the corridors of command through battalion headquarters, brigade, regiment, division, army, general headquarters, and at 10 Downing Street, where Lloyd George sullenly awaited developments.

In those sunny days before the attack, while only the cannoneers dueled, a million British foot soldiers in and near the salient rested and killed time and tried not to think of the future.

Day and night the dusty roads from Ypres ("Mecca of all good soldiers") to Vlamertinghe and Poperinghe were thronged with troops seeking sundry pleasures in towns, farms, and rest areas far behind the front. Soccer and cricket were played on improvised fields. Red Cross canteens were crowded uproariously and good-naturedly as never before, and there was no end to the talk and well-worn phrases. "Hullo, I thought you were dead!" "Are you enjoying the war?" "Got a spare fag?" "Remember me to Blighty!"

In Y.M.C.A. tents kindly old gentlemen in vaguely military uniforms served cake, cocoa, and packets of real British Woodbines. The men swam in the canals and in little lakes such as the Zillebeke and the Dicke-busch, bargained with the farmers' daughters, got drunk, haggled over souvenirs. Far behind the restless front, where the big guns were only a rumble, it was a carnival time for troops who would soon be back at the business of war. In wonder and joy and with aching hearts they absorbed those common sights and sounds so long forgotten—leafy trees, splashes of sunlight on outdoor cafés, green fields, people at work at home and in their orchards. They polished their boots, scraped dirt from their uniforms, and filed into wash-ing sheds singing that immortal ballad:

> *Whiter than the whitewash on the wall,*
> *Whiter than the whitewash on the wall,*
> *Wash me in your water*
> *That you wash your dirty daughter*
> *And I shall be whiter than the whitewash*
>   *on the wall*

and scarcely were they dressed again than a warning itch proved that they would be as lousy as ever next morning.

In such backwater towns as Calais the streets were flooded with soldiers of all Allied nations—Portuguese,

Belgians, a scattering of American engineers, blue-clad French poilus, brawny New Zealanders, French colonials of darker mien, Canadians, reserved Indians, Londoners, Irish, tall, bronzed Australian farm boys not noted for classic discipline, always with soft hats and rolled-up brims. The beer was weak, the food was overpriced, but life was good. Far from the face of war they marched, met inspection, drilled at bayonets, practiced squad maneuvers, dozed, played cards, walked the countryside, crammed the restaurants. By the last week in July most leaves had ended, the carnival was over, and a great influx of returning men had restored front-line battalions to full assault strength. Back at the front nothing seemed to have changed, except that new tensions lay like a shroud over the battle zone and the guns boomed with a greater, grimmer intensity than ever before.

In London, too, everyone awaited the start of Haig's offensive and the good news it was sure to bring. The nation carried on as usual that relatively placid, pregnant summer.

On July 7 the most daring air attack of the war hit the metropolis from twenty four-engine Gothas, killing and wounding two hundred fifty people, most of them in the East End. There was much recrimination in Commons over the poor defenses and the lack of proper warning.

After a naval action the Admiralty reported that the destroyers *Swift* and *Broke* "were fortunate in being able to save the lives of ten German officers and 108 men from the vessels which were sunk," a communiqué which caused intense disgust. The *National News* wrote of the "crassly idiotic words and messages penned by a responsible government official.... Nothing could be calculated to throw contempt on the nation so much as official folly of this description . . . sentimentality . . . weak-kneed . . ."

On July 28 Colonel A'Court Repington, that haughtly analyst of military affairs, wrote, "We played tennis on Sunday, but were driven in later by the rain, and then played Bridge. . . . The guns in Flanders were heard very distinctly on the terrace at Glynde. It was a continuous throbbing, the noise of the heaviest guns occasionally rising above the distant din."

In Parliament Mr. Pringle complained of the lack of discretion in calling-up notices, which had been sent to "the maimed, the halt, the blind, the mute, the mad, and even the dead." A large uproar ensued. Bonar Law insisted that the War Office was making "an honest effort" to carry out the Review of Exemptions Act.

Early in July the *Daily News* editorialized about the Russian offensive: "The remarkable success attending the Russian army is due primarily, no doubt, to the spirit of freedom abroad in it. There is no spur in war like an ideal." Scarcely was this edition on the street when the Russian armies melted away. Now came a sadder and wiser headline, "The Tragedy of Russia," and the writer stated dully, "The Russian army would seem to have ceased to exist as a military instrument."

As the month drew to a close, showery cloudy days spread over most of England—a typical summer's-end cold front that moved slowly from west to east across the Channel and headed for northern France and Belgium.

Here on July 30 Sir Douglas visited General Gough in Fifth Army headquarters at Chateau Loewe and found him "in the best of spirits, and full of confidence as to the results of tomorrow's fight."

The British and French artillery bombardment might be said to have begun in earnest on July 15. By the 22nd it had become ultra-heavy and continuous along the entire Flanders front. There had never before been such shelling—one gun to every six yards of line—and what with the German batteries replying and the flaming streaks of variously colored signal flares it was perhaps the greatest show of fireworks in history. On the 28th counter-battery fire began, but, as we have seen, on the 29th and 30th intermittent fog cloaked the battleground and made it impossible to carry out this final and most important task with much efficiency. It was, in truth, from the looks of things all too likely that rain was coming, and soon.

For three evenings prior to the morning of zero hour the assault brigades plodded toward their advanced assembly areas and then, more stealthily, into the front lines. The tanks rumbled toward their stations. Regiments of mounted cavalry cantered to their assigned

Stretcher bearers in action after the Battle of Pilckem Ridge, August 1, 1917

flank positions. The early night of the 30th was warm and calm beneath leaden skies. As the infantry walked forward a signaler or runner occasionally flashed his lamp; then there would follow angry yells: "Put that blasted light out!" Enemy shelling grew heavier by the hour.

Just before the attack a German machine gun facing 13th Sussex spoke: "Ta-t-t-ta-ta." A British gunner replied: "Ta-ta." The men chuckled. They kept up the game till it got on everyone's nerves. Then a shell dropped into the lines. There was a suppressed commotion.

"Stretcher bearers!"

"Coming up."

"Someone hit."

"Ay."

"Lucky sod. He's saved a lot of trouble."

The stricken man called out wildly for his mother, and a nerve-racked voice grated, "Oh, put a sock in his blasted mouth."

Trembling and with hearts pounding, the men fixed bayonets and touched hands. The youngest man in one platoon insisted on shaking hands with everyone. He was dead drunk. This time the troops had been given not the usual tea with rum before an attack, but tea that was more than half rum.

Sir Douglas Haig, at his advanced GHQ in a railway coach beneath a row of trees nineteen miles west of Ypres, recorded nervously in his diary:

Glass steady. Morning dull and coldish. The bright weather reported as coming is slower in its progress than expected by our weather prophet.

He dozed. At 4:15 he was awakened by the stupendous drumfire of the barrage many miles away and by the ground shaking beneath his railway car. The Fifth Army had, in fact, gone over the top almost half an hour previously.

Field gun bogged at Pilckem Ridge, August 2, 1917

9. The Opening Phase

Essentially the fate of the assault which unrolled that morning—one so monstrous that it appeared beyond the creation or control of the human will—depended on II Corps, commanded by the astute Lieutenant General Claud Jacob, fifty-three years old, born and raised in India and in the Indian Army. He had been handed a most formidable task. That dark-gray morning his three divisions lay poised, armed to the teeth, aimed like a pistol at the scowling undulations of Gheluvelt Plateau. On both sides of this key objective some sixty feet high—a sizable eminence in Flanders—the ground fell away into little valleys. From its top the entire Flemish plain could be seen on a clear day as far west as the French border, occasionally as far north as the sea.

Within II Corps, one might say, everything depended on the 30th Division, composed mainly of Manchester and Liverpool battalions—a slender reed, for it had been hurt especially severely at the Somme last year and at Arras during the spring, and its personnel were not pleased at having been assigned to the deadly direct attack against the ridge. Of this the Fifth Army staff seemed unaware. However Haig's headquarters, somewhat more alert to military realities, had suggested interchanging the 30th with one of its two flank divisions. Perhaps the advice came too late; in any event the switch was not made.

Facing Jacob's young men along a three-mile front was the most domineering sector of the German reception zone—three major defense lines jammed together within less than a mile, dense with pillboxes and lesser machine-gun posts. In the past British infantrymen had learned how to deal with isolated strong points, but here each post defended another, so that men trying to knock one out would be exposed to fire from one or more close by. This entire system of brownish fortifications not only had been well camouflaged but had had the protection of bad weather and was practically intact. Thus the prior bombardment had been firing more or less at random, rather than at specific targets such as these. German light artillery looking down on No Man's Land was massed heavily on the slopes east and south.

Everywhere along the Fifth Army front the ground was exasperatingly soft. Nobody had worried much about the showers of preceding weeks, but they had done their part to gum up the plain through which the infantry would have to pass before reaching the gentle upslopes.

Even Fifth Army planners had been anxiously aware of the problems in their path, and for weeks had bombarded divisional commanders with warnings and data concerning soil conditions and the abnormal intensity of enemy defense preparations. This is not to say that General Gough and his immediate officers anticipated a reverse. On the contrary, past failures had dissolved into nothingness in dark, forgotten recesses of their minds. As usual, they expected to win out after a brisk fight. In Churchill's words, "the hopes of decisive victory . . . grew with every step away from the front line and reached absolute conviction in the Intelligence Department."

The confidence of British brass was matched by that of von Hindenburg:

I had a certain feeling of satisfaction when this new battle began. . . . It was with a feeling of absolute longing that we waited for the beginning of the wet season. As previous experience had taught us, great stretches of the Flemish flats would then become impassable, and even in firmer places the new shell holes would fill so quickly with ground water that men seeking shelter in them would find themselves faced with the alternative, "Shall we drown or get out of this hole?" This battle, too, must finally stick in the mud, even though English stubbornness kept it up longer than otherwise.

Somebody had to be wrong. Either way, the fate of the Third Battle of Ypres would very likely be indicated after the first few days of fighting.

As II Corps advanced due east toward the shrouded highland the men found themselves variously impeded throughout the outpost system by Chateau Wood (8th Division), Sanctuary Wood (30th Division), and Shrewsbury Forest (24th Division). In this pathetic jumble of debris, fallen trees, rusty barbed wire, and shell craters the heavy-laden troops laboriously picked their way to the accompaniment of a tornado of shrapnel. As for tanks, the first messages brought back by carrier pigeons were disquieting: "Direct hit on tank by field gun. One killed, two wounded." "Ditched in German front line. Being heavily shelled."

Along Jacob's front the ponderous, clanking machines tried to advance through three narrow defiles; here they immediately came under heavy artillery fire. Not one reached its final objective. In the heavy going they could barely achieve a speed of one mile an hour, and soon they were left behind by the infantry. In No Man's Land dozens became trapped in soft spots. Their crews got out and tried to pull them free—a sight both pitiful and incongruous, for while the men shoved and hauled at their steel monsters in the midst of this most ferocious battle scene they became the target of everything that could fire at them from land

Field Marshal Paul von Hindenburg, Kaiser
Wilhelm II, and General Erich Ludendorff

and air. Five tanks reached the 18th Division jump-off tapes and tried to push forward. Every one bogged down, and in a flash four were knocked out by unpleasantly accurate shell fire.

The general attack had scarcely begun when part of the 30th Division ground to a halt a few hundred yards up the Menin road, blocked by one enormous pillbox which could be neither captured nor destroyed by heavy guns. One by one the tanks that approached were knocked out by its anti-tank gun. Soon seventeen broken, abandoned tanks littered the ground, some smoldering; and as the men tried to get out they were machine-gunned by Germans within the intact pillbox. Thus was created the famous "Tank Graveyard."

Very soon the 30th Division lost all touch with its barrage, which was proceeding as stolidly as Frankenstein's monster at the rate of twenty-five yards per minute—a complete waste of ammunition—and while the first (Blue) line a few hundred yards ahead was reached early in the morning it began to appear doubtful if the men could fight their way forward any farther without artillery support.

By ten o'clock a sorry situation had developed. The British artillery, still ignorant of the true state of affairs, had commenced its forward creep from the second to the third objective, though the infantry had not even left the first one. At 10:40 the commanding general of the division forwarded a message to II Corps headquarters near Poperinghe that "apparently we are not on the Black [second] line anywhere. . . ." The admission was a serious one, for if after seven hours the 30th Division had only been able to move some five hundred yards through Sanctuary Wood, it might be said that II Corps as a whole was stymied, that the Fifth Army had failed, and that Haig's entire plan had already blown sky-high.

What of the other two divisions in II Corps? Perhaps they had been able to salvage matters. But by late morning the 24th had advanced through Shrewsbury Forest only three or four hundred yards, and the 8th was embedded in the nightmarish wastes of Chateau Wood. Everywhere the story was the same: the pillboxes were far more numerous than Fifth Army headquarters had anticipated, German artillery dominated the field from both flanks, the tanks were valueless except in a few isolated instances, British light guns were firing blindly at nothing that mattered, losses were high, the ground gained was far short of expectations. One brigade got lost altogether and reported that it had captured Glencorse Wood (it was, in fact, occupying Chateau Wood), and such confusion developed along the Menin road that after a few hours eight separate battalions were milling around in the same splatter of shell holes just east of Sanctuary Wood.

II Corps was now really stalled, and, to make matters worse, communications were such that headquarters was unable to straighten out the jumble or even to visualize the tactical situation. Practically every telephone wire had been cut by enemy gunfire, wireless instruments were dead, visual signaling was ineffective in the hazy light, and only pigeons and men were able to relay scraps of information back and forth. By noon every effort to push on had been fruitless and a long, sinister pause took place all along the front from the Ypres-Roulers rail line to Klein Zillebeke.

Elsewhere the news was far better. The French had fought spiritedly—this was strange, for according to Sir Douglas there was little or no spark left in the French Army—and by noon Anthoine's troops had proceeded nearly a mile toward Bixschoote.

XIV Corps up north had captured Pilckem by 1 P.M. and had advanced another mile to the Steenbeke. On its right, XVIII Corps also reached that stream and had even managed to cross it just north of St. Julien.

XIX Corps worked its way forward through the first German defense zone a distance of about a mile, and here again one of its divisions (the 55th) crossed the Steenbeke and pushed on a bit farther.

Below General Jacob's unfortunate brigades the Second Army captured all its modest objectives by noon and then stopped to await further developments, if any, by II Corps on its left.

But all these peripheral profits did not constitute an unmixed blessing, for the deeper the three northern corps of the Fifth Army shoved forward into the German positions the more they constituted a salient (due to the failure of II Corps) into which enfilade fire increasingly poured. Thus as the day crept on and the

British clung to their gains deep in No Man's Land they suffered steady losses of the most exasperating kind from machine guns, mortars, and 77s to their right, emanating from ground which Jacob's men had been unable to occupy. By one o'clock a sizable but dangerous bulge about two thousand yards deep had been created northwest of Zonnebeke. Since this area could not be held at reasonable cost, it was decided to evacuate it.

At one o'clock it began to drizzle. The fighting went on in a desultory way—quite heavily here and there—though by now there was no momentum left along the Menin road and no real hope that II Corps could get forward any farther that day. A west wind swept coldly across the plain. The scudding gray clouds imperceptibly thickened and became a solid mass beneath which a few rickety airplanes still sputtered, trying to glean some information from the colors of the men's uniforms and from occasional signal flares thrown up to identify units stranded far forward, a-waiting the inevitable counterattacks. Thirty British planes were shot down by rifle and machine-gun fire, some by their own men.

At four o'clock the drizzle turned to rain—a heavy, relentless downpour of the kind which gives one the feeling that it will never end. The water in the shell holes, in the blasted canals and shallow streams, slowly and microscopically rose. Very little rain water sank in; it merely lay on the topsoil and began saturating

the thin crust that hid the clay. By dusk the battleground was in the preliminary stages of flooding, and
already all movements were becoming quite laborious.

That afternoon Sir Douglas visited General Gough,
who was seemingly in excellent spirits, agreed with his
superior that the first day was proving a "great success," and reported that over 5000 prisoners had been
taken and that the ground was thick with dead Germans. A communiqué along these lines was issued to
the world by British GHQ. One may only observe that
it bore little resemblance to the realities faced by the
fighting men in the battle zone.

The first of many counterattacks had begun at 9:30
that morning and increased in boldness throughout
the afternoon and evening. The faces of officers in the
concrete dugouts of battalion headquarters were by
now glum and—what is perhaps worse—indecisive.
Farther up front the handwriting on the wall could be
read even more clearly. Most company headquarters
were established in shell holes covered by waterproof
sheets which kept out the rain but allowed the surface
wash to seep in. Slowly the craters filled with scummy
water. Here the junior officers, runners, and platoon
sergeants crouched with flashlights over maps and
messages. Tempers were short. One officer tells how "I
found myself suddenly threatening a sergeant-major
with arrest for some unfriendly view. . . ." There had
long been a legend in the British Expeditionary Force
in France and Belgium that the Germans could make

it rain whenever they wanted to. By this standard, the rain had begun precisely on Boche schedule. It kept pouring. An utterly black evening crept on, lit only by lurid flashes of the guns and reddish-white explosions as the shells whammed into the soft ground.

Most fortunate were headquarters personnel who had set up housekeeping in captured German pill-boxes. But the Germans turned their guns on these as well as No Man's Land. When there was a direct hit against a concrete shelter or an occupied shell hole, hell broke loose in the darkness; the wounded screamed and cursed; the dead were hastily shoved aside; groping, shouting figures milled around in terror and called for stretcher bearers and stared hard into the gloom for signs of approaching Germans. All too often they came, and from St. Julien down the line to Warneton enemy troops kept sliding in and enfilading the Allied positions. Innumerable little brawls developed, with bombs and bayonets, on the order of bar-room free-for-alls. The fighting was dogged and disjointed. As the shell holes, concrete emplacements, and mounds were battled over, attackers and attacked constantly changed places. Casualties among junior officers were heavy, as in all pitched battles of all wars. Sergeants, sometimes corporals, sometimes even privates, became platoon commanders.

It was the classic picture, painted perhaps more somberly than most, of a military impasse along most of the front, particularly on the right. While fortunes changed minutely throughout the day and evening, the new French and British line was little different by midnight from what it had been at noon, except that it had been drawn back or forced back at several places.

As the fighting simmered down, the waste products of the battle, like the precipitate in a cloudy glass, moved rearward—the walking wounded and the stretcher-laden wounded ("very cheery indeed" according to Haig's diary), soaked, bloody, haggard with pain; the shrouded dead; the vague and stumbling shellshocked. One artillery lieutenant had been struck in the throat by a bit of shrapnel. As the blood gushed, he walked a hundred yards to a dressing station near Zillebeke, gasped to a doctor, "My God, I'm going to die!" and immediately did so. The stretcher bearers worked all day and night, helped by German prisoners, who also had begun to filter back early in the day—surprisingly young boys and older, grimmer veterans—all with sunken eyes, sodden clothing, boots full of water that squished at every step.

As the rain continued, traffic was forced to leave the open fields. On the roads sluggishly moving masses of men and machines, mules and wagons congregated— choice targets against which the German gunners now concentrated effectively. But as yet, because there was no need for them, serious counterattacks did not develop. Rupprecht's divisions on and behind the reverse slopes of the ridge sat tight and awaited instructions, while smaller units along the Passchendaele sector, astride the St. Julien-Poelcapelle road and atop the crest of Zonnebeke spur, drove forward through the day and early evening. Preceded by brief, brisk barrages, they attacked strong points here and there along the new line. After actions like these, the silence of the tomb settled forever over many British advance posts, and certain localities such as at Kansas Cross and Schuler Farm had to be abandoned. But the Germans, too, had to wade through mud and water up to their ankles, found the going hard, and often were thrown back with ease by the defenders.

On both sides the losses were already considerable, with the Allies deeper in the red than their opponents. By 10 p.m. the three assault brigades of the 55th (1st West Lancashire) Division had suffered casualties of seventy per cent. This was unusually high, though by the end of the day Gough's army had lost more than a third of its attacking complement in killed, wounded, and missing. The first sobering shreds of this information began to reach Sir Douglas Haig late in the morning. When later he visited Gough he had seemed cool and confident, but that he was shaken is plain from what he said: The attack was to proceed, by all means, but only after heavy bombardment had stunned the defenses and dominated the enemy artillery. For an hour the two men spoke quietly in the huge, ugly La Lovie Château which housed Fifth Army headquarters, while rain slashed against the windows and the air trembled with the incessant roar of guns miles away; and as they talked they awaited further word —perhaps more encouraging—from II Corps. None came, and Haig took his leave.

Shortly before six o'clock Gough received a final situation report: General Jacob's infantry had still not moved and XIX Corps had retreated a mile to the Steenbeke. That settled it. At 8:45 Sir Hubert ordered both corps not to renew the attack for two days, after "several adjustments" had been made.

Concerning the first day's operations, Sir Douglas stated in a note to the War Cabinet that the results were "highly satisfactory and the losses slight for so great a battle."

On the other hand, the fighting of July 31 (known henceforth by the British as the Battle of Pilckem Ridge, because of their comparative success there) was considered by the Germans to have gone clearly in their own favor. The Crown Prince's diary entry that evening was a jubilant one. He was especially pleased because his Group Wytschaete counterattack divisions to the rear of Gheluvelt Plateau had hardly been employed at all.

Thus the following day, August 1, in a phenomenon not rare for wartime, newspapers in London, Berlin, Paris, and Vienna were all claiming the same victory. The *Times* proclaimed:

GREAT ALLIED ATTACK
Ypres Salient Widened
Two Miles' Advance

Everywhere our objectives were attained . . . the beginning is splendid. . . . Thus we have wrested from the enemy the last of the four great ridges which he held opposite our front up to a year ago.

And in another column:

> We have broken the German line on the whole front attacked. . . . Our casualties seem . . . remarkably light.

It would be hard to cram more inaccuracies into a shorter compass. The salient was not widened; in fact, salient-wise, it was a worse one than before. At the point that mattered most the advance was not two miles but a third of a mile, nor was the average gain anywhere near two miles. The objectives were attained only at subsidiary points. The beginning of the battle was not splendid but a cruel disappointment, especially in view of the break in the weather. No ridges were captured. The main German line had not been reached, much less broken; only his outpost area had been penetrated. British casualties were not light; they were sufficiently severe to cause Sir Douglas to caution Gough against further headlong attacks.

Yet with slight embellishments the newspapers published only the news received by their correspondents from Haig's headquarters. Here it was that Brigadier General Charteris handed out soothing opiates to the newspapermen. It can safely be said that from July 31 to the end of the Flanders campaign Charteris lied steadily to the press, to the War Cabinet, and to his own chief, Field Marshal Haig; and his almost psychopathic distortions during that time must be kept in mind in order to understand how and why the operation progressed as it did. That Haig implicitly trusted the man cannot be doubted. Charteris was to Haig what d'Alenson had been to Nivelle. In the words of General Gough:

> Unfortunately Haig placed complete confidence in General Charteris, head of his Intelligence Service. Charteris was a good psychologist—if not a very strong character—and always told Haig something he especially wanted to hear. Thus Charteris would report that there were no Germans on our front, or that they were too exhausted to be capable of serious resistance. These misconceptions of the real situation cost the British Army dearly on more than one occasion.

Lloyd George particularly despised this forty-year-old Regular Army Glasgowman, to whom the news was always good. "He could only be caught by a bright fly," the Prime Minister writes. "That he swallowed up to the gut"; and he refers cuttingly to how the Intelligence officer selected only those figures and facts which suited his fancy, and then issued hopeful reports accordingly. We shall hear much too much more of General Charteris as the campaign progresses.

For four days and nights it poured, and even Charteris, with a humility and despair uncommon for him, writes in his diary:

Every brook is swollen and the ground is a quagmire. If it were not that all the records in previous years had given us fair warning, it would seem as if Providence had declared against us.

The scene that existed has been well described by Sir Douglas Haig himself in a dispatch to the Government:

The low-lying, clayey soil, torn by shells and sodden with rain, turned to a succession of vast, muddy pools. The valleys of the choked and overflowing streams were speedily transformed into long stretches of bog, impassable except by a few well-defined tracks, which became marks for the enemy's artillery. To leave these tracks was to risk death by drowning, and in the course of the subsequent fighting on several occasions both men and pack animals were lost in this way. In these conditions operations of any magnitude became impossible. . . .

On the morning of August 1 Haig instructed a French representative to urge Pétain to attack as soon as possible on his front so as to draw away Ludendorff's reserves from the salient. Haig had claimed to be attacking largely to take pressure off the French; now it was the other way around. There is a whiff of sour grapes in his diary notation that evening, and a non sequitur in the final phrase:

A terrible day of rain. The ground is like a bog in this low-lying country. . . . We are fortunate not to have advanced to the extreme "Red Line" because it would

not have been possible to supply our guns with ammunition. Our troops would thus have been at the
mercy of a hostile counterattack; and a check might
have resulted.

Small attacks and German counterstrokes continued
for three days without changing matters. Gough canceled the big push scheduled for Thursday, August 2.
Pétain promised to deliver his diversion the following
week. A lull set in; even the big guns quieted down.
Haig was in despair as the Germans collected themselves. Air reconnaissance dropped to zero. The officers at tank headquarters, those brash and peppery
young men, issued a typically sharp memorandum:
"From a tank point of view the Third Battle of Ypres
may be considered dead. . . . From an infantry
point of view the Third Battle of Ypres may be considered comatose. It can only be continued at colossal loss
and little gain. . . ." Fogs blanketed the salient sporadically for the rest of the week, and the rain varied
between drizzles and near cloudbursts. Saturday the
Times soared to new heights of euphoria and spoke of
important new gains, 6122 captured Germans, and
enormous enemy casualties. The French communiqué
that day was in stark contrast:

AFTERNOON. The bad weather continues on the whole
front in Belgium.
EVENING. In Belgium the situation is unchanged, and
the bad weather continues.

Both sides settled down to bury their dead and minister to the wounded. Sixty-nine former members of the German 237th Reserve Infantry Regiment were buried in a mass grave while a Protestant chaplain, one officer complained, "uttered offensive platitudes." A Bavarian corporal with one leg torn off and an arm shattered kept crying over and over, "Haven't you got a bullet for me, comrades?" His friends and fellow-wounded smoked their pipes and stared at him in silence. Here and there fallen horses screamed until they died or were shot. The card players resumed their games. Behind the German front long lines of stretcher bearers waited with their burdens to get into the dressing stations.

Near Zonnebeke, Father William Doyle of the 16th (Irish) Division dashed off another of his famous battle notes to the *Dublin Review*:

> All day I have been hearing the men's confessions, and giving batch after batch Holy Communion. My poor, brave boys—they are lying on the battlefield, some in a little grave dug and blessed by their chaplain. Do you wonder that, in spite of the joy that fills my heart, many a time tears gather in my eyes. . . ?

The diary of an English nurse assigned to a field hospital dangerously near the front also tells of the sequel to battle:

> Soaking hopeless rain, holding up the advance; the worst luck that could happen. Poor Sir Douglas Haig . . .

I got to bed between 2 and 7 and slept like blazes. This morning they really don't look so bad—for abdominals. Only 23 deaths . . .

The abdominals coming in are very bad today—both Boche and British. The work thickens as the wards fill up and new wards have to be opened. We are to take Chests and Femurs too. . . . It is getting very ghastly; the men all look so appalling when they are brought in, and so many die. . . .

Can God be on our side, everyone is asking—when His (alleged!) Department always intervenes in favour of the enemy at all our best moments?

And another dispatch from the tireless Father Doyle was scribbled out and rushed to Ireland:

A moment's pause to absolve a couple of dying men, and then I reached the group of smashed and bleed-bodies, most of them still breathing. The first thing I saw almost unnerved me—a young soldier lying on his back, his hands and face a mass of blue phosphorus flame. He was the first victim I had seen of the new gas the Germans are using. . . . Good God, how can any human being live in this! As I hurry back I hear that two men have been hit twenty yards away. I am with them in a moment, splashing through mud and water—a quick absolution, the last Rites of the Church. . . .

And that same day, after many visits from officer friends to whom she served tea, Nurse Luard returned to her duties at the Advanced Abdominal Centre where a boy named Reggie in the Moribund Ward continued to wail, "I do feel bad and no one takes no notice of me." Fortunately that night (his last) he slept like a baby. The rain stopped. An inventory shows that the British and French had lost about 35,000 men up to this point. The average Fifth Army advance was less than halfway toward the objectives planned for July 31. Half the tanks were destroyed. The situation was, in the restrained words of the official British historian, "only relatively satisfactory."

General Gough decided to give II Corps another try on the 9th, with the rest of his army joining in on the 13th, and after a day's delay, due to atrocious weather which had broken in the meantime, General Jacob's brigades jumped off (crept off would be a better description) toward Gheluvelt. The attack this time was spearheaded by the 18th (Eastern) Division, a fresh outfit that had been in reserve. Fit or not, it did no better than the unfit 30th. The operation was a failure; and the grand offensive which followed three days later also accomplished nothing in the way of capturing ridge positions on the vital II Corps southern flank.

So desolate, so meaningless were these August struggles that the record of them in histories and memoirs fills one with a certain weariness. Listlessly the men assemble at the jump-off tapes. Behind the same familiar barrage they advance through the same narrow porridge-like strip of ground. The same hidden machine guns greet them; the same whiz-bangs open

Near Zillebeke, August 9, 1917

up at them. Here and there a strong point is captured, a new outpost is reached, to which a few riflemen forlornly cling. Some of these are held, and occasionally the line is advanced a few hundred yards. Brownish masses of German troops slog forward and everywhere nasty hand-to-hand encounters take place. The men on both sides are lacerated and punctured, bleed and die, in numbers that baffle the imagination. Nameless new beings take their place, but nothing else changes.

Gaunt, blackened remnants of trees drip in the one-time forests. The shells of countless batteries burst deafeningly and without surcease; the dank smell of gunpowder, wet clay, poison gas, and polluted water spreads over the battleground and drifts eastward. The men hardly know what they are doing or how affairs in general are progressing. By mid-August they were told even less than soldiers are usually told: Move up there. Start walking that way. Occupy those shell holes. Wait near the barn. Surround that pillbox. Relieve those chaps (you can't see them from here) behind the canal and wait for further word. After two weeks such was the status of Haig's grand offensive which was to have burst out of the salient, bounded across the ridge, released the prancing cavalry steeds, and with flying banners captured the Channel ports.

And for what the people across that Channel knew, all this did seem to be happening—not as quickly as had been hoped, perhaps, but nonetheless inexorably. Maps in the newspapers showed huge shaded areas captured from the Germans; but a closer inspection of the scale revealed that the gains were measured in hundreds of yards rather than dozens of miles.

The illusions of the times were not all the fault of Charteris and the GHQ press releases, nor were the correspondents entirely to blame. The newspaper moguls, the politicians, the industrialists, the people at large desperately wanted a victory. Almost unconsciously the editorials reflected that inner need, and created wish-dreams out of the copy at hand. The columns of the *Times* sounded like a prayer meeting to bolster the faith of backsliding parishioners. On August 17, under the heading "Ypres Battle Resumed," splendid advances around Langemarck are described despite "stubborn resistance"; and while it is conceded that most German counterattacks were successful, these were "at great cost." The *Spectator's* accounts were exceptionally slavish and inane:

> Certainly we have reason to congratulate the General Staff. The strong and promising new blows which have been struck in the new battle are, we imagine, only the first in a long series.
>
> The fourth year of the war is opening with all the lessons of the past three years being applied not only with science but with resolution. Our Staff work in the field seems to be irreproachable. . . . The infantry, whose losses are said to be comparatively light, march behind the moving curtain of shells and bless the gunners as they go.

And the *Times* righteously told on August 18 of

ENEMY LIES EXPOSED
What the Germans Are Told
Falsification of Battle News
The Lie as a Buttress of Morale

In another column the disappointing action of August 16 was outlined by a war correspondent in this vein:

> Our successes . . . were even more satisfactory than I dared to assume when telegraphing yesterday afternoon . . . slaughter of the Fourth Division of the Prussian Guard. . . . Our progress . . . appears to have been swift and admirably executed.

And contemptuously this writer pointed out that the opposing troops were young Prussians of "poor fighting material . . . undernourished for the last two years before enlistment."

The arithmetic of German casualties was in British numbers so enormous that, from forty years of hindsight, one wonders how any but the most gullible could have been deceived by them. Haig reported an even hundred thousand on August 21 and flatly stated that the end of Germany's resources was at hand—this on the basis of a paper written by Charteris, who, however, protested in his diary (he does not seem to have protested elsewhere), "D. H. has not only accepted *in toto* my report . . . but he has gone much further."

Constantly throughout August the German armies were "visibly cracking." There was "proof that they were preparing for emergencies." They were alleged to be burning some villages; "this might be preliminary to a withdrawal." Lloyd George remarks that even the War Cabinet and other politicians believed the campaign was going well, and again he attributes this to the evil genius of General Charteris, to Haig, and to Kiggell:

> It naturally pleased Haig to have carefully chosen and nicely cooked little tidbits of "intelligence" about broken German divisions, heavy German casualties, and diminishing German morale served up to him. ... He beamed satisfaction and confidence. His great plan was prospering. The whole atmosphere of this secluded little community reeked of that sycophantic optimism which is the curse of autocratic power. ...
> As for General Kiggell, the Chief of Staff, he had the air of a silent craftsman, whose plans, designed and worked out by his art in the seclusion of his workshop, were turning out well and proceeding inexorably without a hitch to the destined end.

To the disgust of Sir William Robertson the Prime Minister, sensing the debacle in Flanders, revived on August 23 before French and Italian dignitaries his old scheme of attacking the Austrians. Furthermore, he vowed, the Belgian operation was positively to be stopped in ten days. (Foch agreed that matters were hopeless on the Western Front.) "Wully" wrote Haig

After the battle

that Lloyd George "is a real bad 'un. The other members of the War Cabinet seem afraid of him. Milner is a tired, dyspeptic old man. Curzon a gas-bag. Bonar Law equals Bonar Law. Smuts has good instincts but lacks knowledge. . . . The rain is cruel luck but it will get fine in time."

And when Haig heard that the Prime Minister had been questioning Foch about British strategy he commented heavily, "I could not have believed that a British minister could have been so ungentlemanly."

Meanwhile *Punch* continued to divert its readers with cartoons showing groups of cringing Germans throwing up their hands and quavering "Kamerad!" to nonchalant individual British privates. The public was happy. At last the war was going properly; all records were being broken in the manufacture of British munitions; the Yanks were coming; and if there were any among the masses of the people who doubted the gladness of it all they were not to be quoted in the periodicals of the day.

Yet as early as August 7 general headquarters had questioned whether the original objectives were any longer obtainable. Suddenly it was suggested that the plan was not, after all, to reach the Channel coast but mainly to wear down the Germans. Should not, therefore, the breakthrough idea be abandoned in favor of the original May step-by-step plan? To this, Rawlinson, for one, still twiddling his thumbs near Nieuport, agreed enthusiastically. In a written summary of his views he remarked that the British army in the west had never really tried to carry out a campaign of attrition, had never issued orders to the effect that limited objectives reached after a series of hard, fast blows were not to be exceeded. Furthermore, he continued pointedly, if the enemy morale were to be broken by such methods it would become common knowledge—"not a matter of conjecture built up on the reports of prisoners and deserters"—plain to every Britisher as well as to the Germans themselves. He urged that the high command stop assuming airily that the German Army was breaking down. Further efforts should never again be undertaken without full artillery cover. Never again, he insisted, should the infantry be assigned targets beyond their physical capacity.

Gough went even farther. In a sudden fit of revulsion and pessimism he advised Haig to close down the campaign altogether. Success was no longer possible, he said, except at the price of disproportionate losses.

But Plumer wanted to continue, and the fighting went on; though now Haig tacitly sanctioned step-by-step methods. He instructed Gough to attack again. On August 22 Sir Hubert did so, but in an extremely limited fashion—just enough to comply technically with orders but not enough to bring about another blood bath. So all August every day there was fighting, intense and otherwise, and the rains continued in unprecedented quantities—it turned out one of the wettest Augusts in thirty years—and by late that month the line had been pushed forward another few hundred yards on the northern flank, though II Corps

General Sir Hubert Gough

lying at the base of Gheluvelt Plateau was still as stationary as ever.

Sir Douglas, perturbed over Gough's failure on the
22nd, made a radical decision that afternoon when it
became clear that Jacob's corps was getting nowhere
at the usual high cost in men. He drove to Second
Army headquarters near Cassel to visit General Herbert Plumer. A delicate conversation followed. The
commander in chief spoke of the regrettable delays in
capturing the high ground to the east and the importance of doing so before the larger plan could be realized. Would General Plumer, who knew the salient
so intimately, consider extending his frontage northward to include the II Corps sector? The rotund little
officer had suspected what was coming, had discussed
the matter previously with Gough, and was not
thrilled. He had been in the salient for two miserable
years, he grumbled, and had no desire to push himself
into another. Taking over the main advance along the
Menin road seemed like a fine way to ruin one's reputation. To throw good money after bad is a thankless
and hopeless business in war or peace. He suggested
that they talk it over with Gough. Later that day the
three men met at GHQ and the decision was consummated: Plumer would take over, and in three weeks
would begin a new drive founded upon a series of meticulous, strictly limited operations.

That Gough was relieved, in both senses of the
word, there can be no doubt. He was glad to be rid of
his wretched chore even at the risk of his professional

standing. And there were others who were happy to see the Fifth Army leave. As usual, criticisms had mounted concerning Sir Hubert's headquarters. Philip Gibbs, the war correspondent, stopped to talk to a group of officers leaving the salient. "You must be glad to leave Flanders," he said, and bitterly one man replied, "God be thanked we are leaving the Fifth Army area!"

But under the conditions that now existed to the east of Ypres, could General Plumer do any better?

On the 24th there was another attack, this time toward Inverness Copse. It failed. (The *Spectator* reported next day, "This has been for the Allies the greatest week of the war.") On the 27th another try was made. It also failed. Between these efforts, and after them until the end of the month, and before them incessantly on dates not mentioned in this narrative, there were more attacks all down the line by Frenchmen, Irish, English, Welsh, Scots, Australians, New Zealanders, Canadians—all for nothing, under hateful conditions, persisted in for no reason that anyone (outside GHQ) could any longer discern. Over and over the Germans counterattacked. Inverness Copse changed hands eighteen times. The senselessness of it all grew like a cancer in the minds of the Allied troops. One historian writes that "these strokes, aimed at the morale of the German army, were wearing down the morale of the British." In the past Crown Prince Rupprecht had been impressed by the coolness of British captives, but on August 16 he was surprised to hear one say that he and his comrades would have been happy to shoot down the officers who made them attack. The following week Rupprecht noted in his war diary that British captives were still bitter against their officers, and that officer prisoners were now blaming the staffs. On August 25 he was advised that the once tenacious British were now surrendering easily. All these reports were passed on to Ludendorff. He knew how badly his own troops were suffering; but the Germans, at least, were winning most of the August battles.

It was during this month, therefore, that Ludendorff felt free to transfer some nine divisions away from Flanders to help the Austrians. Though General Gough was discouraged he tried to put up a good front at Fifth Army conferences. Baker-Carr, one of the tank specialists, has told of the many times that Gough opened proceedings with a statement such as this: "Gentlemen, I have just come from an interview with the Commander-in-Chief and he tells me that everything points to a complete breakdown of the enemy morale and that one more hard thrust will crumple up his defenses"; but the younger officer comments that "there was not another single member of the Conference who did not know how grotesquely inaccurate this statement was in fact."

One trouble was that most generals were too distracted by the pressures of staff work to find time to

visit the battle zone. During August Baker-Carr delivered a tank lecture at the Staff College Course at
GHQ, and after lunch he candidly amplified his views.
The fighting, especially as it concerned tanks, he said,
was "as dead as mutton," and had been precisely that
ever since August 1. His words were met by stony
silence. After lunch Brigadier General John Davidson,
Haig's director of operations, asked to see him in his
office. When Baker-Carr arrived he found the general
seated at his desk with his head in his hands.

"Sit down," he said. "I want to talk to you."

Baker-Carr complied.

"I am very upset by what you said at lunch, Baker.
If it had been some junior officer, it wouldn't have
mattered so much, but a man of your knowledge and
experience has no right to speak as you did."

"You asked me how things really were and I told
you frankly."

"But what you say is impossible."

"It isn't. Nobody has any idea of the conditions up
there."

"But they can't be as bad as you make out."

"Have you been there yourself?"

"No."

"Has anyone in O.A. been there?"

"No."

"Well then, if you don't believe me, it would be as
well to send someone up to find out."

Yet there was, perhaps, more behind it all than met
the eye. The Germans too were being hurt—not as

badly as their attackers, but enough to worry Crown
Prince Rupprecht. As for Ludendorff, here we find a
discrepancy. In August 1917 his words and actions
were those of a man who had no qualms, whereas in
his later memoirs he writes:

> The costly August battles imposed a heavy strain on
> the Western troops. In spite of all the concrete pro-
> tection they seemed more or less powerless under the
> enormous weight of the enemy's artillery. At some
> points they no longer displayed that firmness which
> I in common with the local commanders had hoped
> for. . . . I myself was being put to a terrible strain.
> The state of affairs in the West appeared to prevent
> the execution of our plans elsewhere. Our wastage
> had been so high as to cause grave misgivings and ex-
> ceeded all expectation.

But the British and French had lost some 74,000
men between July 31 and the end of August; while
German casualties were about 50,000.

In the *Daily News* H. G. Wells asked, "Why . . .
does the waste and killing go on? . . . The declara-
tions of public policy (on both sides) remain childish,
vague and disingenuous. . . . They chaffer like happy
imbeciles while civilization bleeds to death."

For one blinding moment the evil sorcery, the taboo,
about discussing peace was broken. August 16 Pope
Benedict XV sent from the Vatican a note to all belligerent governments crying out against the war: "Shall,
then, the civilized world be naught but a field of
death? And shall Europe, so glorious and flourishing,

rush, as though driven by universal madness, toward the abyss, and lend her hand to her own suicide?" He suggested broad means of ending the conflict and settling the issues. The *Times* denounced the note as "pro-German and anti-Ally . . . permeated with German ideas." Every major power on both sides rejected it. The fighting would go on till somebody won. At Birkenhead Lloyd George estimated in an impromptu speech that "we shall just win," to which the *Nation*, that irreverent organ of the Left, innocently asked, "Win What?"

August ended as it had begun—with new torrents of rain. Battalions in reserve, such as those at St. Omer, waited apprehensively for orders to return to the front. Rumors drifting back from the salient were indeed chilling. The told of subhuman grappling in swamps, of tanks shattered by the hundreds, of careless plans and alarming casualties, of furious generals, of stubborn attacks doomed before they began. The *B.E.F. Times* tried to keep spirits up—how successfully we shall never know—with humor, verse, and satire such as the following "want-ads" of August 15:

WANTED.—To rent for the winter season, DRY WARM DUG OUT. Must be commodious and in healthy locality; untroubled by hawkers and Huns. . . . Apply— Reggie, c/o of this paper.

FOR SALE.—TWO TANKS. Slightly soiled. Price moderate. Or would exchange for a pair of rabbits. Apply— 41, Dammstrasse.

FOR SALE.—PLEASANT COUNTY ESTATE, situated in one of the nicest parts of Belgium. Heavily wooded. Has been shot over. Owner desirous of leaving. Apply—Feddup, Glencores Wood.

Late in the month Father Doyle was killed. Nursing Sister Luard reported in her diary August 27 that three of her men would die that night and that one boy "who's had a leg off . . . is to lose an arm and an eye tomorrow." As the month closed Sir Douglas inscribed a familiar entry in his own diary: "Glass falling slightly. Weather unsettled. Heavy showers of rain fell throughout the day."

Philip Gibbs wrote of new enemy counterattacks and reported that although Inverness Copse had changed hands for the nineteenth time, and was now held by the Boches, fighting continued at the usual pitch of sublime British courage. The *B.E.F. Times* advertised a great "Special Attraction: Haig's Company in a Stirring Drama, Entitled: PILCKEM'S PROGRESS."

Gradually the great guns became silent. On the chessboard of Flanders the opening phase had ended. The pawns lay still, filled with forebodings. The grand masters stroked their mustaches, surveyed the deadlock, and plotted their next moves.

10. The Intermission

EVER SINCE the war began, frustrated generals on both sides had largely based their failures on a shortage of artillery ammunition. In England these complaints had been to some degree justified and during 1915 had led to the famous "shell scandal," one result of which was to raise Lloyd George to the Ministry of Munitions. (Winston Churchill assumed this post in July 1917; at the same time, Sir Edward Carson entered the War Cabinet and Sir Eric Geddes became First Lord of the Admiralty.) After the Somme the same outcry had arisen: If only the Allies —the French especially—had been supplied with enough heavy-caliber shells they never would have been stopped.

And on September 2, 1917, in a report to the War Cabinet, Sir Douglas Haig grumbled again that his batteries had been limited in ammunition during August, and that this plus the terrible weather, neither of which was his fault, had affected adversely the first phase of his campaign. He hoped that both conditions would soon be rectified and expressed regrets that operations would not be resumed for about three weeks. But "the best, if not the only, way to surmount the crisis and the temporary inaction of the French Army was to continue the campaign with all available resources." Generally, however, his report implied that the August fighting had gone as planned. The Germans were demoralized. They had lost vast numbers of men. Valuable terrain had been captured. The Allies held a strong initiative. The spirit of his troops was still excellent. Casualties suffered had been reasonable, and only here and there had there been small setbacks.

Lloyd George was not impressed. Whatever else Sir Douglas may have thought of him, the Prime Minister could read a map and he could plainly see that a month of terrific fighting had produced almost no gain in ground. He also doubted Haig's other claims. By now he was definitely alarmed. How was he, the Prime Minister of the Empire, to fulfill his mandate to win the war if Haig persisted in killing off the British Army? "Blood and mud," he repeated dismally, over and over, "blood and mud, they can think of nothing better." Flatly before his associates he berated himself for having allowed the Belgian offensive to begin. As for this bland report from the field marshal, Lloyd George considered it an insult to his intelligence.

Its tone was indeed reminiscent of a regrettable phrase once uttered by Joffre which had contributed to his downfall; the Frenchman had said that he was "nibbling at the German line." With the exception of Carson, who at this stage was fully backing the military, the War Cabinet was in an uneasy mood. Even Parliament as a whole, knowing nothing of Haig's earlier promises and less of what had really happened thus far, showed signs of doubt as to whether military affairs were progressing as admirably as claimed.

One reason for the uncertainty was the flood of rumors that had begun to engulf the home islands. Wounded soldiers returning to England told grisly stories, often exaggerated, of the condition of the battlefield and the number of dead, captured, and stricken. Like all bad news it traveled fast. Others who found ways of drifting away from the fighting zone and of circulating tales of disaster diligently did so, in the age-old manner of such men. The impression gained ground that British armies had suffered an inexcusable slaughter in Flanders and that the authorities were trying to hush it up; and these suspicions were not confined entirely to gullible or disillusioned members of the masses, for they were felt by many in Parliament as well.

The same young women from the East End continued to walk to and from Charing Cross in the same little groups, but they no longer sang their shrill patriotic songs. Now they came silently to greet the ambulance trains and to watch the ambulance lorries load up and chug away with their never-ending loads of wounded men. Day after day—and mostly night after night, for it was deemed more circumspect then—the trains discharged their mutilated cargoes. Soon it was whispered that Britain had taken a quarter-million loss since July 31. During the first week in August people had believed that a great and inexpensive victory was being won. In the first week in September the bubble inflated with hot air had already burst. While publicly the politicians and the press made a fine show of optimism, Sir Edward Carson admitted that "a great deal of very loose and mischievous talk about peace" was in the air.

The police and engineers went on strike. The whispering continued. "Wully," it was said, was to be sacked. Plumer would be the new Chief of the Imperial General Staff. Haig was finished too. His successor would be Sir Henry Rawlinson. Robertson himself was depressed; and this was no mere rumor. He admitted to Colonel Repington during luncheon at the Bath Club that fighting conditions in the Low Country "were pretty horrible," that the rain was giving Rupprecht plenty of time to reinforce his troops and to string up new masses of barbed wire. It was hard luck—"on Haig." But, he added helplessly, what else was there to do but to go on? "Haig thought that he was killing a lot of Germans." Plainly Sir William was backsliding again.

On September 3 he wired Haig: "General Foch arrives London . . . to press British War Cabinet to agree to his sending 100 heavy guns from French First Army (Anthoine) to Italy at once; if, as I suppose, this will affect your plans, it is very desirable that you should come over and see War Cabinet." The commander in chief needed no urging and arrived in England that evening.

The following day a meeting was held in Robertson's room at the War Office. Both he and Haig were on a bad spot. The War Cabinet had agreed to the offensive on condition that it would progress more or less as the general and the marshal had promised, and that it would be broken off if it showed signs of failure. How were they to evade their perfectly plain obligation to redeem the face value of the insurance policy they had sold their government in July?

Morosely Lloyd George summarized matters. The Russians were through. The French were recuperating. The Americans would not arrive till next year. The British had been stopped. The Italians had just started another offensive on the Isonzo and needed big guns. Therefore all operations on the Western Front should cease for the time being, and a hundred heavy pieces should be rushed to Cadorna.

Foch agreed. Bonar Law was, in Haig's words, "as usual, very weak." Carson and Smuts disagreed. Lord Cecil of the Foreign Office stood aloof. The Prime Minister would not back down. He insisted that the case was open and shut and kept referring to Haig's previous promises. Robertson—that impolite, intolerant, formidable, beloved hater of politicians—was unusually excited. He intended not to give an inch. When he spoke, his h's disappeared. Concerning Ca-

dorna's new effort that was to work wonders, he grated
caustically (as so often in the past), "I've 'eard different." Haig refused to release a single gun or to abandon the initiative. Neither he nor Robertson argued
that the first Flanders phase had been successful. They
said nothing of the infinitely distant Channel ports,
nor did they dwell upon the distasteful fruits of attrition. They merely emphasized that abandoning the
offensive might allow the Germans to strike either the
French or British an "overwhelming" blow.

The military had a weak case, but again won out.
For the record, Douglas Haig agreed to "review" in his
own mind, and perhaps some day with Pétain, the ad-
visability of during some future month sending some
guns to Italy. Meanwhile operations in Belgium would
continue. But how long would Lloyd George continue
playing Haig's game?

Sir Henry Wilson, now in charge of the Eastern
Command, looked on sardonically and confided to his
diary a series of biting comments:

> This is unfortunate, especially as Haig is not going to
> do anything really serious at Ypres this year. . . .
> Haig, Robertson and Kiggell are running the maxim
> of superior forces at the decisive point, etc., into the
> ground. . . . I believe that Lloyd George, knowing
> that Haig will not do any good, has allowed him to
> keep all his guns, etc., so that he can, later on, say,
> "Well, I gave you everything. I even allowed you to
> spoil the Italian offensive. And now, owing to gross
> miscalculation and incapacity you have entirely failed
> to do anything serious except lose a lot of men." And

in this indictment he will include Robertson, and then get rid of both of them.

We do not know whether the Prime Minister was indeed plotting in this satanic fashion, but we learn that he had begun taking steps to reduce the flow of manpower to the Western Front where, in his opinion, Haig would only get them uselessly killed off anyway. In this indirect way he hoped to curb the commander in chief, even if he could not stop him altogether. Already "Wully" was complaining that less than eight thousand drafts would reach France in September. Such skimpy rations would only replace "normal wastage," in the rather repellent technical phrase, much less replace the abnormal casualties suffered in August and anticipated for subsequent stages of the campaign. Cylists, clerks, and other noncombatant personnel, already in Europe and beyond the clutches of the Prime Minister, were being "combed" and rushed to the front. But this sort of thing had its limits, and by early September the fifty-two British divisions on the Western Front were each running alarmingly near an average of two thousand men short.

From now until the end of the campaign there was to be a constant tug-of-war between the civilians and generals concerning the release of troops for duty in Belgium. Recruitments had fallen off almost to nil. Without volunteers, only draftees remained. But other than youngsters gradually attaining military age, who could any longer be drafted? The rock-bottom requirements of the civilian economy had to be met. Lloyd George refused to weaken industrial capacity by calling up any more essential workers. Sir Eric Geddes, the new First Lord of the Admiralty, even advised subtracting riflemen from Haig and putting them to work in the fields and factories. To this Sir Henry Wilson replied that he too wanted "to take troops away from France during the mud months, not to grow cabbages here, but to beat the Turks." Sir Douglas and Sir William would have none of this nonsense. They wanted all the men they had and at least 85,000 more. It was, they insisted, the only way to keep up the pressure and thus ward off a knockout blow against France.

This in turn raised a basic question late that summer, while the fighting died down and the warlords wrangled: How weak *were* the French? Was it true that they were even incapable of defense? After all, five full months had passed since the Nivelle affair. Lloyd George conceded that they might be unable to mount a grand offensive, but he believed that they could surely hold their own on French soil. Pétain, ever gloomy (*"trop négatif, trop timide,"* in Joffre's words), and perhaps trying cynically to keep Haig attacking, told the latter that he had not a man upon whom he could rely between Switzerland and the British right. Even Sir Douglas accepted this statement with reservations, though he was delighted to be implored to continue his offensive. *Someone,* at least, saw things his way. So weak was France in manpower and fighting spirit, Pétain continued, during his visit at British GHQ, that his Government might even demand a separate peace rather than face another German attack. This remark Haig passed on to the War Cabinet. It was received doubtfully. Pétain, it was suspected, had rather a predilection for throwing in the sponge. Yet his assertions could not be altogether overlooked.

While the above version of events is generally accepted, most of it is mythical. Pétain did not implore Haig for help on September 19. He was in Paris at the time and did not visit GHQ until October. Haig's own diary mentions no visit from him. Not once—by any contemporaneous record—did Pétain request continuing, major British assaults, to screen the French army. Publicly on several occasions he had even derided Haig's campaign.

Haig began the myth in subsequent letters and conversations. The British official historian, General Edmonds, perpetuated them. He was 87—and either confused or deceptive—when in 1949 he wrote of Pétain's nonexistent threats and pleas.

Still, there was no doubt that France was enervated that summer. Aside from her precise degree of military incapacity, which will forever remain a matter of argument, it was well known that her civilian morale was lower than that of Britain. Even from as far away

as Germany's triumphant Eastern Front Max Hoffmann wrote in his diary on September 14:

> The news of the domestic situation in France sounds
> excellent. The country is sick of the war, and the ac-
> counts we get from responsible and impartial people
> in Switzerland are most encouraging, from our point
> of view.

Matters had not been helped by a division of 17,000
Russian soldiers who had fought with Nivelle on the
Aisne and then had been unwisely retained in France.
Wherever they were stationed they preached revolution. An attempt had been made to ship them back to
Russia, but Kerenski did not want them. In time they
had become so Bolshevik in sentiment, so trouble-
some, that it was decided to ask them to surrender, as
though they were enemy troops. Only 57 did so. The
rest dug trenches and put up barricades. While the
civilian population hurriedly departed, a final ultima-
tum was issued on September 14. It was refused. Next
day their food was cut off and they were encircled. On
the following day they were attacked. After being defeated they were disarmed and shipped to ports on the
Black Sea. The incident did its part to infect France
with stop-the-war propaganda, not only in itself but
because of the widespread publicity it received.

Late in the year, and increasingly after the war was
over, Haig used the argument of French weakness up
to the hilt. How worthy it was, and how much of it he

actually believed in his own heart, is a continuing riddle. Certainly Lloyd George thought little enough of Haig's opinion; he considered it a convenient device used for the purpose of furthering rash military dreams. He was fed up with the bickering. More and more his thoughts dwelled upon a supranational governing board which would run the Allied war effort from such a lofty, unassailable height that field commanders such as Haig, Pétain, and Cadorna would simply do what they were told, rather than fight on in solitary confusion, coordinating nothing, arguing incessantly with their respective chiefs and with one another, and getting nowhere. It was early this month that he first proposed an Allied Joint Council, to be composed of three members of each nation: the supreme civilian leader, one cabinet member, one general. Painlevé and the British War Cabinet approved informally, and President Wilson evinced interest. Thus, tentatively and embryonically, the Council came into being.

As every Tommy knew, the Germans could make the rain come and go at will. Accordingly it had stopped early in the month; and now there set in a period of brilliant, warm, dry days. Slowly the swamp-like aspect of the salient disappeared. Moving men, machines, and mules stirred up a fine, whitish dust. Much water in the shell holes evaporated, and from a distance they seemed dry as a bone. By mid-September only some hollows in the lower-lying ground remained waterlogged. To Australians the broad crest of the ridge recalled the rocky, broken spurs of the Libyan desert where they had recently trained. So hard became the thin upper crust of the ground that bullets often ricocheted on it.

These were perfect days for an attack. The Germans braced themselves, but their enemy did not come. On the 12th Crown Prince Rupprecht wrote in his diary, "The Flanders fight seems actually to have ended," though von Kuhl, his chief of staff, doubted that the "stubborn British" had stopped for good. Rupprecht insisted "the enemy was regrouping in order to attack at another place." In this belief he was supported by several British prisoners who had lied splendidly; the Flanders offensive was over, they said, and the next attack would take place farther south. On the 13th von Kuhl changed his mind and recorded his "inmost conviction that the battle of Flanders is at an end." It seemed almost inconceivable to the Boches that even the peculiar British would fight in the rain and rest in the sun.

The early September days dwindled. Splotches of green covered large portions of the sunlit salient, a few flowers teetered in the breeze which drifted inland and even, in rare moments, smelled saltily of the North Sea. Some of the charred tree stumps put out a forlorn leaf or two—the most poignant note of all. For a fortnight the sky remained almost cloudless by day;

and under the level stare of the sun the soldiers per-
spired and the birds hopped and twittered among the
ruins of nature and the debris of man.

The Germans waited and wondered. Was this the
end of the fight? Would Haig and his Tommies try
again? "They are paper tigers," ran the ancient
Chinese adage, "fierce to look upon, but they melt in
the rain." Had they indeed melted?

There was astounding news along the British lines
about the so-called "Admiral," a middle-aged volun-
teer ambulance driver who had been allowed to tarry
in the area wearing the badges of an Army captain and
the crenellated rings of a Navy lieutenant. Here he invented weird gadgets and bombs with which to mor-
tify the enemy. Earlier he had devised a bulletproof
body shield, and to prove its worth had walked past
Crossroads Farm and Forward Cottage in daylight,
unfortunately forgetting that he had no flank cover
and that he was in a salient. After recovering from his
bullet wound he had invented and set a new booby
trap into which he had just fallen—so flashed the spectacular report.

At the Hôtel du Sauvage in Cassel, last civilized stop
on the way to Ypres, men thronged for dinner and
wine at tables covered with real linen, while candles
flickered against the dim walls, their shadows trembling delicately at the far-away rumble of the guns.
Here reigned old Madame, and behind the desk sat
Mademoiselle Suzanne, "a dainty rogue in porcelain";

and seldom was it that the laughter, the singing, the tinkling of Madame's piano ceased. But only officers— and not those of the Air Force, who had proved too boisterous—were allowed in this pleasant rendezvous.

On the other side of the hill the Huns partook of similar fleeting interludes, similar pleasures, similar yearnings. And there were those who waited with longing for the lull to end and the war to be won. On September 10 one Helmut Zschutte wrote:

> I am restless. I hate the kitchen table at which I am writing. I lose patience over a book. I should like to push the landscape aside as if it irritated me. I must get to the Front. I must again hear the shells roaring up into the sky and the desolate valley echoing the sound. I must get back to my Company . . . live once more in the realm of death.

Soon enough Corporal Zschutte would return to the realm of death, never again to leave it.

Time was running out, too, for Lieutenant General Sir William Birdwood's I Anzac Corps (1st and 2nd Australian Divisions) for these were the men selected by General Plumer to handle the coming main assignment. In the streams they fished with homemade hooks, shot at the fish with their rifles, and even set off Mills bombs to stir up the fish so that they could be caught. The villagers complained, and headquarters sternly ordered all such bombing to cease. Sports were organized almost every day after training. Again the tall youngsters from down under congregated in the towns and hamlets of France and Belgium, as hundreds of thousands had done before them. They ransacked the countryside for firewood (enough coal was never issued); chairs, sheds, and ladders were pilfered by the soldiers to heat their tea and bully beef, and countless were the suits for damage brought against the British Army by the outraged Belgian citizenry. In the cool and peace of the evening the card players grimly waged their pasteboard wars for stakes ever more astronomical.

Occasionally fighting flared up, in accordance with Haig's instructions that the Fifth Army harass the enemy in the direction of Poelcapelle. The plan was to distract the enemy from the vast preparations under way by the Second Army. Accordingly two divisions attacked on September 6 and 7, and one on the 10th. All three assaults neither won ground nor harassed the Germans, and about a thousand British casualties were suffered. In disgust Sir Douglas advised Gough to discontinue such operations, and additional ones scheduled for three subsequent days were also canceled.

The weather was ideal for flying. Twenty-six squadrons of the Royal Flying Corps were aloft day and night along the front of the Second and Fifth Armies; and slightly more than this amount had been allotted to the area by the German high command. Among the latter was Captain Manfred von Richthofen's dread "Flying Circus," led by the phlegmatic twenty-three-

year old killer who was to become the greatest ace of
all. By the end of August he had already accounted
(officially) for 59 Allied planes, and one day early next
month, soon after breakfast, flying a spanking-new
bright-red Fokker triplane, he somewhat ingloriously
nailed his sixtieth, an R.E.8 observation model:

> I approached and fired 20 shots from a distance of 50
> yards, whereupon the Englishman fell to the ground
> and crashed near Zonnebeke. It is most probable that
> the English pilot mistook me for an English triplane,
> because the observer was standing upright in his
> plane and watched me approach without making use
> of his gun.

These were the halcyon days, days of glory for the
greatest aerial heroes of World War I; and above the
salient most of them fought duels the romance and
terror of which will never be forgotten. Every day the
human moles below peered up into the blinding sky
and watched the virtuosos fight and die in their agile
little machines: Albert Ball, he of the suicidal methods; Richthofen, the master; that impersonal mur-
derer, James McCudden; Billy Bishop, the Canadian
sharpshooter; gay Ernst Udet; Mick Mannock, dogged
and hate-filled; the great Werner Voss; Hermann
Goering; even sometimes the fabulous, brooding,
deathly ill Georges Guynemer, France's greatest ace.
Overshadowed by these world-famous fighters flew
the two-seater crews—pilot and observer—doing the
less spectacular but vital photographing, observing,

bombing, and artillery spotting. Throughout early September the Flemish air was peppered with planes in tight-knit formations of concentrated firepower; for the air war was no longer a potpourri of derring-do and life-and-death gambles but a crucial adjunct to the more desperate drama unfolding below.

The keynote of Plumer's plan can be expressed in the word concentration. The main attack against Gheluvelt Plateau would be conducted by four divisions. (Gough had used three.) The frontage of the attack would be 4000 yards. (Gough's three divisions had been spread over 6200 yards.) The ratio of mass, therefore, was more than two to one in Plumer's favor. Along the decisive front from Klein Zillebeke and Westhoek, Plumer had almost 1300 guns. (Gough had employed less than 900.) Almost half of Plumer's batteries were in heavy and medium categories. (Gough's fraction was only a third.) Plumer's batteries were to fire three and a half million rounds before the actual attack and on the first day. (The density of Gough's fire was under a million rounds for the comparable period.) Plumer planned to capture the high ground in four steps, with about six days of meticulous preparation and consolidation between each. (Gough had vaguely figured on perhaps reaching the fourth German defense line, three miles away, in the first day or two.) In other words, Plumer hoped that his vastly greater power, concentration, and planning would in three weeks pay out an advance such as Gough had envisioned for the first day alone.

All these differences are so remarkable and revealing that they call for little comment; though one might observe that Herbert Plumer and "Tim" Harington intended to fight the battle of Messines again, while Gough had expected to capture the ridge in the same whirlwind way that Sherman had roared into Atlanta.

The total front of attack would be eight miles. Studious arrangements were made for the almost instant relief of all primary attacking battalions. On the left the Fifth Army would, it was hoped, advance a thousand yards toward Poelcapelle and Gravenstafel. To the right of I Anzac, the X Corps with two divisions would push southeast nearly a mile. Farther south one division (the 19th) would hold up the right flank and attempt to proceed a few hundred yards toward Belgian Wood. All other divisions between this point and the Comines canal would stay on the defensive; and while the French up north were to make a large uproar they too were to stand pat.

Thus, in effect, the entire scheme had been compressed—not only the basic drive toward the eastern highland, but the total front of attack—into a slow-motion charge half as wide and twice as intense as that which had taken place on July 31.

In all this there was the irreducible minimum of imagination, subtlety, and surprise, and not a single tank would be used.

The bombardment began on September 13. Each day it was turned on more heavily, and twice daily the barrage scheme was practiced—deadly, earnest practice that inched across the German defense zone causing losses to enemy machine gunners and leaving the remaining defenders wondering when the false alarms would prove to be the real thing. Any German doubts that a new attack was coming in the salient were now ended. On September 17 Sixt von Armin's headquarters announced that it was, after all, imminent; but as yet these gentlemen did not know that the exact moment was to be 5:40 a.m. of the 20th—the very earliest, it was calculated, that an infantryman would be able to see two hundred yards ahead of him.

On September 18 all attacking brigades of the Second and Fifth Armies regretfully left their training areas and moved up close behind the front. This was the day Bonar Law wrote to Lloyd George, who was in Wales:

> Treasury Chambers
> Whitehall, S.W.
> 18, September, 1917
>
> My Dear Prime Minister,
> . . . The only thing at all new is that, in speaking to Robertson yesterday, I said to him that I had lost absolutely all hope of anything coming of Haig's offensive and though he did not say so in so many words, I understand that he took the same view. I do not know when the next attack is supposed to take place but I believe it may happen at any time. It is evident, therefore, that the time must soon come

when we will have to decide whether or not this offensive is to be allowed to go on. . . .

Yours sincerely,
A. Bonar Law

It was too late. The following day, with the sun set-
ting behind the massed troops and sending streaks of
pale light against the rising ground to the east, the
final approach march began. Smoothly and silently the
vast armies (squeezed together as they marched, to
avoid casualties from long-range, probing shell fire)
moved across the open fields, leaving the roads clear
for traffic on wheels. As the men trudged forward they
were greeted by the usual comments from onlookers
and those being relieved: "There go the cemetery reinforcements!" and solemn warnings that "there's a
shortage of coffins up there."

The very moment darkness set in, it began to drizzle. An hour before midnight rain was falling heavily
and slowing everything down, especially in the soft,
untracked fields. By now General Gough was distraught—he had become neurotic about rain, and with
good reason—and rang up General Plumer. Stop the
attack, he recommended. Plumer was equally worried
but wanted first to confer with his weather expert and
corps commanders. They in turn, after much indecision during which even the divisional generals were
phoned for their views, told him that although the topsoil was muddy the rain was expected to stop. The
consensus was recorded: "Very difficult to form an

opinion. Conditions not good but promising better things. Rain decreasing and wind rising. General opinion slightly in favour of continuation." Birdwood was especially strong for carrying on. Plumer asked him to call Gough back and say that the attack would go on. At 12:10 the rain ended.

At 3 a.m. an Australian machine-gun officer lost his way in No Man's Land and, after a wild struggle, was captured by a German patrol. As they were taking him to the rear he was detected trying to destroy his papers; these were extracted from him and turned out to be the Second Army operation orders. The German 121st Division issued a tense report "that about two Australian divisions are to attack on either side of the Ypres-Menin road and about one kilometre south of the Ypres-Roulers railroad. The date of the attack not definitely to be ascertained, but apparently for today."

Enemy artillery was ordered to lay down "annihilation" fire. A wireless alert was sent to all 4th Army divisions. Starting at 4:30 heavy fire opened up from German batteries against the starting positions of I Anzac. A shower of brilliant rockets soared from the enemy lines at 5:36. It was perhaps a coincidence, but one suspects that Sixt von Armin had somehow learned the exact time of zero hour. Four minutes later the barrage burst in all its brutal splendor, and in the swirling fog that had followed the rain the first British riflemen, "like spectres out of the mist," fell upon the Teutonic defenders.

11. The Menin Road

THE DATE seemed an important one at the time: September 20, 1917; and the event was given a grandiloquent name: The Battle of the Menin Road; and in truth it was the first measurable, big-headline victory since Messines, three and a half months before. And like most other calculated advances thus far in World War I, it was essentially an artillery coup. Fully a thousand yards in depth, the great barrage screened the infantry flooding into the greasy battlefield. The air saturated with drumfire seemed to scream in pain, the mighty drone of the big shells high above blending with the screeching trajectory of the smaller projectiles below. Thousands of shells slammed against the ridge, which appeared to burst into flames. Cherry-red patches flickered and fused along the enemy positions from No Man's Land well back into the rising ground where the heavier masses of German troops lay in wait. For miles along the opposing front yellow, white, red, and orange flares pierced the sky. Within minutes, a grayish pall of smoke had begun drifting over the salient.

To German eyes the oncoming British seemed maddeningly cool. Languid, unhurried, they trudged toward the ridge in broad, straggling lines. Antlike, they engulfed the extreme forward posts of the enemy as they went. Here and there a flamethrower worked over a German target in a spectacle of solitary splendor. The khaki-clad Australians appeared the most disinterested of all, the most confident. Some carried their rifles on their shoulders. With sticks in hand, officers walked about and conferred.

When the British swarmed into an isolated German shell hole or barricaded emplacement near the jumping-off line the defenders often panicked and yelled as they tried to escape, *"Die Tommies . . . raus, raus, die Engländer!"* Inexorably most of these suicidal advance posts, already shaken by the unparalleled cannonade, were gobbled up. As the slow sweep continued, signalers worked feverishly to run their lines through the craters and mud. Stretcher bearers began to move gravely amidst the pandemonium. The Lewis gunners slipped and fell and swore, and their heavy, clumsy weapons often became choked with mud.

Farther back, dense columns of supporting battalions shoved forward. The rear zone now swarmed with troops moving up front. Teams of little donkeys hauled at the guns and wagons, their dainty hoofs slipping in the slime. Uncomprehendingly they labored in the din, ears flapping and sad of eye, and seemed to wonder (like many a soldier) what they had done to deserve their fate.

From shell holes, and while they walked, and from the jump-off tapes where the relief units awaited the signal which would send them forward, the men watched the drumfire, fascinated by the innumerable petals of flame that flowered against the enemy lines. Anxiously they peered, not at the immediate front positions—they knew that little opposition was left in this zone—but at the terrain farther back where the danger really lay. Were the howitzers and field pieces scoring there as well?

The 18-pounders belched in a hysteria of rage. New rearward batteries, formerly hidden and silent, now came into action. When a small copse was caught in a fury of shells the trees flew uprooted through the air like a handful of feathers; in a flash the area became, as in a magician's trick, as barren as the expanse around it. The artillery officers stood near their guns pensively, smoking cigarettes, instructing their men from large unfurled maps that flapped and crinkled in the brisk morning breeze.

Black rolls of smoke, like that which rises from factory chimneys, spread majestically and rolled skyward. As the riflemen disappeared into the haze and shell holes a certain amount of confusion developed. Officers worked ceaselessly to locate and re-form their outfits. Occasionally toylike silhouettes of Germans were outlined against the dirty sky; then, almost at once, they too were swallowed up again by the landscape. Here and there haggard men leaned stolidly over one of their wounded or dead companions, collecting his papers and identity disks.

The attack possessed a certain ghastly beauty, especially in the virulent pillbox area of the woods to the south where the explosions, the wretchedness of the ground, the density of attacking and defending troops, the madness of it all, were accentuated to a degree rare even for the Western Front. Here the air was dense with strands of hissing steel from the machine guns ahead. As the men groped forward many fell, touched by an unseen wand. The remainder moved on rigidly, instinctively, gripped by fear. Over their heads airplanes whizzed like black hornets, strafing the enemy and in return drawing clusters of anti-aircraft shrapnel that floated feebly above the battleground.

The barrage had made possible the contemplated advance. By 9 o'clock the Australians had passed through Glencorse Wood. Later they entered Polygon Wood and swept over strong points at Carlisle Farm, Black Watch Corner, and Northampton Farm. They waited and rested for two hours before proceeding to their second objective. During this strange interlude one officer sent up bundles of newspapers and cigarettes. The riflemen turned the pages and smoked, like gentlemen of leisure, while the shells roared back and forth over their heads. Then they tossed aside their cigarettes, picked up their guns, and went forward.

Many deeds were performed, all monotonously similar and astoundingly heroic. . . .

Lieutenant Colvin and his platoon cleared one dugout after another, and he alone took about fifty prisoners.

Private Inwood invaded a strong point, killed several Germans, and captured nine.

After Lieutenant Glanville worked his way up to the entrance of a pillbox, nine Germans emerged, and in so doing were all killed by the lieutenant's men.

Lieutenant Birks rushed a machine-gun nest singlehanded and killed the entire crew with one bomb.

Corporal Egerton volunteered to neutralize a stubborn German blockhouse, dashed in under heavy fire, shot three Germans, and came out with twenty-nine prisoners.

When an Australian officer was shot through the head in trying to take a pillbox from behind, his men swarmed forward, and, though these Germans too tried to surrender, the former "went mad," so it was told, and "filled the place with bombs until, growing tired of the killing, they allowed a remnant—an officer and 40 men—to go to the rear as prisoners."

One section, having run into some old concrete artillery shelters, was in the process of eliminating their garrison when a German emerged with his hands up. Another, behind him, fired between his legs and wounded a sergeant. An Australian Lewis gunner yelled, "Get out of the way, sergeant, I'll see to the bastards." He fired bursts into the crowd until almost every German was dead or wounded.

By early morning the "Diggers" were digging in and a 2nd Australian Division captain was reporting:

> I have just returned from a tour round the whole of our country and everything is absolutely *très bon*. 9th (Bn.) just a bit disorganized . . . but all right now. They are getting no machine-gun fire from the enemy on the very front line, and will quite easily take the two final objectives and then will have enough men there to hold all the German divisions on the whole front.

That afternoon, September 20, 1917, the Battle of the Menin Road virtually ended. The main attack had gone practically according to plan except for a single holdup at Tower Hamlets, a mile west of Gheluvelt. The average gain, from the Comines canal on the south to the Ypres-Roulers rail line, was about nine hundred yards. Gheluvelt itself was now only a half-mile away. The gain along the Menin road was a full mile. Gough's Fifth Army had also proceeded according to instructions except at the extreme north toward Poelcapelle and in the center in the direction of Gravenstafel, where checks had occurred. During the fading sunlight German counterattacks started, but nowhere were they successful.

Over 3000 prisoners were taken. Total British casualties were 22,000. On the other hand, writes an official historian, "the losses on the two sides were about equal, or the British loss even slightly in excess of the German."

Who had won? The British line had been shoved forward in general half a mile, and gloomily the German official history states, "The new English method of attack had proved its effectiveness." Yet in Paris Lord Bertie, Ambassador to France, summed up in his diary a broader view: "We have done a good offensive which is much appreciated. But will it lead to anything really important?"

It is a commentary on the way of thought of Haig and his officers, after three unbroken years of heartbreak, that they were electrified by the day's action and spoke as though it were the beginning of the end of the war. Knowing nothing substantial concerning enemy casualties, they jumped to remarkable conclusions and came to believe that they had slaughtered the Boches wholesale. About the disappointing bag of prisoners they said, "We are killing the enemy, not capturing him." (In all this one discerns the fine Scottish hand of General John Charteris.) Though it later developed that British losses exceeded those of the Germans, and though the average gain in ground was little more than the length from tee to green of St. Andrews' Long Hole which Sir Douglas had played so often, the Battle of the Menin Road was labeled and filed by the British high command as an outstanding victory.

But the problem was not whether it was, in fact, a decisive triumph, or a small victory, or an equal encounter, or what it really meant in terms of ultimate victory. The question at general headquarters was merely whether this conquest, this hammer blow, could be repeated the following Wednesday—September 26—preparations for which were even now under way from St. Julien on the north to the newly occupied ground just west of the Gheluvelt ridge.

Mr. David Lloyd George could not have been less entranced. For one thing, he believed hardly a word of General Charteris' Intelligence summary concerning the alleged victory. For another, he was furious over the latest development from Italy. On the day after the fight Cadorna had dispatched a note to his allies expressing regret that his present offensive was to be curtailed, and that the Italian armies would have to go over to the defensive. His reason (it developed a month later that it was an ominously good one) was that he feared a heavy attack reinforced by German troops drawn down from the Eastern Front. Another reason, which he did not state, was that his own offensive was faltering. In any event, the British Prime Minister was much perturbed. Cadorna had promised continuing attacks and for weeks had been boasting about his magnificent accomplishments. The British high command also came in for its share of scorn from 10 Downing Street. Note what has now happened,

Lloyd George remarked, because of the fact that Haig
and Robertson had refused to support Cadorna even
with guns. Naturally the man had to stop attacking.
What else could he do without mortars and heavy
artillery? Everybody knew that the Italian Army was
rich only in field pieces, but thus far Haig had consented to deliver the grand total of one 9.2-inch how-
itzer to that front.

Robertson being in London and Haig in France, the
former had to take the brunt of the Prime Minister's
onslaught. A couple of tempestuous days ensued during which, "Wully" wrote Sir Douglas on September
24, the civilian's mind had been "very active":

> I have had to knock out a scheme for operating in
> the Aden hinterland involving the employment of not
> less than a division. I have also had to destroy one for
> landing ten divisions at Alexandretta, all of which
> would have had to come from you. Further, I have
> had to fight against sending more divisions to Meso-
> potamia. Generally, all round, I have been quite suc-
> cessful, although the expenditure of energy which
> ought to have been otherwise employed has been a
> little greater than usual. The whole Cabinet are anx-
> ious to give the Turk as hard a knock as possible this
> winter; they have heard that he is sick of the whole
> business. . . .

Haig was also sick of the whole business. Would
there be no end to Lloyd George's mad schemes to undermine him on the Western Front? The commander
was visited by Mr. Gardiner, editor of the *Daily News*,

who told him that the Prime Minister "never reads anything or thinks seriously." Haig listened with sour pleasure and in his diary that evening exclaimed,

> How unfortunate the country seems to be to have such an unreliable man at the head of affairs in this crisis. I thought Gardiner much above the usual newspaper man who visits France.

For his part, Lloyd George considered it a calamity that Sir Douglas was at the head of affairs in France and Belgium. It was his dream to fire the man. But how? A frontal assault was impossible, nor was it in keeping with the Prime Minister's methods. Were Haig to be summarily dismissed, Robertson would quit in sympathy and the entire country, Parliament, even the War Cabinet, would hit the ceiling. Firing Haig would also imply that the Empire was losing the war, would encourage the enemy, and was certain to strike a heavy blow at Allied morale. No, he could not remove Haig and Robertson outright. He would have to find another way. He began in September to put his mind seriously to the problem.

He visited Haig at his French chateau around this time and wrote:

> I found there an atmosphere of unmistakable exalta-tion. It was not put on. Haig was not an actor. He was radiant. He was quiet, there was no swagger. That was never one of his weaknesses. . . . The politicians had tried to thwart his purpose. His own

commanders had timidly tried to deflect him from his
great achievement. He magnanimously forgave us all.

Sir Douglas and his staff told the Prime Minister of
the wretched caliber of German prisoners now being
taken—proof that the enemy was scraping the bottom
of his barrel. Lloyd George asked to see some of them.
The officers hesitated. Would he not prefer to drive to
Vimy ridge for a fine view of the enemy lines? Lloyd
George replied in the negative, and since there was no
stopping him GHQ surreptitiously phoned one of the
Fifth Army corps headquarters and gave instructions
to remove all able-bodied prisoners from the com-
pound before the Prime Minister arrived. When he got
there he was forced to agree that "the men were a
weedy lot. They were deplorably inferior to the manly
specimens I had seen in earlier stages of the War."

Lloyd George's contempt for the military was
graphically expressed in this short trip to the Fifth
Army. He did not tell General Gough he was coming,
and the latter became aware of his distinguished vis-
itor only by catching sight of him pass by his window,
accompanied by General Charteris. Sir Hubert was
astounded, sent an aide to find out why Lloyd George
was there, and was told that it was for the purpose of
examining prisoners. The civilian did not condescend
to drop in, and the general let him continue on his
way.

The ostensible purpose of the trip was to get Haig's
personal views, which were duly delivered: 135 of the

147 German divisions on the front were broken by their losses. The offensive was making good progress. The British troops were "elated and confident." The Germans were depressed. It was beyond question that the attack had to be continued up to the limit, especially since the enemy's manpower, at its present rate of annihilation, would run out by the following spring.

"Then," in Lloyd George's words, "came the usual stuff from the Charteris stillroom," except that the latter placed the number of German divisions at 179, of which 154 were classified as inferior and getting worse. The Prime Minister considered the appraisals of both Haig and Charteris fantastic and implied that they were nothing but propaganda:

> G.H.Q. could not capture the Passchendaele ridge, but it was determined to storm Fleet Street, and here strategy and tactics were superb. The Press correspondents at the front were completely enveloped and important publicists and newspaper proprietors in this country were overwhelmed. Lord Northcliffe had, ever since 1916, been the mere kettledrum of Sir Douglas Haig, and the mouth organ of Sir William Robertson.

But such a view contradicted what he had said earlier. Haig did sincerely believe that he was on the verge of shattering the enemy front. Immaculate in his service khaki uniform, his field boots glistening like a mirror, gesturing stiffly with his forearm, the field

marshal tried hard to prove his point. The Prime
Minister listened politely but was not convinced. He
returned to London more certain than ever, as he
remarked to Robertson, that he was "backing the
wrong horse."

Autumn arrived that week and bathed all of Western Europe in sunlight and warmth. It was proving to
be one of the driest Septembers on record; but as the
beautiful days crept on Haig's offensive appeared
stalled no less than in August. Feverishly work continued for the attack of the 26th. The artillery made its
forward moves. Sir Douglas issued his final orders for
the second step of twelve hundred yards up the Gheluvelt Plateau, to include the capture of the entire Polygon Wood and the town of Zonnebeke.

On the 25th, behind a vicious barrage, the sup-
posedly shattered German Wytschaete Group surprised the 33rd Division with a heavy attack between
the Menin road and the edge of Polygon Wood, drove
it back, and exposed the southern flank of the Australians directly above them. Coming when it did, the
enemy move was most embarrassing and threatened
to dislocate Plumer's thrust intended for the following
morning. While Rupprecht knew it was due, the success of his own stroke led him to believe that the
British would have to hold off for a few days. He left
for Munich on personal business. But immediately
after the Crown Prince's departure it was learned
through English prisoners that Plumer was, after all,

going to attack on the morning of the 26th. All German front-line divisions were placed on the alert. A special artillery concentration was organized.

The Battle of Polygon Wood took place as scheduled, after a frantic last-minute patch-up job to repair the damage to the timing caused by the German stroke of the preceding day. In general along the five-mile front all objectives were obtained. Most of Zonnebeke village was captured, Polygon Wood was almost completely cleared and occupied, and I Anzac and V Corps pushed forward for an average gain of a thousand yards. British losses in infantry and artillery personnel were 17,000, very nearly the same as the German. Throughout this day and the next the enemy counterattacked, but gained not a yard of the ground they had given up.

The two attacks of September 20 and 26 annoyed Generals Ludendorff and Rupprecht. Their losses, too, had been considerable, and it was becoming difficult to reinforce their lines through the west Belgium rail bottleneck. It was not a matter of lack of troops—they had at least a million fighting men in or near the salient, and there was no end to the divisions available from Hoffmann's front—but it was a problem to keep them flowing into tactical position during periods of incessant combat. On the 24th the Crown Prince had noted in his diary, "It is to be hoped that another attack will not follow too quickly, as we have not sufficient reserves behind the front."

Erich von Ludendorff begrudged the enemy his

Near Pilckem, October 10, 1917

small gains and the fact that he had "managed to adapt himself to our method of employing counter-attack divisions." The trouble was that the German technique of elastic defense had the defect—more psychological than anything else—of almost automatically surrendering the thinly held advance zone. The German high command decided to make some changes. In the future they would strike back the day after a British assault, instead of throwing in their *Eingreif* divisions piecemeal from the beginning. Therefore their front-line defenders were allotted more machine-gun crews, in a partial reversion to the prewar German motto, "One line and a strong one." The importance of these minor alterations was not great, but they did reflect German irritation over the incessant denting of their front starting with the Messines affair sixteen weeks before.

Yet one may wonder whether the customary pessimism of the Bavarian Crown Prince and the quarter-master general was warranted here. It can hardly be said that the British had burst out of the salient since July 31. At the point of farthest advance—toward Zonnebeke—the gain was three miles. Elsewhere it was a good deal less, and in some sectors on the extreme flanks the line had hardly been carried forward at all. The salient was now a different one, indeed a deeper one, but essentially it was still a salient transposed slightly to the northeast. What of the ridge? In this respect, too, the Germans stood fairly well despite

the violent pounding to which they had been subjected. Only the bottom third of the arc had been
wrested from them, and they still held the long seven-
mile sweep of elevations from Gheluvelt through
Broodseinde and Passchendaele to the outskirts of
Westroosebeke. "Counting heads," they had taken a
heavy toll of the British and French, though Ludendorff did not know that to date the ratio of casualties
was five to three in his favor.

Many an English dream had faded since July. The
Channel ports of Ostend and Zeebrugge no longer
beckoned; they lay quietly in the German embrace.
Near Nieuport Lord Rawlinson and his army fretted
and squatted and waited for the command which they
now suspected would never come. In the Thames and
the waters of the North Atlantic Admiral Bacon's ships
and sailors carried out other tasks and thought no
more of amphibious landings. On the flanks of the
salient the cavalrymen and their steeds rested; no gap
had been opened for them to pour through. Even the
ridge itself, which Sir Hubert's legions were to have
overrun many weeks ago in the early stages of the
campaign, still commanded most of the Allied positions lying in the shallow bowl below.

Sir Douglas was forced to concede all this. But, he
asserted, the fundamental strategy was to wear the
enemy down; and he claimed and perhaps believed
that he was doing so. Mr. George Bernard Shaw was
one of many doubters:

The war dragged on; and I sedulously assured everyone who discussed it with me that it would last thirty
years; for the war of attrition, as it was called, attrited
both sides impartially, the great offensives always
petering out just before their consummation, and the
momentary successes producing no more decisive results than the tediously protracted failures.

Such an attitude was to be expected of Mr. Shaw
that communist, but one is more surprised to find Sir
William Robertson writing Haig on September 27 in
much the same vein:

> My views are known to you. They have always been
> "defensive" in all theatres but the West. But the dif-
> ficulty is to *prove* the wisdom of this now that Russia
> is out. I confess I stick to it more because I see nothing
> better, and because my instinct prompts me to stick
> to it, than because of any good argument by which
> I can support it.

What bothered Sir William was a feeling, which he
never quite crystallized into words, that the Third
Battle of Ypres was only a fragment of the same old
siege-war mosaic. Nothing had really changed. During
the first half of 1915 the French had attacked incessantly in Champagne and Artois. Late in 1915 the
British had attacked day after day at Loos, and the
French had again attacked week after week at Champagne. For four months in 1916 the Allies had attacked
on the Somme. In early 1917 Allenby had attacked in-

terminably around Arras, and Nivelle on the Aisne. All these operations had cost the attackers far more than the entrenched defenders, and they all bore a disquieting resemblance to what was now going on in Flanders. No rational person, and Robertson had more than his share of brains, could fail to notice the similarity.

The high command had gradually shifted their perspective from the forest to the trees. If it cost them 20,000 men to advance a thousand yards they consoled themselves with Intelligence estimates which proved that the enemy had lost even more. It did not seem to occur to them that General Charteris could not possibly know the enemy's casualty figures, nor that such victories were essentially Pyrrhic, nor that tales of woe from Ludendorff and captured privates did not really indicate an enemy breakdown. British prisoners also complained, and so did many a British general on occasion; but the German warlords were more sophisticated than Haig and paid them little heed. The enemy seemed more capable of facing facts. After the war Captain Liddell Hart, the military analyst, in his essay "Two Appreciations," demonstrated incisively the difference between Haig's wishful reasoning and the cold realism of the German Supreme Command's Operations Section. GHQ in France had a tendency to resent negative facts and adverse opinions. With their eyes riveted on the little salient in Flanders they ignored the slings and arrows of outraged amateurs such as Winston Churchill, who pointed out:

A policy of pure attrition between armies so evenly balanced cannot lead to a decision. . . . Unless this problem can be solved satisfactorily, we shall simply be wearing each other out on a gigantic scale and with fearful sacrifices without ever reaping the reward.

And, concerning the new goddess of attrition that had sprung into being Minerva-like that September, Lloyd George had this to say:

Our men advanced against the most terrible machine-gun fire ever directed against troops in any series of battles, and they fell by the thousands in every attack. But divisions were sent on time after time to face the same slaughter in their ranks, and they always did their intrepid best to obey the fatuous orders. When divisions were exhausted or decimated, there were plenty of others to take their places.

Haig insisted that this time the Germans really were crumbling. The operations of September 20 and 26 had turned out splendidly. Another one was set for the first week in October. Who could deny that it would be equally successful? The problem was to define the word success.

The countless human moles that made up Haig's armies could hardly agree that they were winning the war. To them the passing days were a crazy-quilt of blood and thunder. July 31, August 16, September 20, September 26 were not isolated battles; for between these dates local attacks occurred (or were endured) again and again. The front-line soldiers saw no victory, no end to the war. At times they were exhilarated by a tiny creep forward; a day later they sensed that peace and normal existence were as far away as ever. They understood, if the high command did not, the enduring superiority of the defense and the true meaning of the impersonal concept of attrition. They knew that only the rats grew fat on attrition; they were everywhere throughout the salient, so glutted with the flesh and blood of soldiers that they hardly bothered to move aside—"loathsome, bloated creatures, half-blind and as big as cats." When the *Times* reported that "we have broken, and broken at a single blow, in the course of some three or four hours, the German system of defense," not one British or German rifleman could possibly have known that the reference was to the incident at Polygon Wood.

British morale had begun to dip, and this was reflected in the increasing number of arrests and executions for desertion. Philip Gibbs, the press correspondent, writes

about a young officer sentenced to death for cowardice (there were quite a number of lads like that). He was blindfolded by a gas-mask fixed on the wrong way round, and pinioned, and tied to a post. The firing-party lost their nerve and their shots were wild. The boy was only wounded, and screamed in his mask, and the A.P.M. had to shoot him twice with his revolver before he died.

And he continues to say that he encountered more and more "deadly depression" in the ranks, among men who could see no future except more bloodshed. They shrank from what was to come, they cursed the luck that had brought them to Flanders while other more fortunate fellows were in Palestine, on battle cruisers in the Atlantic, at desks in London, playing at war in Greece, counting boots and cartridge cases at French ports, or a hundred other cushy places; and above all they hated the salient with a despair reflected even in the place names: Suicide Corner, Dead Dog Farm, Idiot Crossroads, Stinking Farm, Dead Horse Corner, Shell-trap Barn, Hellfire Crossroads, Jerk House, Vampire Point.

The scene in No Man's Land these final days of September was indeed a chilling one. The one-time barns were litters of rocks and moldering timbers. The ridge was a faint, featureless rise that hardly disturbed the endless expanse of rubble. Farms were deserts. Woods were empty fields marked by what seemed to be a few short poles stuck into the ground. In many places weeds tried to grow among the gravel, between the shell craters, and around the faintly protruding concrete blockhouses. But while the landscape was not a thing of beauty it was at least dry; and from a strictly military standpoint it was capable of supporting men, horses, guns, and tanks. It was the British high command's intention to capture more of this wretched lowland with Plumer's next "bound."

The specter of rain pressed against the brains of the British generals and filled them with a sense of urgency. They had been abnormally lucky in September, just as they had been unlucky in August; but their luck could not hold up indefinitely. Sir Douglas Haig, however, seemed less worried than other officers about the race against time. On September 28 he conferred with Generals Gough and Plumer concerning the forthcoming operation and explained how, after the probable collapse of the enemy's resistance, the reserve formations, the tanks, and the mounted cavalry were to rush in pursuit and turn the enemy's flank. He asked Gough and Plumer by what tactical methods they intended to do this, and what their matériel requirements would be.

The two army commanders were rather taken aback. Gough thought that Haig's views were "somewhat optimistic," and though he too was encouraged by recent events he doubted whether they could actually plan on pushing ahead with unlimited objectives in view.

Plumer questioned Haig's estimate that German casualties thus far had exceeded the British "not improbably by a hundred per cent," nor did he see eye to eye with him concerning large-scale exploitation of purely siege assaults.

Both generals then responded in writing to their chief's exhortations. They rejected the idea of a breakthrough and suggested that, in any event, the ridge

would have to be captured first. Gough could not understand, he explained politely, how step-by-step
methods which would leave the enemy's artillery intact could suddenly lead to conditions of open warfare.

On October 2 the three generals met again. Haig
back-tracked slightly, but still insisted that they
should be ready to plunge forward if the opportunity
arose. It was decided to bring ten more divisions to the
salient front, and five new tank battalions. The attack
would take place at dawn, October 4. Gheluvelt, that
exasperatingly tough nut, would be bypassed; and the
main effort would be made farther north by I and II
Anzac Corps, their targets Broodseinde and the Gravenstafel spur respectively, both roughly a mile away.
As for the Fifth Army still farther up the line, its objectives were more limited and included the ruins of
Poelcapelle and certain modest heights.

While Plumer and Gough were not as sanguine as
Haig, they too felt certain stirrings of hope. The last
two moves had, after all, acquired the intended
ground. Perhaps the next one would also do so, and
perhaps—if the weather held up—more of the same
kind of gains might follow. While other individuals,
high and low, considered a major triumph out of the
question in Belgium that autumn, most British generals thought otherwise; and the atmosphere at the
highest levels of command was redolent with impending glory.

Early on October 3 Haig's weather prophet announced that rain was en route, and scarcely were the words out of his mouth when a fine drizzle began to fall. The assault brigades began their approach march, the Australians leaving Ypres through the remnants of the Menin Gate. The sun sank gloomily, for by now brisk, sporadic showers were falling and the sky was overcast with low clouds running hard to the northeast before winds of gale force.

Across the North Sea another moonlight raid had just taken place on the City, causing much commotion and some damage. As usual, thousands took refuge in the tube stations—among them, the *Morning Post* reported, "swarms of aliens" who "push women and children aside and generally act like brutish beasts." Several dozen people were killed by the bombs; in the euphemisms of the day they were "knocked out," or "went out of it."

There in that far-off land the shortage of butter was causing much indignation. The restaurants were thronged, and endless queues outside the music halls were the despair of nearby shopkeepers. The cinemas rolled in customers and wealth, and servicemen on leave (reported the *Nation*) rushed after "purchasable satisfaction, and the Bishop of London utters his voice in vain." A horrid rumor spread that some kind of a khaki uniform was being considered for all war workers, a term which by September 1917 included practically everyone.

Meanwhile Sir James Barrie's play *Dear Brutus* was

playing to enthusiastic audiences, and so was Henry Arthur Jones' new production, *The Pacifists*, which berated all those who pursued an ignoble peace. The sensational trial of Lieutenant Malcolm had just ended with his acquittal for murdering Count de Borch who, during the lieutenant's duties at the front, had tried to seduce his wife; and the joyous echoes over the jury's decision had not yet died down.

Alone in his quiet room at the War Office, that day in London before the attack, Sir William Robertson scrawled out a glum message for transmittal to Marshal Haig. It was to the effect that the War Cabinet had "approved in principle" the British army's taking over more front line from the French, and it meant that the civilians had finally given up hope that the Third Battle of Ypres would accomplish anything. "Wully" knew what Haig's reaction would be, especially since the latter had not even been consulted. Now it was more important than ever for the future of the campaign—from Sir Douglas's point of view—that tomorrow's great battle should be a winning one, an absolutely decisive one, unmistakable proof that he was on the right track.

12. Haig's Decision

OF THE THREE blows delivered by the British and French starting September 20, that of October 4 was the largest and presumed to be the most telling; and after its conclusion the air was filled with groans, both from German wounded and from the German high command. Ludendorff grumbled that "we only came through it with enormous losses. It was evident that the idea of holding the front line more densely . . . was not the remedy." The German official historian summarizes: "The new battle scheme had not stood the test on the 4th October." Prince Rupprecht's chief of staff wrote: "Crown Prince Rupprecht found himself compelled to consider whether . . . he should not withdraw the front in Flanders so far back that the Allies would be forced to carry out an entirely new deployment of Artillery." Another enemy monograph referred to the Battle of Broodseinde as "The Black Day of October 4th." Foot

Guard Regiment No. 5 considered it "the worst day yet experienced in the War."

On the other side of the hill, British comments were joyous. In his diary Haig speaks of "a very important success." Even more cheery than usual, Charteris thought the Germans had been so mangled that they possessed "few more available reserves." He turned to Harington and exclaimed, "Now we have them on the run—get up the cavalry!" The Australian official historian writes, "An overwhelming blow had been struck, and both sides knew it." For the London press Philip Gibbs reported, "It has been a bad defeat for them and they did not hide their despair." British officers claimed a record number of dead Germans littering the captured area. New Zealanders spoke of unusually heavy casualties dealt the enemy and boasted that their division alone had taken 1159 captives. General Plumer called it "the greatest victory since the Marne."

All this seems to indicate a triumph beyond argument or carping, despite the deteriorating weather.

Yet an examination of the map shows that the physical gains were even smaller than in the two previous attacks. The former towns of Gravenstafel and Poelcapelle were captured (the latter not entirely), the remnants of Polygon Wood were occupied, Broodseinde was taken, and so was the remaining half of Zonnebeke village. One mile in the center was the point of farthest advance. Averaging out the gains over the entire front from Tower Hamlets to the

Ypres-Staden railroad, one learns that the dividend was some seven hundred yards. The price of this investment was nearly 26,000 casualties, half of whom were killed or missing. And this figure does not include scattered losses suffered by the French up north.

The Germans had been hurt no worse; and despite the complaints of their commanders that they were still finding it hard to fling reserve divisions into crucial sectors exactly when needed, their defensive wall was intact. They had, however, lost more of the ridge, especially around Broodseinde. They had taken a terrific battering which they could ill afford, for the legions of America would soon counterbalance the Russian defection. They had given up 5000 prisoners as compared to the British 3000. Yet, all in all, one cannot fully accept the view of British officers who thought they had handed the enemy a crushing defeat.

A further inspection of the official map shows that along half the front of attack objectives were not quite reached. The New Zealand historian admits that Broodseinde was only a partial success, since German counterattacks on the extreme right flank had regained most of the ground which the 5th and 21st divisions had initially won.

The Boches showed little sign of any deep-seated demoralization around midday, when both Plumer and Gough attempted to exploit their gains. After a few hours of trying without avail to get their attacks rolling again, both generals gave up and turned their attentions to the more negative business of merely warding off enemy counterstrokes. The victory, if one cares to interpret it as such, thus fizzled out as soon as the British tried to fan the flame.

"Long ere now it had become but too clear that the strategic aims of the Ypres offensive were incapable of realization," writes one authority, and he blames the worsening weather and the "brave and skillful" enemy for the meager fruits of Haig's program.

But had it never rained in Flanders in the fall, and had not the Germans always been brave and skillful? The front-line soldiers muttered about the Germans' unusually powerful show of artillery. But the Royal Flying Corps, the eyes of the guns, had been grounded all day because of the high winds (a serious flying factor in those times), the rain, and the low clouds.

In his dispatch to the King, Sir Douglas, after pointing out that one of the most important segments of the ridge had been taken, proceeds as follows:

> The year was far spent. The weather had been consistently unpropitious, and the state of the ground, in consequence of rain and shelling combined, made movement inconceivably difficult. The resultant delays had given the enemy time to bring up reinforcements and to organize his defense after each defeat. Even so, it was still the difficulty of movement far more than hostile resistance which continued to limit our progress, and now made it doubtful whether the capture of the remainder of the ridge before winter finally set in was possible.

And lamely he continues:

> On the other hand, there was no reason to anticipate
> an abnormally wet October.

But these words were written in retrospect. On the
day of the attack he, as well as his fellow generals, was
exultant. It seemed to them that they could continue
their progress indefinitely. Haig decided to move up
the next attack by forty-eight hours, and was annoyed
when General Anthoine told him that he could advance the schedule by only one day. Always prudent,
General Plumer suggested mildly that perhaps they
had encountered only forward units of the enemy defense as yet; he too, however, thought affairs had gone
wonderfully up to 3 p.m.; and Gough was also in favor
of shoving on with all possible speed.

There was an air of suppressed excitement that afternoon at GHQ. Two miles on the average had been
gained in two weeks. A calmer observer might have
reasoned that at this rate Berlin could not be reached
for nine years; but the generals were not calm. Tensely
they projected their gains in ground westward toward
the Channel, they told each other of the decay of
enemy morale, they computed his present and eventual gigantic losses in men. They felt that if the weather
held up (and what could be more sensible than always
to concede the possibility that it might not?) British
troops faced the possibility of a really big success.

General John J. Pershing sent Haig a message congratulating him on his gains, which "give a striking answer to weak-kneed peace propaganda."

From London Lord Derby wrote him, ". . . congratulations on your great successes. You cannot imagine how it has bucked up everybody here."

And Sir Douglas, in his grave and impassive way, was the most exhilarated of all. He decided not to send Gough the Canadian Corps of some 60,000 men. They despised this officer for the way he had driven them at the Somme last year; and in any event Plumer was spearheading the present drive and needed them more. On the afternoon of October 4, while heavy fighting continued, hurried planning got under way for the blow scheduled at dawn, October 9.

Colonel Repington was in France that week, and he too thought Haig's offensive might as well keep going on the same old lines, though his views were more cynical and far-reaching:

Since nations counted money no more than pebbles on a beach, and all would probably repudiate in one form or another at the end of the war, there seemed no reason for stopping, especially as so many people were growing rich by the war; the ladies liked being without their husbands, and all dreaded the settlement afterwards, industrial, political, financial and domestic.

So among everyone but spoilsport civilians such as Lloyd George and certain French officers there was a willingness to continue the big push. Perhaps Haig was right, after all. Perhaps it was natural for the generals to congratulate one another and for their staffs to work out brilliant new assaults. But only the weather refused to cooperate; and while it was true that October 4 was a turning point in the Third Battle of Ypres it was not of the sort that the buoyant generals had in mind.

It had been drizzling and gusty all morning during the main attack, but at noon conditions took a turn for the worse. Now the wind shifted slightly to a northerly quarter and heavy showers broke. For three days it rained. On the 7th the showers changed to a heavy drenching downpour, and after a meeting Charteris suddenly made this personal note: "Unless we get fine weather for all this month, there is no chance of clearing the coast. . . . Most of those at the conference would welcome a stop."

The rain created extreme problems in the frontal zone. For one thing, the duckboards reached up only to the previous line. Beyond that it became almost impossible for anything or anybody to move. Carrying parties, trying to get supplies to the new forward positions by working their way through the untracked morass, were soon exhausted by their labors. The system for evacuating casualties collapsed. In captured pillboxes the badly wounded men lay, while those less hurt crouched outside on the muddy ground, exposed to the weather and shell fire. The majority had to be left unattended for the better part of a day. Ambulance cars often careened off the slick tracks and overturned into the shell craters on either side. Even the horse-drawn ambulances skidded and crashed, at least one of them with a full load of wounded troops inside.

The more it rained the more it became a puzzle how the light artillery was to be moved up. Some battalions ran completely out of duckboard planking. Soon the heavily trodden mule paths were in ruins. Water lapped at, and often covered, the duckboards; inch by inch the crests rose in the shell holes where many thousands of riflemen held on, chilled through and utterly soaked. Far away in Paris Marshal Foch, temporarily stripped of his field command and surveying the military scene from his lofty but impotent status as chief of the French general staff, said when interviewed, "*Boche* is bad, and *Boue* is bad, but *Boche* and *Boue* together—ah!" and he raised his hands in a warning gesture.

There was much unhappiness among the tank people. They had been squandered in small packets here and there for the past two months and had accomplished precious little. Their casualties had been severe, and they were sick of being wasted under hopeless conditions. They felt that they held the key to victory on the stalemated Western Front, for there was no way around and they alone were capable of breaking through; and they insisted that their formations be employed only on dry ground at a time and place of their own choice. The revolt was accepted without much concern at GHQ. In relief, armored commanders settled down to examine microscopically the British front for a sector they could later exploit; and, as we shall see, they found one.

After the battle and counterattacks of October 4 a relative peace descended upon the salient. The rain came and went; but mostly it stayed—hypnotically, almost caressingly, murmuring as it splashed into the saturated, semi-liquid ground, tapping ceaselessly against the steel helmets of the warriors. Tea, bread, and jam were served for breakfast, and farther back the soup kitchens did a thriving business. As the fighting died down, salvage crews scoured the area for arms and equipment that might be used to fight another day. Redcaps directed the men to the rear along roads and trackboards that led into open fields where bivouac sheets were raised. For two days despondent stragglers kept shambling in. Each night, in silence, rum was issued and the companies settled down as best they could. And up ahead less fortunate people brooded in the flooding craters, weapons at hand, unable to sleep, almost under the muzzles of enemy machine guns a few hundred feet away. These at the moment were the last insurable men on earth: the extreme front-line infantry soldiers of Great Britain, clinging to the outer rim of the most lethal battle zone in history. And as they did so they pondered two questions— Were the Huns coming? When would they be put back into reserve?

The meeting held at the commander in chief's French château on the evening of October 7 was a far cry from that glad occasion three days earlier. The heavens had thrown cold water upon the salient and upon the spirits of two of the conferees; but the third, Sir Douglas Haig, was as grimly determined as ever to proceed with the attacks scheduled for the 9th and 12th.

He started by asking Generals Plumer and Gough to state their views. They responded flatly that the campaign should be stopped. Haig refused to do so, and one wonders why the conference was called; but since the decision made here was one of the most serious in the annals of the war it may be pertinent to consider his motives. By any normal standard, the campaigning season was over. Haig certainly knew that proper preparations, rested troops, and full artillery coverage were no longer possible. His armies were groping and floundering. With the Westroosebeke ridge now barring their way even to Passchendaele, it seemed that only two rational possibilities existed, both of which meant that the field marshal would have to abandon his strategic plan sold to the civilians in London many weeks ago—first, to stop where they were and simply try to hang on for the winter along a very bad line; second, to retreat to a decent line. The latter was more logical, but nightmarish. Not even Gough and Plumer could face up to the prospect of writing off nearly 200,000 casualties (the total since Messines) and going back where they had started from, or even farther.

After the Somme, Joffe had said coolly to another officer, "I shall be sacked, you shall be sacked, we shall all be sacked." The uproar that would take place if the British armies should retreat, as though admitting failure, was one that for personal reasons, among others, the generals absolutely refused to consider. Haig insisted that they at least try to capture more of the Westroosebeke-Passchendaele sector of the ridge. If they could do so, he argued, they could then overlook the valley of the Steenbeke (for whatever value that depressing sight might be worth), and the men would be able to rest on higher, dryer ground for the winter.

And there were other reasons. One which requires no comment was that capturing the ridge would "tranquilise public opinion." Then there were the French. It had been decided in London on September 25 to have Haig take over six divisions of their line. The idea was that spreading out his armies more thinly would keep him from attacking. But Haig turned the scheme upside down. If the French were so weak, he explained, that they could not even hold their assigned frontal breadth, then it was essential to keep attacking so as to save *them* from attack. It was the same tune in a different key. Furthermore, Pétain had promised to deliver a strong attack at Malmaison on October 23. To some this might have seemed a contradictory note, but Haig looked upon it as still another call for continuing the teamwork at his end.

Italy too was a factor. All signs pointed toward a

combined Austro-German blow at Cadorna's front in the near future. Haig would not agree to reinforce that line. Rather, he insisted, the best means of cooperation was to keep Ludendorff busy in Flanders.

As for the weather, he had hopes that it would soon change for the better. Concerning the terrain, it was "not yet impossible." To delay would only give the Boches extra time to strengthen their defenses. Sir Douglas had an answer for everything. The campaign would continue, and when it would end nobody could any longer guess. There were many who now considered Haig obsessed by a conviction that he could defeat the Central Powers singlehanded. Memoranda summarizing his attitude, delivered to Robertson and the War Cabinet next day, seem to lend some weight to that growing contention:

He would refuse to take over more of the French line, and would "adhere resolutely to that refusal, even to the point of answering threats by threats if necessary."

He claimed that the French were not capable of a serious military effort, but appraised them as "staunch in defense" and "may be estimated as fully equal to an equivalent number of German divisions"—a rather astonishing admission, for it seemed to undermine his own basic argument for the Flanders offensive.

He asked for more drafts to replace his wastage and that the War Cabinet should have faith in the outcome of his plan. Neither request was granted.

He felt that Russia would stay in the war and would

continue to contribute the same number of divisions as at present. Two months later the Russians quit.

He claimed that the Germans would be able to place only 179 divisions on the Western Front in 1918 as a result of their losses in the present campaign. The number turned out to be 210—a difference of some half a million men.

He felt that the enemy was collapsing and might soon "gladly accept such terms of peace as the Allies might offer"—provided, of course, that the pressure in Belgium was kept up.

For the sake of argument he admitted that Russia might break down, but that even so Germany could transfer only "the 32 more efficient divisions" to the west. But Germany had already switched to Rupprecht's front more divisions than Haig had envisioned "at the most." By the following April they had, in fact, brought down 300,000 more men than Haig had estimated.

He said nothing about a possible German offensive, even aided by Hoffmann's divisions, which might some day counteract his own. The following spring Ludendorff went over to the attack and smashed through Haig's line.

He predicted that if Russia dropped out the pressure on Italy might increase, but that the latter "should still be able to hold her ground unaided." Sixteen days later the Italian army was crushed at Caporetto.

There was to come a time when Haig would throw open the door of his room of dreams and enter the

gray corridor of reality; but that day was six months
distant. Meanwhile the War Cabinet and even
"Wully" received his assurances uneasily. They had
that tone of dull, relentless optimism which over the
years they had come to associate with the man. As for
Broodseinde, the civilians did not believe it was a
great victory. Lloyd George sarcastically calls it "still
another smashing triumph a few hundred yards
ahead." Haig had cried wolf once too often. The politicians were generally convinced that his offensive was
buried in a sea of mud, nor were they impressed by the
Times' claim that October 4 had seen "the most important British victory of the year. . . . The particular task which Sir Douglas Haig set his armies has been
very nearly accomplished." Next day the *Times* went
even further. Now, in truth, "our object is already secured." The British armies were said to be in sight of
Bruges, and the correspondent praises the marshal's
"calm, unhurried persistence which compels the admiration of the world. . . . With each successive stride
the arrangements grow more exact, the results more
certain, the losses lighter."

And Philip Gibbs in his report the day after the
battle evoked even more thrilling vistas:

> One of the prisoners, a professor . . . thinks "it will
> not be long before Germany makes a great bid for
> peace by offering to give up Belgium. By mid-winter
> she will yield Alsace-Lorraine; Russia will remain as
> before the war, except for an autonomous Poland;

Italy will have what she has captured; and Germany will get back some of her colonies."

Marshal Henri Pétain, for one, was less sanguine and to Colonel Repington said that "Charteris killed off the Germans too quickly. . . . He and Davidson egged on Haig to believe that he was winning the war." And he remarked of the British generals that they were "very tenacious of their ideas, kept a straight course, but ran in blinkers." He held his hands up to his eyes to show Repington what he meant and added that he could not consider the Flanders attack good strategy—this despite the Frenchman's recommendation the previous day that limited British operations might usefully be continued, and that Pétain's troops would cooperate with local attacks.

Nor was Pétain alone in questioning on the basis of original strategy, Haig's October 7 decision. For one thing, the submarine menace was subsiding. From the beginning many had derided the alleged need for re-capturing the Belgian ports. Now the dispute was academic. In April one-fourth of all British merchant-men leaving the United Kingdom had never come back; but the convoy system (resisted heretofore by the Admiralty and put into effect at the insistence of Winston Churchill) had started the following month and had worked wonders. The April losses of 874,576 tons were cut in September to 351,105, only one per cent of which was in convoy. The sinkings were lessen-ing month by month and would surely continue to do so. Therefore the naval significance of Zeebrugge and Ostend had become quite negligible.

Over the months, and under the wise tutelage of Henri Pétain, the French Army had largely recovered its willingness at least to resist. And while it was conserving its strength it was in 1917 inflicting nearly as many casualties as the British upon the enemy in the west.

What of the United States? Haig had not considered the entry of that country when he had first formulated his plans, but by October the new giant had been in the war for six months. Her weight would soon be felt and would make eventual victory certain. Already nearly 100,000 Yanks were in France; and this number could if necessary be increased to 5,000,000—and, behind the men, the wheels of the greatest industrial establishment in the world were revolving ever more prodigiously.

In his published papers Haig refers to America only once during the Flanders fighting: his June 10 diary reads in part, "There must be no thought of staying our hand until America puts an Army in the field next year." The marshal's utter indifference to United States power (he was at heart militarily indifferent to all Allied nations but his own) must be rated one of the strangest phenomena of the campaign. Now, four months after the entry above, various invoices were coming due.

Haig had promised the politicians that he would close down the offensive as soon as it showed signs of foundering. It was doing so. He had sworn that the French would cooperate in strength. They were not. He had assured Lloyd George that his campaign would be predicated upon achieving decisive results before the notorious Flanders weather broke. The results to date were meager, and the weather had broken with a vengeance. The German line showed no sign of cracking. The amphibious plan involving Rawlinson's Fourth Army and the Royal Navy had been finally and quietly shelved. The British cavalry was marking time; there was no opening for them, nor could they operate in mud. Russia's virtual collapse meant unending new reserves for employment on the Western Front. Italy needed help. The element of surprise was irretrievably gone. Haig's own generals wanted him to stop. The politicians had lost their last vestige of faith in his campaign. The morale of his own armies was sinking into the swamps of the salient. What Haig still hoped to achieve that day of decision in early October, and what he was trying to prove, are perhaps questions more appropriate to a psychiatrist than to the student of military science.

German diplomacy was currently in the hands of the brilliant young Baron Richard von Kuhlmann, who as Foreign Minister had decided to make another try at a negotiated peace and in September had established contact with Great Britain through neutral offices in Madrid and Brussels. These overtures were formal and serious, and aroused much alarm among the Allies. Among other things, von Kuhlmann offered to return Alsace-Lorraine to France, to restore Serbia to her prewar status, to make territorial concessions to Italy and colonial concessions to Britain, and to clear completely out of Belgium. Monsieur Painlevé was dismayed. If the terms were genuine, as they appeared to be, how could his nation be induced to go on fighting?

Lloyd George was uninterested on general principles. He wanted a military victory, so that peace terms could be dictated to the Central Powers rather than negotiated. For once he and Haig were in accord. The latter put his views in writing. They were to the effect that Germany would be defeated even if Russia left the war, provided that he be given all the men and munitions he needed in Flanders, and that "accepting an unsatisfactory peace" at the moment would lead to dire consequences in the future. The ambassadors of Great Britain, France, America, Japan, Italy, and Russia convened in Paris on October 8 and drafted a somewhat evasive reply to the irritating German minister which, however, indicated a willingness to discuss matters further. Unfortunately von Kuhlmann backed off from his previous pledge concerning Alsace–Lorraine, and the episode led to nothing.

The fact is that Lloyd George, despite his disappointment over Haig's military progress, was really in no great hurry. Like Pétain, he was waiting for the Americans and the tanks. Meanwhile he urged the War Cabinet on October 5 to back his request for an offensive in Palestine. That evening he sent for Sir Henry Wilson, and a discussion followed which the latter summarized in his diary:

> Lloyd George is mad to knock the Turks out during the winter . . . his difficulty being that Haig was hostile (which he thought natural) and Robertson was mulish, which he thought maddening. He wanted to know my advice. I repeated . . . that, if a really good scheme was thoroughly well worked out, we could clear the Turks out of Palestine, and very likely knock them completely out, during the mud months, without in any way interfering with Haig's operations next spring and summer. . . .
>
> Lloyd George has no illusions about Haig's "victory" of yesterday. At the same time I again insisted on Lloyd George giving Haig *all* the men and guns that he possessed, up to the time of the mud, to which he agreed. The fact is that Lloyd George is profoundly dissatisfied, but does not know what to do.

But "the time of the mud" had already and quite definitely arrived, and the Prime Minister was at least clear on what not to do. He still hoped to curb Haig indirectly—by withholding drafts, by extending and thus thinning out his front, by shifting emphasis to the Holy Land and thus killing time rather than Englishmen, and by denying him the moral support of the War Cabinet. But all this was a slow process, and in the interim Haig was pushing his offensive with feverish haste. The tortoise had too much of a head start and could not be caught by the hare.

And though Haig still stood fairly well in the estimate of many members of Parliament, Robertson's star had begun to decline. Unlike the former, who was literally and figuratively remote, "Wully" was too close to the politicians for comfort. They resented his never-ending demands for more men to be sent to the charnel houses of France and Belgium, and they reacted in natural fashion to his plain contempt for politicians. They felt, in Winston Churchill's words, that Sir Douglas at least "acted from conviction; but Sir William Robertson drifted ponderously." Mostly he backed Haig with passion, but often and in public he questioned whether endless battering at the ridge was truly worth while. The civilians had begun to wonder whether the chief of staff really knew his own mind. His egregiously poor manners did not help. And, as Haig's campaign proceeded down the muddy road to extinction, the career of Sir William followed in kind.

In Flanders prospects were a shade brighter. The rain ceased on the evening of the 7th, and a flurry of activity ensued. Plumer phoned Lord Birdwood, commanding I Anzac Corps, and asked his opinion. Birdwood still thought the attack should be canceled. He was overruled. Charteris was galvanized into a new fit of elation: "With a great success tomorrow, and good weather for a few more weeks, we may still clear the coast and win the war before Christmas." Gough rang up to say that Lieutenant General Cavan (XIV Corps) was in favor of attacking as planned, but that

Lieutenant General Maxse (XVIII Corps) was opposed. Haig was brought a message from the Frenchman, Anthoine. It was not enthusiastic—according to the Scot's diary that evening:

> a very mean document. He is evidently keen to save himself and to place the risk of failure on me. I am ready to take the responsibility and have ordered him to carry on and do his best. The French seem to have lost their chivalrous spirit if it ever existed out of the story books!

General "Tim" Harington, that guiding spirit of Plumer's Second Army, held a conference with the war correspondents. His army was invincible when it came to limited, step-by-step attacks, he assured them; and tomorrow would be the same story as in the past. He said he was not concerned with certain lugubrious views emanating from the Fifth Army. His officers were determined to attack. He still hoped to fling the cavalry through the gap. The sandy crest of the ridge, he claimed, was "as dry as a bone."

But this was said when it was raining again, and raining heavily. The newspapermen listened to the general with alarm; had he too lost his perspective? One of those present recorded his impressions in a despondent passage:

> I believe the official attitude is that Passchendaele Ridge is so important that tomorrow's attack is worth making whether it succeeds or fails. . . . I suspect

that they are making a great, bloody experiment—a huge gamble. . . . I feel, and most of the correspondents feel . . . terribly anxious. . . . These major-generals . . . are banking on their knowledge of German demoralization. . . . I thought the principle was to be "hit, hit, hit, *whenever the weather is suitable.*" If so, it is thrown over at the first temptation.

It was not so much that it rained but that it seemed to rain, by a maddening coincidence, nearly every time an attack was due. If only the beautiful weather earlier that day had persisted!

13. The Slough of Despond

SOME FIFTEEN hours before Harington's uneasy press conference, along the disjointed line of shell craters and shallow ditches which constituted the new British front line in Flanders, a balmy and brilliant autumn day had been born. And the sight which greeted the front-line men that sunny dawn of October 8 was impressive indeed. Thousands of shell holes, many of which overlapped each other, were at least partly full of water and many of the smaller ones were already overflowing. The canals, the "bekes," and the intricate system of drainage ditches torn by months of shelling were everywhere spreading their waters horizontally throughout the low-lying and level plains, for the molasses-like topsoil could neither absorb it nor allow it to sink through. All these conditions were especially prevalent in front of the Fifth Army lying to the south of Houthulst Forest.

Looking northward from the front, one was afforded an unusual view indeed. One observer

> through what might have been a porthole of a ship . . . saw as still a sea as any sailor gazed on . . . watched the blessed sun dawning on still another sea of mud. And that too was beautiful! Sunrise, gold and orange fading into an ultra violet that the eye could not discern, and under it mud and swamp and brimming shell-holes, all reflecting the gaudy colours of the sky. . . .

That morning of the 8th a strong wind came up, and hopes lifted; but by late afternoon the rains had begun again in torrents worse than before, accompanied by an icy wind that screamed across No Man's Land, lashed the rain into horizontal sheets, and turned the Flanders plain into a frenzy of little waves. Field Marshal Haig's forecasters had correctly predicted no immediate end to the storm, and by dusk it had settled down to an ordinary downpour. It was now that the assault brigades started their march to the jumping-off line.

The attack that would begin the following morning at 5:20 was to be a double blow with objectives of roughly a mile each. The major task was assigned to General Plumer's Second Army. The II Anzac Corps, composed of the 49th and 66th divisions, would advance along two parallel spurs toward the flattened village of Passchendaele. The corps commander, Lieutenant General Sir Alexander Godley, had allotted two brigades from each division for this purpose. There was no chance of the sections' offering each other flanking support, because between their respective ridges lay the valley of the Ravebeke; this was described in an Intelligence summary as "saturated ground. Quite impassable. Should be avoided by all troops at all times."

Below II Anzac stood I Anzac Corps, Lieutenant General Sir William Birdwood commanding, an officer who deeply mistrusted the coming operation but because of his minor role in it had decided to say nothing of his opinions to Haig or his staff. From here the 2nd Australian Division had been designated to furnish a flank for the 66th. Operating from around Broodseinde, its advance was to be in the nature of a small, shallow smoothing out of the line. Simultaneously the 66th would advance to the first cottages of Passchendaele, about half a mile short of the ruined church. And finally the 1st Australian Division to the south would provide a tiny diversion, using less than a hundred men, of whom more will be said later.

The Fifth Army to the left under General Gough had been assigned a far more modest task from the standpoint of material gain: they were merely to proceed almost due north through Poelcapelle and stop near the outskirts of Houthulst Forest. This flat, low-lying six hundred acres of broken stumps and wreckage—once a forest—was really a swampland now. In appearance it resembled a large junkheap. It possessed a minimum of tactical value, and the Germans had made no serious attempt to fortify its approaches.

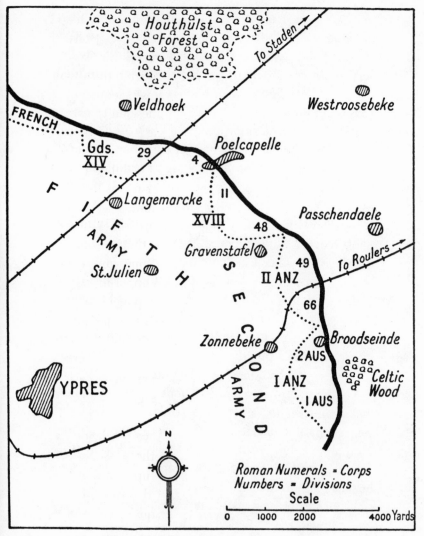

The Allied front line, October 9, 1917

Two British corps would advance in that direction—
one brigade each from the 11th and 48th divisions,
XVIII Corps, under Lieutenant General Sir Ivor
Maxse—farther north five brigades total from the 4th,
29th, and Guards divisions, XIV Corps, Lieutenant
General Earl of Cavan commanding. These units were
to be assisted on their left flank by the First French
Army under Anthoine.

It cannot be said that the offensive of October 9 involved any striking innovations. Rather it was in the
established tradition of the Western Front: masses of
artillery would pour forth a prior bombardment which
would in theory stun and disorganize the front-line
troops of the enemy, knock out his machine guns, cut
his wire entanglements, neutralize his opposing batteries, and (incidentally) eliminate any possibility of
surprise. Afterward the infantry would advance behind a creeping barrage and occupy the ground. As for
tanks, there would be none in action this day; there
was no chance at all that these feeble, primitive Mark
IVs could make progress through the gluey battleground.

The past history of the war had proved, provided
the shelling was heavy enough, that methodical operations like these did work successfully, up to a point.
The system had even been dignified by a little
formula: average depth of advance equals width of
assault divided by two $(D = \frac{W}{2})$, assuming that the

artillery was of maximum density and that this intensity of fire could be maintained all along the attacking front. On October 9 that front, from the French near the forest to the Australians just south of Broodseinde, would be eight miles wide and the theoretical advance would therefore be four. Needless to say, this was neither assigned nor anticipated. However, it was hoped that a little more of the ridge could be bitten off to the south and that Poelcapelle could be wholly occupied by Gough's brigades. And then, if further advances of even a few hundred yards could be attained near the forest by Plumer and the French, all this would add up to a small achievement that might be capitalized on in drier weather for capturing the entire Passchendaele–Westroosebeke–Staden ridge.

Thus the operation that took place October 9 was minor, routine, and conservative in its aims. About 31,000 British troops would participate in the direct attack, and 6000 French. On the other side of No Man's Land the German Fourth Army lay in wait, a hundred yards away in some places (such as in the village of Poelcapelle, held jointly by both sides), fully a mile away in others. As for the British front, it was nothing more than a collection of joined shell holes. The only trenches, so to speak, were messy affairs that joined the shell craters, and they could be dug only about two feet deep, at which point permanent underground water was reached. The biggest holes were used for batallion headquarters. Lesser holes were occupied by company headquarters. The smallest holes each housed one or two forlorn men.

Let us now unravel what happened to the six attacking brigades of I and II Anzac Corps, Second Army.

The 66th (2nd East Lancashires) was an untried division that had arrived in France a few months previously. Since this was to be its first serious test it had been assigned a front along which there was no enemy barbed wire—this, at least, was the understanding of Second Army Intelligence. In view of the inexperience of the unit and the lamentable ground conditions, Plumer's chief of staff, Harington, had suggested assembling the men about two and a half miles from the front and starting them on their march at 7 p.m. Conservatively assuming a rate of half a mile per hour, they would arrive at the jumping-off tapes at midnight, and would be able to rest for five hours before zero hour. The 49th Division started from its assembly area east of Ypres at the same time. Nine thousand drenched troops began their forward march at dusk in full battle order—water bottle on the right hip, haversack moved rearward, an extra fifty-cartridge bandolier over the right shoulder and under the left arm, and a Mills bomb in each side pocket.

Immediately grave difficulties were encountered. The engineers had not been able to improve the infantry's sorry duckboard tracks beyond marking them with tapes and lamps (it had been deemed more essential to make roads for the heavy guns) and by nightfall conditions were such that the men could barely walk. The boards were now coated with slime, or submerged, or shattered every few yards. The heavy-laden troopers (sixty pounds of clothing, equipment, and weapons were carried per man) kept slipping and colliding. Many toppled into shell craters and had to be hauled out by comrades extending rifle butts. And falling into even a shallow hole was often revolting, for the water was foul with decaying equipment, excrement, and perhaps something dead; or its surface might be covered with old, sour mustard gas. It was not uncommon for a man to vomit when being extricated from something like this.

Worse yet, the 66th encountered unexpected swampy areas in the direct and unavoidable line of march. Here it was necessary to walk in liquid mud at least knee high—the kind of autumn terrain in this area well known to Napoleon, whose remark, "God—besides water, air, earth, and fire—has created a fifth element—mud!" was well known throughout the salient.

Throughout that wretched evening the wind slapped the rain against the numbed faces and hands of the wading troops. By midnight, five hours later, only a little more than a mile had been covered. Everyone could now see that it would be touch and go whether the 5:20 attack would be mounted on time. One thing certain: the right-hand brigade (197th) could not possibly make zero hour, and staff officers were sent forward with instructions to get all able-bodied men to the front in time and let the stragglers jump off whenever they arrived—a remarkable arrangement made necessary by circumstances. (As it later happened, the bulk of the outfit arrived twenty minutes after the attack had started, whereupon without pause the men fixed bayonets and kept walking.) One junior officer, lurching back along the greasy duckboards with his head bandaged, said to a reporter:

> Ah doan' know what our brigade was doin' to put us in after a twelve hours' march—twelve hours from beginning to end. We had no duckboards like these—we plugged through the mud. We didn't know where the tapes were, and by the time we arrived there our barrage had gone on half-an-hour. The men were so done they could hardly stand oop an' hold a rifle. We didn't know where our starting position was, but we went on after the barrage. I'm sorry for the Australians, and it was our first stoont too. We're a new division, ye know.

Meanwhile the 49th (1st West Riding) Division had been encountering similar problems. Both its brigades barely made it on time, and the men who arrived at the jumping-off tapes (the tapes themselves were studded with aluminum disks to keep them from sinking under the mud) could hardly be recognized as civilized creatures. From head to foot they were daubed with slime. Their faces were clay-white like those of corpses. Many had tied strips of sacking around their boots. In the words of one correspondent they looked "like men who had been buried alive and dug up again." In the inky darkness and driven rain they had been able to see scarcely a yard in front of them. Meanwhile the Germans were shelling the roads, mostly with their heavier guns, causing hundreds of casualties. Every man fell not once but a score of times en route.

"Where are you, Bill?" one soldier shouted.

"I'm bogged. For God's sake, give me a hand, old lad!"

The troops splashed and slogged toward the front at an average speed of four hundred yards per hour.

One man recounted, "My pal Bert fell in deep and then sank further in. 'Charlie!' he cried. Two of us, and then four, tried to drag him out, but we slipped down the bank of the crater and rolled into the slime with him. I thought we should never get out. Some men were cursing and some were laughing in a wild way, and some were near crying with the cold. But somehow we got on."

Moving shells to the advanced field batteries was a difficult chore. It could be done only by mules; and they too required about eleven hours to arrive at the battery sites, except for those which slid off the planks and suffocated in the bottomless mud on both sides. In one official history there is a picture taken during the day, captioned "Bogged," of a mule in a shell hole. His hindquarters are deep in the mud; only his head and shoulders protrude. In utter despair his head rests in the mud, eyes half closed. Many mules had panicked,

Bogged down, October, 1917

had fought merely to stand on visible portions of the planking, and could be made to move only with much coaxing and punishment. And most shells that did arrive at the batteries were covered with mud and had to be cleaned, one by one, before they could be fired.

As for the guns themselves, it is not known to this day what proportion of the Allied light batteries got into action that morning. From what ensued one might guess no more than a third of those assigned. The main trouble was that the gun roads had not been adequate. Again the mules and pack horses had scrambled aboard any part of the tracks before they were finished. And very few of the gun platforms themselves could be properly laid in position; they either sank under the mud or simply floated away on the surface water in the manner of an episode in Alice in Wonderland. A few of the light pieces were supported in one makeshift way or another, but most were left up to their axles in mud while their helpless crews awaited the signal to open fire. With each shell thrown, the recoil forced them deeper, often up to their muzzles. Their barrels began pointing upward at increasing angles. Accurate aiming was impossible, and the range of many guns was so reduced that they could not reach the enemy lines. So although the heavy artillery well back was able to operate according to schedule, the preparatory 18-pounder bombardment before 5:20 was exceedingly feeble as a whole. Would this be true of the covering barrage also? That question began to loom larger as the hours passed.

To the north, XVIII Corps' two attacking brigades were also trying to get up to the front. And it was fortunate that these 4000 men had started early the previous afternoon, for they needed fully fourteen and a half hours to arrive. In the pre-dawn morning many fell asleep during rest periods and had to be prodded awake and pushed forward by their officers.

Cavan and his XIV Corps had better luck—their terrain was not so badly torn up—and this collection of five brigades arrived at the tape lines well in advance, as did the French to the extreme northwest of everybody.

So now by that morning in Flanders, October 9, 1917, almost all Allied troops had in one manner or other splashed up to their assigned positions. Bayonets were fixed. Pale and silent, the infantry kneeled in their shell holes or lay nearly prone in shallow, oozing trenches awaiting the beginning of the covering barrage. There were some whisperings and final arrangements. Everywhere platoon officers slithered along the tape and repeated, "Wait for the whistle now, boys, and keep in touch."

Many was the man whose nerve now gave way, or who developed diarrhea, or whose legs collapsed beneath him in fear. The advance would have to go on without such as these. They would be dealt with later. Cases involving commissioned and noncommissioned officers posed a problem of leadership. Somebody would have to lead. Hurried consultations took place, and these occasional difficulties were ironed out. In one instance (Lancashires of the 66th Division) a corporal went to pieces and an ex-corporal was ordered to command the section. He refused.˙A squabble developed, and the platoon officer himself had to take over.

The rain continued. And from thousands of pillboxes and other observation posts German eyes surveyed the wasteland and the enemy front. Almost untouched by the futile bombardment, suspicious of certain signs of an impending attack, quite rested, the German Fourth Army patiently waited for what was to come.

When the barrage exploded at dawn—none too convincingly—the Second Army advanced, followed later by stragglers from the 197th Brigade. Immediately it was found that Intelligence had erred in assuming that no wire existed in front of the 66th Division. Twc continuous belts of dense entanglements did in fact bar the way. The prior bombardment had been too weak to break it up, and had left enemy personnel almost untouched as well.

As the British walked forward the classic drama of the Western Front was again enacted, in this instance even more graphically—the scene that will forever haunt Western civilization—for as they did so the rain perversely stopped and in perfect visibility German machine gunners began to play upon the advancing waves of men, their bullets lashing and spurting from the pillboxes and from behind parapets. In the flame and clamor and greasy smoke the British slogged forward deliberately, almost unhurriedly. They moved from crater to crater, but even in the craters they were not safe, for the German gunners streamed bullets against the edges of the holes and wounded many men lying near the rims. As the British walked, some seemed to pause and bow their heads; they sank carefully to their knees; they rolled over without haste and then lay quietly in the soft, almost caressing mud. Others yelled when they were hit, and grabbed frantically at limbs or torso, and rolled and tumbled. In their fear of drowning beneath the slime they tried to grip the legs of their comrades, who struggled to break free.

The first wave almost melted away, the second one splashing forward also seemed to dissolve, the third wave melted into the chaos of the first and second, and later waves blundered into the remnants of the others. By now the remaining troops of the Second Army, exhausted and soaked, had dived panic-stricken into the shell holes of No Man's Land. There they waited for instructions, or more supporting artillery, or nightfall; but as for advancing, there would be no more of that.

The stretch of uncut wire had stopped the inexperienced 66th and would have stopped anybody. Many of these newcomers to war had tried to pick their way through it. As they struggled to free themselves, German machine guns worked them over. Their limbs jerked when the bullets smacked home. Some ripped off their clothes and when killed were almost naked, and often they were accompanied in death by friends trying to help them get loose. The great trouble was that the artillery had failed not only in its pre-dawn bombardment but in the creeping barrage that opened up at 5:20. If aircraft—eyes of the artillery—had been able to operate effectively, matters would have been improved, but the high winds, rain, and clouds had made practically all air operations impossible. A few single-seater fighters did get under the low ceiling to attack the German trenches and batteries, but not enough to help appreciably.

Germans were killed by British guns that day, but due to the pinning down of most of the Second Army at the outset it was reported that not a single enemy soldier was found dead of shell fire on the battlefield; "there was no curtain of fire at all, and it was impossible to see where the edge of the barrage was supposed to be." The few field pieces in position to cover the advance were worked with extra fury by gunners mostly stripped to the waist despite the cold wind. The noisy little guns rattled and roared without let-up, and surrounding the gun positions was a litter of dead horses, refuse, scattered shell casings, live ammunition, stranded wagons.

By superhuman heavings some of the bogged-down

guns were twisted into position and fired from where they lay. Meanwhile efforts were still being made to get more 18-pounders up near the front, and sometimes it was actually possible for a failed or knocked-out gun to be replaced. Casualties to field gunners were severe that morning, for when the rain stopped the Germans could clearly see the exposed British batteries in action below, and turned their guns on them with devastating effect. And, finally, because of the weird or nonexistent gun platforms, parts of the barrage fell short. One battalion of the 66th found itself under protracted bombardment simultaneously from enemy and friendly artillery. Afraid to move in any direction at all, the men huddled in craters and waited for at least one side to leave them alone. And, as one historian reports, "similar occurrences were noted by other units."

An unfortunate feature of the artillery debacle on October 9 was that the British high-explosive shells either failed to detonate in the mud, or, if they did go off, were smothered so deep under the surface that their effect on the enemy was minimal. While this was true of German heavy artillery also, the British needed their own big guns far more than the enemy that day.

Yet for a few hours there had been some isolated gains. The 198th Brigade had jumped off exactly on time, its left flank on the flooded Ravebeke, its objective seven hundred yards short of Passchendaele. Scarcely had the men been slowed down by several water-filled, unexpected derelict trenches when they were caught in enfilade by machine guns working from pillboxes a few hundred yards away. The men flopped into craters and awaited developments.

At about this time the overdue 197th troops began their attack along drier ground to the right, and made some progress up the main ridge. Around 11 o'clock one officer's patrol actually entered the outskirts of Passchendaele itself, found that section of town deserted, and after a few wary moments retired to their companies. By now, in fact, advance units of this brigade had already reached their "red-line" objective. Then these men discovered that they possessed no support on either flank. They swung back on both sides as a precaution. Those in the center observed the men on their right and left withdraw, assumed that for some reason the entire brigade had been ordered to retreat, and did the same. This was about 1 P.M.

Thus the one brigade which had managed to carve out a respectable gain, and more, of higher ground was now back in contact with the stationary 198th and with the 2nd Australian Division to the southeast.

What had happened to the Australians who had been assigned the simple task of merely flanking the 66th near Broodseinde? By late morning the commanding officer of the 66th, Major General H. A. Lawrence, was complaining bitterly that the Australians had not yet appeared, as far as he or anyone could see, and he was right. The reason goes back several days. Both attack brigades of the 2nd Australians had foolishly been pressed into laying cables and plank roads during the 6th, 7th, and 8th. Each evening they had returned to find their crater homes full of water, and there they had slept. Their historian reports that "under such treatment the 6th Brigade, and the 7th also, simply faded away. Hundreds were evacuated through exhaustion, hundreds more with incipient 'trench feet.' By October 9th the 6th Brigade was down to 600 available men, and the 7th to 800," and it was suspected that there had been a certain number of desertions.

This abbreviated division had been stopped cold by German infantry in shell holes and pillboxes. Observing large enemy reinforcements moving up, the Australians read the handwriting on the wall and withdrew another half mile.

As for the 49th Division farther north (the left unit of Plumer's army) its attempt to advance was marked by one mishap after another. First was the Ravebeke, a little canal shown on maps to be only five feet wide. Today it had spread to one hundred fifty feet, with water waist-high in the center. One of the two brigades (except for a few men) never did get across. This left the 146th Brigade. These men crossed farther north and advanced several hundred yards, whereupon they were staggered by shrapnel and heavy machine-gun fire from pillboxes on the higher ground ahead. Messenger pigeons released to bring word back to headquarters were so terrified by the din that they fluttered about and refused to leave their bearers. Next the British encountered a hundred feet of low barbed-wire entanglements which lay intact across the entire line of advance. Even each pillbox was encircled by an apron of wire. The men took potshots at the apertures and tried to formulate a plan of attack. Lewis guns rattled tattoos around the loopholes. Sometimes a man charged forward; in most cases he was hit long before arrival. Other bombers actually arrived at the emplacements and crouched down by the apertures. One has been described:

> Suddenly his helmet seems to be knocked off by an unseen hand. We wait to see his arm swing up and deposit its messenger through the little slit; instead it sags limply while blood commences spouting from his neck. His face has disappeared, leaving him practically headless in a kneeling position, one hand resting on the concrete wall, the other hanging down still clutching the bomb—so near and yet so far.

And in some cases (though this was a particularly futile day for the 49th) an attacker did get through, and did drop his Mills bomb into the pillbox, or accepted the surrender of the inmates, or killed them one by one as they emerged with their hands up, shouting "Kamerad!"

And finally what one reporter calls "the main resistance" was met in the form of rifle and light machine-gun fire from hundreds of shell holes scattered through the zone of attack. Eleven men in one platoon of Yorkshiremen were shot down by one German sniper. A special party was detached to find him, but failed. By ten in the morning an impasse had been reached; the German 16th Rhineland Division was master of the field.

Back at division headquarters Major General Perceval paced and fretted. What was the reason for the hold-up? Reserve troops were sent forward to get the attack moving. Something resembling a traffic jam seems to have occurred on the Gravenstafel spur west of the Ravebeke where the assault had collapsed. There was much hole-to-hole milling around, indecision, and cynical waiting, while groups of officers, noncoms, messengers, and telephone men crouched in the sloppy craters and argued over what was to be done next. Some units were stubbornly ordered forward into the same trap as their predecessors', and were similarly handled by the enemy, but local officers stopped most companies from trying to advance, despite orders from higher up and farther back. And, as the interlude dragged on, the men's water began to give out, water parties were ordered up, and there began to be much stealing of water canteens from the corpses underfoot; for war is a thirsty business even in rain and swamps. By early afternoon both brigades had returned exactly to where they had started from.

When this withdrawal of the 49th Division became apparent to the officers of the 66th on the former's right, the latter also retired slightly, so as not to protrude, and to avoid being enfiladed by the same enemy machine guns and light field pieces which, from north of the Ravebeke, had harassed and decimated II Anzac Corps all day long.

German counterattacks were few and small. There was really very little for them to counterattack. The Second Army's original meager objectives were in no sector reached or even approached. The 49th Division had suffered 2585 casualties and had not advanced at all. The 66th Division had lost 3119 men, had attained five hundred yards of No Man's Land, but had not even dented the main enemy positions atop the ridge. The 2nd Australians had received 1253 casualties and had not advanced their line.

One more bit of action completes this day's story of the Second Army. It will be recalled that the 1st Australian Division on the extreme right of the line was to furnish a diversion in hopes of tricking the enemy into broadening his artillery fire somewhat away from the attacking front. To accomplish this, 85 men had raided Celtic Wood—an area southeast of Broodseinde alive with pillboxes—exactly at zero hour, 5:20 a.m. What the men lacked in experience they possessed in enthusiasm. Briskly they entered the edge of the wood; at once they came under attack from the 448th German Infantry Regiment. Fourteen Australians returned, unwounded. To this day nobody knows what happened to the missing men. They were never heard from again. Their names were never listed as prisoners by the Germans. The German regiment never reported the attack in its records. After the war the Graves Commission found no trace of their bodies. Australian stretcher bearers carrying Red Cross flags who tried to enter the wood in search of survivors were themselves shot down.

Thus ended the efforts of the Second Army in the fields of Flanders October 9, 1917.

Some miles to the northwest the Fifth Army under General Gough, flanked by the French under General Anthoine (that enormous, genial Santa Claus of a man), were simultaneously carrying out their end of the day's bargain. Let us sketch briefly the fortunes of the various divisions concerned.

First in line, just above Plumer's people, stood Major General Fanshawe's 48th (1st South Midlanders), one of the two divisions in Maxse's XVIII Corps. Opposed to this was the crack German 16th ("Iron") Division with instructions to cover and hold the Passchendaele high ground at all costs. Fresh, rested, outstanding in quality, this latter unit had advanced its machine gunners during the night to shell holes so close to the British jumping-off tapes that the barrage of the latter fell far behind them. As a result the British, when they advanced, were surprised almost instantly by sheets of bullets that forced them back to their starting lines. And here, for all practical purposes, was where they spent the day.

Next came the 11th Division. Exhausted by the

fourteen-hour march to the front, the Yorkshiremen were able to capture only the remaining half of the long village of Poelcapelle that had formerly been in German hands. In this wreck of a town there was savage fighting, especially around the brewery held by fanatic German machine gunners. In these operations, and to buy this one victory, Maxse's corps paid over 2300 men.

XIV Corps under the Earl of Cavan was more fortunate. His 4th Division, attacking along an eight-hundred-yard front with one brigade, advanced precariously a quarter-mile on atrocious ground, but nonetheless advanced, and might have gone even farther had it not been that Maxse's men on the right were unable to get past Poelcapelle. So after losing about half its men in casualties the brigade consolidated its position where it was, a little to the east of that town.

The central division of this corps was the 29th, attacking directly toward the south rim of Houthulst Forest with two brigades. Here the main worry had been the flooded Broembeke, which lay astride the line of advance. However, the men, under cover of an efficient barrage, slowly waded across without using the planked bridges which were ready to be laid down if necessary. Then, behind a hail of machine guns that unceasingly swept the swampland before them, the British sloshed through light opposition (the enemy made no more than token attempts to defend this ground) and reached their "Red" objective about a mile away. It was still early in the morning. Casualties were 1112.

Last of the participating British troops was the Guards Division. Their experience was similar to that of the adjacent 29th. Protected by an outstanding mortar barrage, they too forded the Broembeke and advanced against token defenses. Only the 1st Coldstream battalion on the extreme left flank was held up to any extent—this by a pillbox near Louvoir Farm. Eventually all forty of its occupants surrendered, except for one officer, whom it became necessary to bayonet. The Guards captured a mile and a half of ground in front of the forest; in so doing about one-third of its personnel were killed, wounded, or missing.

And, finally, the French First Army to the left of the Guards also advanced about a mile to the edge of the forest.

By the end of the afternoon the French and the Fifth Army were occupying the bog they had captured and repelling without difficulty the slight counterattacks of the enemy, who seemed to show little interest in the ground and possibly considered it more of a liability than an asset. It was in the dreary depths of blasted Houthulst Forest itself that the Germans would make their stand, as everybody well knew. It was there that pillboxes studded the ground like hobnails on a boot, where other machine-gun emplacements had been built by hundreds, and where the enemy had stationed great masses of elite troops.

The advance of Gough's and Anthoine's troops, plus the tiny but more significant progress of Plumer's men up the Passchendaele ridge, had cost the allies over 13,000 men, of whom some 4000 were dead. Possibly due to British artillery difficulties German casualties were unusually low that day—only about half those of their opponents. An official British historian refers years later to the battle as a "comparative success"—for the Germans. But at the moment the latter did not entirely recognize the efficacy of their new defenses (they had held forward positions lightly and forced the attackers to advance through shrapnel and harassing fire in depth before reaching the main defense lines), and a comment added to their record complains that "the sufferings of the troops bore no relation to the advantage gained." One suspects that the day was no picnic for them either. Sir Douglas Haig in his Government dispatch refers to "stiff fighting," "unfavourable conditions," and the advance of the line by Gough and Anthoine. He has little to say concerning the virtual stalemating of Plumer's army against the ridge. And his entire diary entry for the day reads:

> Tuesday, October 9. A general attack was launched at 5:30 a.m. today from a point S.E. of Broodseinde on the right to St. Janshoek on the left (1 mile N.E. of Bixschoote). The results were very successful.

In England and the United States the newspapers also described the attack as a victory. It is true that their correspondents billeted in Cassel were in a difficult position, both for observing and reporting. Censorship was rigid. Negative attitudes were frowned upon. Military Intelligence officers headed by Brigadier General Charteris exerted great pressure upon them. GHQ resented aspersions upon its omniscience and efficiency, nor did most of these officers see any reason why the war had to be reported anyway. Measures were taken to keep the civilian writers in line. Top men such as Perry Robinson of the *Times*, Philip Gibbs of the *Daily Chronicle*, and Beach Thomas of the *Daily Mail* knew their jobs and what was happening. But the most they could do was refer to the patience and suffering of the men without implying that affairs were disgraceful or impossible. Yet behind the brave headlines these and other war reporters gave a fairly plain impression that, in the words of one officer attached to the press corps, "to fight the whole German army, on that narrow strip of land between the Belgian inundations (on the north) and the industrial valley of Lys (on the south) in torrents of rain, was almost hopeless."

The New York *Times* headlines read:

BRITISH AND FRENCH SMASH THROUGH
Wide German Front North of Ypres

All Haig's Objectives Gained

Attack Launched at Dawn, with
Allied Airplanes Co-operating
Effectively in a Clear Sky

And the London *Times'* special correspondent at GHQ reported as follows, beneath a headline referring to the joint British-French effort:

SIDE BY SIDE TO SUCCESS

. . . conditions of extraordinary difficulty and discouragement . . . seem to have made no difference. The blow has been struck as surely, and with results as decisive, as any of the former blows. . . . The story is the same story I have had to tell so many times, the story of an attack pushed with perfect determination and gallantry to final and complete success. The Germans on the whole fought badly.

But in his memoirs, General Gough writes:

Still the guns churned this treacherous slime. Every day conditions grew worse. What had once been difficult now became impossible. . . . No battle in history was ever fought under such conditions. . . .

In the aftermath one correspondent wrote:

It was on the Menin Road that I first noticed the condition in which our men were coming back. A couple . . . passed us, going very slow. They were white and drawn and detached, and put one foot slowly in front of the other, as I had not seen men do since the Somme winter . . . but these men looked whiter.

There were hundreds of cases referred to, often contemptuously, as shell-shocks, which in later years would be diagnosed not wholly in terms of reaction to artillery fire but as serious neuropathic disorders resulting from a total experience beyond their capacity to assimilate. Such men, tramping stolidly back from No Man's Land along the ankle-deep duckboards, could not always be recognized as mental casualties unless they were crying uncontrollably, or giggling, or muttering under their breaths, or falling prone at every explosion or sharp command. Some were, in fact, outwardly quite normal. If you asked one his name he knew it, and if you told him rations were down he might very well wander off to meet them, and if you asked him his outfit he might tell you plainly. He would know where he was and did not seem too distressed. But he would be vaguely confused under more pointed questioning, and perhaps a little too anxious to leave; and as for futher fighting he would be plainly far beyond that—perhaps even beyond defending himself.

In that war men in this condition were scarcely dignified by the term casualty. "Casualty" meant a physical wound or a complete emotional collapse. There was no doubt about the former when the battle ended. They came streaming back soaked in blood and carelessly plastered in field dressings (those who still lived, or could walk, or were lucky enough to be picked up by stretcher bearers) by the thousands for the next three days. Wounded or not, their eyes smoldered in faces that no longer seemed human. They craved whisky—even those who had never touched it before—as though by instinct. The bearers of British rum rations were grabbed as though they alone carried the flame of life, and there was no satisfying the demand for their wares.

The stretcher bearers retrieved first the seriously wounded British; then the moderately wounded British; then the British dead; then the German lightly wounded. The German seriously wounded had to be mostly ignored, and enemy dead in No Man's Land were never touched by British bearers except for souvenirs. While on an individual basis the campaign was fought by both armies with reasonable decency, sometimes hopelessly mangled men were administered the *coup de grâce* by their opponents. In one reported instance a British officer scouting the area came across a horribly wounded enemy soldier. "Shoot him," he said unhappily to his enlisted runner. The German lay watching them in a stupor of agony. The runner unslung his rifle but could not fire, nor could another enlisted man in the little patrol. The officer drew his own pistol, stared in gloom at the German writhing on the ground below, and could do no more. Later he said savagely, "Damn funny, wasn't it? And we just left him there, so I suppose he'll die in the mud tonight."

One photograph shows six stretcher bearers carrying one wounded soldier back from the front. The bearers, up to mud from one's ankles to another's hips, seem to be smiling almost apologetically. All day the walking wounded in their bandages drifted back, punctured and lacerated in the usual ways of war, trudging along the porridge-like roads in their heavy boots which resembled nothing but blobs of mud. (Some got lost at night and walked the wrong way—directly back into the wire.) At regimental aid posts only a few hundred feet rearward doctors worked swiftly at routine first-aid or serious amputations required on the spot. Then the men were passed back to another dressing station, except for those still needing surgery, who were moved to a casualty clearing station. At these collecting points the ambulances lined up by the hundreds like taxis at the Waldorf—waiting and loading and rattling through the area all day and night with their sodden cargoes. The men moaned or lay half-stunned during the clattery ride back to hospital, where they would variously find peace or permanent disability, or an anticlimactic death after all.

But many of the lightly wounded were more cheerful, and joked about small injuries which meant a soft life for months, perhaps a permanent assignment in "Blighty." Unlike these gay chaps were the majority of silent, brooding ones who sat covered with whitish clay, staring at charcoal stoves and waiting for ambulances. In some the spirit of soldiery sometimes still flickered, and at least one remarked sullenly, "Only the mud beat us. We should have gone much farther except for the mud."

At the roadside dressing stations danger was not yet past, for still the Germans probed the roads and intersections with their long-range guns. Doctors themselves were killed there, and the wounded were sometimes wounded again, or finally finished off for good. At these collecting points around Broodseinde, Poelcapelle, along the Menin road and besides the Ypres-Staden railroad the wounded congregated, crying and moaning so that the sound rang in everyone's ears all day and destroyed many an appetite. And later in the day and evening some of the dead began to be hauled back in mummy-like blankets ready for burial. Pitifully small they seemed, hardly half the size of the cursing, burly fellows (four per corpse) that slid and stumbled down the tracks with their tolerant burdens.

In No Man's Land the wounded still lay in the mud. Their shouting and sobbing kept everyone's nerves on edge. Those in shell holes generally drowned there. Slowly they slipped down the muddy banks into the water below, too weak to hold themselves up. Their feeble whispers often could not be heard by comrades passing by. As time went on No Man's Land thus became converted into a vast limbo of abandoned dead and dying. Each shell hole with blood on its water usually meant another corpse entombed below.

Unfortunately the harried stretcher bearers had encouraged the wounded to try to make their own way back. Hundreds started off, but could not keep going. Exhausted and losing blood they crawled into shell holes, only to learn that this blunder would cost them their lives. Battlefield deaths of this kind are described by a survivor:

. . . a khaki-clad leg, three heads in a row, the rest of the bodies submerged, giving one the idea that they had used their last ounce of strength to keep their heads above the rising water. In another miniature pond, a hand still gripping a rifle is all that is visible, while its next-door neighbor is occupied by a steel helmet and half a head, the staring eyes glaring icily at the green slime which floats on the surface almost at their level.

The drier portions of the battlefield held more orthodox collections of dead. One German was pinned to the ground by a bayonet around which his hands had stiffened as he tried to withdraw it. A corporal's trousers had been blown off and his belly ripped open up to the chest. The top of a machine gunner's head was missing, and his shoulders and gun coated with blood. One corpse was so strangely battered that nobody could understand what had happened. Many hundreds bore tiny perforations not visible beneath their uniforms. Machine gunners lay scarcely relaxed beside their machines—hard, grim fighting men still facing the enemy British. A few were fearfully butchered by near hits of large shells. The faces of the dead everywhere were brown and aghast, their white teeth always showing.

The action of October 9 (known as the Battle of Poelcapelle, though the capture of the upper half of this town was a minor item) was over; but desultory shelling, machine-gun fire, and patrol work continued throughout the 10th and 11th. One Englishman scouting the area wrote before he died, "I was lying out in no man's land. A little German dog trotted up and licked my British face. I pulled his German ears and stroked his German back. He wagged his German tail. My little friend abolished no man's land, and so in time can we."

But at the moment it was necessary to prepare for the attack of October 12. And as usual Sir Douglas Haig was plagued by the most abominable luck, for on Thursday night of the 11th it began to rain again after two dry days. Then the weather cleared for a few hours. But at exactly six the following morning, as the troops went over the top, showers began to fall. Soon torrents of rain were pelting the mud, the brimming craters, the planked roads, and the British infantrymen again advancing warily and half-crouched across the forward zone of the salient.

14. Journey's End

I<small>N</small> L<small>ONDON</small> the ladies were agog, for the fall fashion shows were the most exciting, the most fabulous, in generations. Outside the salons private motorcars swarmed; within, closely packed throngs of women watched as gorgeously attired models toured the rooms. "Is there a war?" inquired Lady Sarah Wilson testily in the *Tatler*. But it was the war that had created the craze. Middle- and lower-class women were earning more than ever before and had turned from the plain clothes of yesteryear to more thrilling modes—ninon and crepe de Chine blouses, taffeta and velveteen dresses, cobweb stockings, fancy shoes. It was regrettably true, as Colonel Repington had pointed out, that many people seemed to be enjoying the war. A new set of bureaucrats entrenched in minor power was fearful that peace might break out, and there were cries of treason when the *Nation* reported in October that five million pamphlets on peace negotiations had been dropped into letter boxes.

For millions the war was a provocative change and a huge game, as well as source of profit—though the pound note had shrunk in value to the equivalent of ten shillings before the war. The aerial bombings went on. ("Don't you think our gun sounds jolly when fired in raids?" one woman asked a writer.) Waste paper was diligently collected, and odd bits of wool and cotton, for they were said to be valuable in making shells. Everyone seemed to be gardening for victory: and potatoes and cabbages and peas bloomed where once there had been green lawns. Crystal gazers and palm readers were the rage; but the muffin man, tray on head and forlornly tinkling his little bell, was seen no more.

Society too was changing; the classes were at least superficially mixing. Even upper-class ladies toyed with war work, if only (it was whispered) to show off their clothes. So-called mixed marriages were vastly on the increase, and betrothals of young people "above" or "below" their station were causing much dismay among the titled strata. It was practically Bolshevism in action. Saturday-night crowds in the City were enormous; in restaurants, night clubs and theaters, earls and seamstresses, welders and landed gentry intermingled with increasing naturalness. Perhaps the pleasures were nervous ones as 1917 waned, the laughter too brittle, wages and prices and fun equally inflated; and perhaps beneath the excitement, the self-conscious committees, the love-making, the proud headlines, the drinking, and the heavy spending there flowed a riptide of pain and disillusionment, anxiety and overwork.

Thus in London the days passed feverishly, and fewer and fewer could pretend to remember why the war went on. The populace worked and played blindly; and in the center of this human bee-hive stood the symbolic Statesman who, as sketched by the *Nation*, directed it all:

> He has a musical and sonorous voice . . . the unaggressive gesture of authority, a gaze of unquestioning but extremely well-bred confidence. . . . War and peace, kingdoms and dynasties, settlements and unsettlements, shrink to items in his notes. The fantastic shapes of struggling armies and the cries of dying men fade away. What remains solid, indisputable, contemporary, is that aristocratic figure, so free from any vulgarity or self-assertion, so practised, so confident, so traditional. . . . He has always stood just in that place between the Abbey and the Thames.

It was at this time that Siegfried Sassoon's case was angrily aired in Parliament and in the pubs, for this lieutenant after receiving the Military Cross for gallantry had decided that he would fight no longer: "I believe that the war is being deliberately prolonged . . . has become a war of aggression and conquest. . . ." But *John Bull* raved: "The Huns—vicious in victory, cowards in defeat—deserve no more consideration than a mad dog or a venomous snake. . . . To Hell with pacifists. . . . We're out for War—let it be War to the death!"

The internecine struggle between Easterners and Westerners reached a new pitch, the former emboldened by the bogging down of the Flanders campaign. From the War Office Robertson wrote Haig:

> . . . I gather from Lord R. Cecil that you are perhaps a little disappointed with me in the way I have stood up for correct principles, but you must let me do my job in my own way. . . . He [Lloyd George] is out for my blood very much these days . . . intolerable conduct during the last week or two. . . . He has got my Future Policy Paper and your Memo. A Cabinet is now sitting. He will be furious and probably matters will come to a head. I rather hope so. I am so sick of this d----d life.
>
> I can't help thinking he has got Painlevé and Co. here in his rushing way so as to carry me off my feet. But I have big feet!

Events moved along the road to Passchendaele. The Prime Minister told Sir William cruelly that "the patient, after a three years' course of treatment not being yet cured, thinks it advisable to call in another couple of specialists." At a meeting of the War Cabinet on October 11 he suggested turning to Sir John French and Sir Henry Wilson for consultation at this "turning point of the war." Robertson derided the medical analogy. The two new doctors were not to discuss symptoms with the old but were to stay severely apart from the latter. Furthermore, a rank layman in military medicine, Mr. David Lloyd George, would then take it upon himself to make a final diagnosis and decide what was to be prescribed. The idea was not only stupid but insulting, "Wully" snorted. He wanted to resign, but Haig dissuaded him.

As for Sir Douglas, he had no intention of stepping down. His job was that of commander in chief in the West, and in his dour way he liked it. If the civilians wanted him out, they should sack him; he would never voluntarily abandon his plain duty to the King. But he was bitter, and wrote in his diary concerning Lord French, "Never before, perhaps, has a Commander-in-Chief, who has been superseded on account of failure, been invited by his government to criticise his successor." As for Wilson, he was a mere court jester "busily ingratiating himself with the Prime Minister, who appreciates his vivid conversation and lively humour."

The views of the two advisers ran along predictable lines. Haig calls French's paper "a poor production . . . evidently the outcome of a jealous and disappointed mind." It spent twenty out of twenty-six pages questioning Haig's strategy and recommended going on the defensive until the Americans arrived. Wilson's memorandum was similar, and he, like French, suggested that a supreme inter-Allied war council be put into motion to control strategy in general and, by implication, Haig and Robertson in particular.

The controversy dragged along for weeks, throughout most of October and early November, settling nothing, and creating even more strain between the two factions.

In Flanders the weather had improved during the 10th and 11th, worrying the troops, who were beginning to feel that they would be thrown back into heavy fighting whenever the rain ceased for an hour. Efforts were being made to clear No Man's Land of British wounded who had fallen during the Poelcapelle affair and still lay there famished and suffering. But a new attack was about to start almost immediately.

Those two days were cold and bleak; and as the assault brigades trudged forward they seemed, to observers, unusually depressed. When they arrived at the front the New Zealanders could see with sobering clarity great masses of unbroken wire facing them. A fine drizzle had commenced, greasing the upper inch of ground which had previously started to dry. One of this division's generals wrote in his diary: "We all hope for the best tomorrow, but I do not feel as confident as usual. Things are being rushed too much. The weather is rotten, the roads very bad, and the objectives have not been properly bombarded. . . ."

Sir Douglas had tea at Château Loewe with General Gough, who expressed concern whether the Second Army was not over-committing itself.

Next Haig had another irritating discussion, this time with the visiting M. Poincaré, President of France, who could speak only of the British taking over more line. Haig thought he was "a humbug," try-

General Sir Herbert Plumer, Major General H. A. Lawrence, and Haig

ing to get as much as he could out of the British. He told the Frenchman that his only plan was to attack, and to keep on attacking.

On the morning of the 11th there were more dissonant developments:

Plumer, who had confidently expected to take Passchendaele next day in a brisk leapfrog operation, was told of the formidable wire entanglement facing both the New Zealand and 3rd Australian divisions. It was thirty yards in depth and could not possibly be cut by shell fire within twenty hours.

Something simply had to be done, it was also suggested, about the hundreds of wounded men stranded in the mud between the lines, being leisurely sniped at by Germans on the slopes to the east. Could the attack really go on in spite of them? Pillboxes up ahead were overflowing with casualties, and outside them the dead lay piled in heaps. The latter were no problem any longer, but what of the living? Sir Herbert was noncommittal; he turned his face aside; the attack would go on.

Then, too, the present line, it turned out, was not at all where the generals had thought it was. After Poelcapelle it had been assumed that the 66th Division had reached the fringe of Augustus Wood. The new barrage plan had been based on that understanding. Now, it was learned, Lawrence's people were precisely where they had started from the morning of the 9th. What now? It was decided, somewhat negligently, to work out a minor change in the rate of advance of the barrage and to make the best of it.

Next artillery officers of the New Zealand Division reported that they could not get their batteries across the Steenbeke—which was no great surprise—nor could they promise artillery support, in any event, due to the instability of their gun platforms and the excessive range. The announcement was an unpleasant one. If the history of warfare on the stalemated Western Front had proved anything it was that troops attacking without surprise, and without the heaviest possible barrage, had no chance.

Haig called for Charteris, who could always be depended upon for an encouraging word; and one suspects that as usual he delivered it; but that evening the Intelligence chief wrote thus in his diary:

> He was still trying to find some grounds for hope that we might still win through this year ·. . . but there is none. . . . Moving about close behind a battle . . . when one is all keyed up with the hope of great results, one passes without much thought all the horrible part of it. . . . But when one knows that the great purpose one has been working for has escaped, somehow one sees and thinks of nothing but the awfulness of it all. . . .

It was a remarkable and distraught admission coming from Charteris, even though made privately. But the time had come for Haig, too, to make some veiled concessions. Before a meeting of press correspondents that afternoon at GHQ he first asserted that "we are practically through the enemy's defenses" and that there were no more blockhouses in his army's path— this despite the fact that they could be clearly seen by front-line soldiers—and then proceeded: "It was simply the mud which defeated us on Tuesday. The men did splendidly to get through it as they did. But the Flanders mud, as you know, is not a new invention. It has a name in history—it has defeated other armies before this one."

That evening Gough phoned Plumer and asked him to postpone the attack. Sir Herbert declined. It took place after dawn along a six-mile front and gained an average of four hundred yards. For lack of a better name it was called "The First Battle of Passchendaele," though in that direction the crater front was pushed forward only a hundred yards. The New Zealanders were badly mauled. The 2nd Brigade, especially, had been trapped astride the Gravenstafel road as they pressed on to the entanglements under a torrent of small-arms and machine-gun fire. This wire was totally unbreached except for a single lane along the sunken road. Through it the men poured, desperate at the sight of their comrades caught and yelling on both sides; but as they shambled down the road they were cut down by concealed machine guns, and not one escaped.

So thin had been the barrage that the men could hardly believe that this brief, almost casual shelling of the ridge actually constituted their artillery support. After the war an official historian coldly asked whether "any of the higher commanders [were] aware that in these operations their infantry attacked virtually without protection." The episode had, in fact, almost crossed the line which divides war from murder. Thirteen thousand men were lost in a few hours, and the New Zealand brigadier who had been so pessimistic before the event now wrote:

> My opinion is that the senior generals who direct these operations are not conversant with the conditions, mud, cold, rain, and no shelter for the men. Finally, the Germans are not so played out as they make out. All the attacks recently lack preparation, and the whole history of the war is that when thorough preparation is not made, we fail. . . . You cannot afford to take liberties with the Germans. . . .

Few rations arrived up front that day and next. It was still raining and supply difficulties had reached the breaking point. Darkness and chaos on the duckboards forced the carrying parties to work by day—a risky procedure, in plain view of enemy field gunners. Horses and mules were in desperate shape. Exhausted and balky, they were showing signs of panic. Yukon packs were tried—a Canadian invention which had worked at the Somme—frames of wood and canvas supposed to hold over a hundred pounds; but here in Flanders they failed, for the weight simply dragged the animals down into the mire. The scene along the

A Mark IV tank, October 12, 1917

Steenbeke was an incredible one. That stream, once only a few feet across, had overflowed to a width of a hundred yards. The gentle slope leading down to it was now packed with abandoned guns and a weird collection of floating and embedded equipment. The road stopped 150 yards from the front. Supply animals had to attempt this interval in saturated clay, and few of them made it.

By now most of the wounded from October 9 were dead, but some still lingered, and a new crop had blossomed. On the 14th an informal truce took place. The enemy allowed British stretcher bearers to clear the area in peace, and for hours they moved about the battleground bringing back those who were still alive. The Germans watched from the nearby heights and shot any man carrying a gun. An Australian officer reconnoitering the line near the Ravebeke reported:

> The slope . . . was littered with dead, both theirs and ours. I got to one pillbox to find it just a mass of dead, and so I passed on carefully to the one ahead. Here I found about fifty men alive, of the Manchesters. Never have I seen men so broken or demoralized. They were huddled up close behind the box in the last stages of exhaustion and fear. Fritz had been sniping them off all day, and had accounted for fifty-seven that day—the dead and dying lay in piles. The wounded were numerous—unattended and weak, they groaned and moaned all over the place. . . . Some had been there four days already. . . .

And later:

> I shifted to an abandoned pillbox. There were twenty-four wounded men inside, two dead Huns on the floor and six outside, in various stages of decomposition. The stench was dreadful. . . . When day broke I looked over the position. Over forty dead lay within twenty yards of where I stood and the whole valley was full of them.

And finally:

> Anyway we are out now and I don't mind much. Only I'd like to have a talk with some war correspondents —liars they are.

Thus ended "another fine bit of work by our gallant men." The *Spectator* reported "a great week for the Allies in Flanders. They have dealt two more hammer strokes." On the morning of October 15 Haig and his staff met at Second Army headquarters in Cassel and decided to halt all further attacks pending an improvement in the weather which would, at a minimum, allow the artillery to cooperate properly. Whether this resolution, which was beginning to have a familiar and empty ring, would be adhered to remained to be seen. In a bizarre development never thoroughly understood, Lloyd George took this unfortunate occasion to send an ardently false telegram to Sir Douglas congratulating him on his achievements since July 31. "I am personally glad," he concluded, "to be the means

A trench near Westhoek, October 17, 1917

of transmitting this message to you . . . of renewing my assurance of confidence in your leadership. . . ." The field marshal was astounded, if not convinced, and laboriously copied in his diary the entire message —the first of its type he had received from the new Prime Minister since taking command.

On the 22nd there followed a curious, half-hearted attack by the French and elements of the Fifth Army in which almost a thousand Allied troops were lost. A few yards were gained, some of which were retaken later in the day by enemy counterattack. Next day the Canadians, making their first appearance in the salient, demonstrated briefly in the direction of Passchendaele. It was their turn now. They had relieved the utterly spent II Anzac Corps five days previously; and until the end of the campaign the sputtering torch would be carried by these brawny youngsters from the farms and forests of the northlands across the sea.

Germany had made a habit of crushing one of her lesser opponents each autumn—in 1915 Serbia, in 1916 Rumania. Now it was Italy's turn. On the morning of October 24 the Austrians, reinforced by six German divisions brought down from the Russian and Flanders fronts, struck at Caporetto. Completely surprised, enfeebled by endless attacks on the Isonzo which throughout the years had accomplished nothing, the Italian Army melted away in twelve hours. Winston Churchill was relaxing at his home in Kent when

Lloyd George telephoned and asked that he drive at once to Walton Heath. There he was shown telegrams which cautiously indicated that the worst disaster yet to overtake the Allies was in progress. The Prime Minister was palpably shaken. The two men discussed the situation quietly and sketched out a plan of action to salvage whatever might be left of the wreckage.

Sir Douglas had claimed that Italy could hold her own unaided, had not conceded that an attack was coming, and had refused to reinforce Cadorna's front —not that it really mattered; for under the autocratic mishandling of Cadorna the Italian Army had long been a shell in all but numbers. By October 27 even this vast quantity was seriously reduced. When the headlong eighty-mile rush for safety had ended, 800,000 Italians were out of the war through wounds, death, capture, and desertion. A defensive front was hastily rigged up behind the river Piave. Cadorna, before being sacked, sent out a melancholy cry for help.

Haig's published diaries omit any mention of Caporetto. When requested on the 27th to send two divisions to Italy he merely noted, "If the Italian Army is demoralized we cannot spare enough troops to fight their battles for them." The military demise of both Italy and Russia had, it seemed, less effect upon him emotionally than the loss of a mile of mud in Belgium. But others were not so ready to write off the Italian Army. Sir William Robertson immediately left for talks with the Italian General Staff. Sir Henry Wilson insisted that more than two divisions be sent, and quickly. In his diary he wrote, "We may lose this war yet if we try," and next day after a talk with Winston Churchill:

> I quoted also my example of the different strategies— ours and the Boches': 1, We take Bullecourt, they take Rumania; 2, we take Messines, they take Russia; 3, we don't take Passchendaele, they take Italy.

The War Cabinet was alarmed at the genuine possibility that Italy might ask for peace and decided to dispatch not two but five of Haig's divisions to the river Piave. This was a blow to Sir Douglas. He rushed General Kiggell to London to protest—a poor choice, for Lloyd George despised the man—but it was a heaven-sent chance for the Prime Minister to cut Haig down to size. He would have snatched twenty divisions away if he could. Within a few weeks the 23rd, 41st, 7th, 48th, and 5th divisions, in that order, had been trundled through the tunnels under the Alps and were standing beside the remnants of the Italian Army on the plains north of Venice.

If nothing else, Caporetto had proved that the Allies could not go on much longer without coordinating their war efforts. The idea of each nation's general staff fighting its own war in something resembling jealous secrecy, telling each other what they were doing the day they did it, ignorant of each other's Intelligence data, free to formulate local strategy of any dimension without regard for the others, made no sense at all;

and practically everyone but Haig and Robertson was now ready to agree that a supreme control had to be set up for 1918. No doubt Lloyd George hoped that an inter-Allied control council would also control Sir Douglas Haig—something the Prime Minister freely admitted he was unable to do. For even as the Central Powers were smashing through at Caporetto and driving the Italians southward like leaves before a winter wind, general headquarters on the Western Front had completed plans for yet another attack in Flanders on October 26.

In wars of other days, troops attacking at daybreak knew they would win or lose by nightfall. In Flanders there was no such expectation. Each day was like the one before, and the pattern of hopeless suffering seemed to have no end. Old-timers wondered how long their luck would hold up. Replacements, many of them boys in their teens who had never seen a German soldier, tried to put on a casual show; but their spirits were quickly deadened by the unnatural atmosphere in which they found themselves. Apathy and a large measure of cynicism hung heavily in the air. There had never been such a silent army. Too morose even to complain, the men masked their emotions and seemed to wait with equal indifference for death or deliverance; and their sullenness chilled the new men, who had expected to be received with traditionally coarse but friendly banter. After one hour under shell fire in a watery hole or a shallow trench of pure mud, among filthy, unshaven men who resembled the living dead, each neophyte knew the salient well, and was gripped by nameless fears.

But there was little tension left among the veterans who had been in and out of the line constantly since Messines and were fairly accustomed to the never-ending battles and cannonade. When a signaler called out, "Raid a complete success, fifty casualties," their reply was at best, "Success my bloody backside"; at worst, they neither reacted nor replied. Stolidly they formed up for each attack or raid, and carried it out as best men could who found it more tolerable to fight than to desert, or feign illness, or self-inflict a minor wound, or allow themselves to be slightly gassed. Casualties among them had become so numerous that most old friends were gone and they fought beside strangers. Only among fresh units such as the Canadians was there at least a sense of familiar unity. Yet the dogged courage of the British infantrymen persisted—a phenomenon almost beyond the understanding of neutral observers separated from the event by a long span of years. With no remaining hope for the success of the campaign, they nonetheless advanced on schedule and to the limit of their abilities. Long ago they had written off the glamour of war as a fairy story for the ears of children; yet in hand-to-hand encounters they fought ferociously. By and large what gains they carved out they held, as though the gains were precious; by and large they faced death obstinately, if not cheerily. Sir Douglas Haig was in a sense fortunate to possess this army; and one is entitled to doubt whether any other would have demonstrated such dour bravery in the fields of Flanders that appalling year.

Mustard gas thrown nightly into the back areas and the valley of the Steenbeke had, in the words of Lord Birdwood, "virtually finished off the Australian attempts on Passchendaele Ridge." Casualties from trench foot were rising alarmingly, and while the ailment was no joke it was welcomed by many as a way out. Dysentery was commonplace. Almost everyone was sniffling and sneezing; colds and influenza were practically endemic and were accentuated by respiratory irritations caused by gas which had settled everywhere in the shallow basin of the salient and had affected every man to some degree.

Half the terrain was so flooded that it resembled a natural lake. By late October this water had become icy cold. While it was only a few inches deep it was impossible to traverse, for nobody knew when he would step into a submerged shell hole. On the broad surface of these pools floated the debris and filth of the battlefield. Calling for the Royal Navy to come and take up the fight had become a standard quip.

In most sections of No Man's Land, where wooden tracks did not exist, even the strongest men could barely move. During raids and larger attacks they were easily picked off by snipers. Bogged down, they could not out-maneuver the pillboxes. Gough wrote that "the state of the ground had been frightful since the 1st August, but by now it was getting absolutely impossible." Shells exploded three feet below the surface of the mud. Instead of steel splinters, only clay and water whipped through the air, and to kill a German or knock out a machine gun an almost direct hit was needed.

The demoralization and growing callousness of the men were reflected in their treatment of the dead. After each attack the souvenir hunters got to work. Gradually the corpses were picked over, the whites of their pockets turned out, their tunics and shirts undone. Revolvers were the best prizes; but money, watches, rings, and the crosses of Catholics were also in demand. An artilleryman examining German corpses for revolvers was observed (by a writer at the front) giving one a vicious kick and snarling, "The dirty barsted, somebody's bin 'ere before me." Frontline soldiers were quickest in the pursuit of loot, artillery and labor troops slower and more methodical. Letters and photos were ignored; these fluttered limply in the mud or floated away on the water.

By that week some British shell holes were on the western slopes of the ridge. Though dangerously exposed, they were not entirely flooded, and by the pathetic standards of the time and place were considered fairly habitable. The men who huddled there, and some who attacked, kept their rifles and Lewis guns wrapped in cloth; and many a soldier too late in unwrapping his weapon paid a severe penalty.

It was this October that the *Spectator* performed

another of its many services for morale by reprinting the poem "Christ in Flanders" in leaflet form and offering to send out copies post free at a price of 1s. per hundred.

Sir Douglas Haig decided that the campaign had proceeded almost far enough for the time being, though he still hoped to capture Passchendaele and the Westroosebeke ridge. In the letters, diaries, and communiqués of the German defenders as October slipped by and winter approached (when not even Haig could dream of attacking) one senses a new confidence and calmness. A Bavarian officer wrote typically that "although the battle rages constantly in uncomprehensible confusion round Poelcapelle and Passchendaele, there is nothing frightening about that. We have been fighting the last summer flies, which attack one so unkindly, almost as much as the English. The *moral* of the men appears to be excellent. . . ." And General Sixt von Armin had this to say when interviewed by a representative of *Korrespondenz Norden* on the 24th:

> They occupy the southern part of the heights which encircle Ypres, while we are in possession of the northern part . . . a dozen kilometres from the acknowledged goal of the English—namely Ostend, Ghent, and Zeebrugge—without the possession of which the battles of Flanders, in spite of their partial successes, remain bloody defeats for the English. Thanks to the tenacious bravery of the English, they have succeeded in pressing us back further in the

Ypres bend, and have driven a wedge in the center of that bend, but that is all. There is no danger in this because, so long as the enemy continues his pressure at this point, he is exposed to our flanking fire and to the danger of being threatened from all sides in the rear, and he would be brought into the same sort of position that we were in when holding the Wytschaete bend.

Lloyd George could not have put it better.

October 25 had been a beautiful day, but at midnight a continuous rain began to fall. At 2:30 in the morning General Gough phoned "Tim" Harington to ask Plumer to stop the attack. At that moment Sir Herbert walked into Harington's smoky little room, jam-packed with corps commanders and members of their staffs. He waited until Harington put the phone down, listened to the message, and then turned to each general for his opinion. Morland and Currie, of X Corps and the Canadian Corps respectively, stated that in their opinion three hours was not enough time to get cancelation orders through. Plumer picked up the phone and put through a call.

"Is that you, Gough?" he shouted.

The reply came almost inaudibly over the crackling wire. "Yes, this is Gough."

"The attack must go on. I am responsible, not you. Good night and good luck."

It began at 5:40, and by nightfall the Canadian Corps had won five hundred yards. X Corps gained nothing. Two French divisions moved about a tenth of a mile closer to Houthulst Forest. In the Fifth Army, XIV Corps got nowhere; and as for XVIII Corps the *Official History* says, "Here, too, the mud, knee-deep, checked progress to a crawl of rather less than a yard a minute. The barrage was lost, rifles became quickly clogged, and the men fell back, if they could, to the starting line, or were cut off." In this caricature of a military engagement 12,000 British and French were lost.

Though Haig confessed in a dispatch to the King that "the persistent continuation of wet weather had left no further room for hope," he continued mysteriously that "in view of other projects which I had in view it was desirable to maintain the pressure on the Flanders front for a few weeks longer." He intended to halt only for the winter and to pick up the offensive again next spring, and said so quite frankly to Colonel Repington, who was touring the front. The sense of his divine mission continued to envelop the commander in chief. Conceding momentary setbacks, he knew that in the long run God was with him. With the sure instinct of a sleepwalker (to use the later phrase of a German of note) he ignored circumstances and advice which would have given pause to another man. His cause was just, his plan the only one that led to victory. He pitied those who were less inspired, for he was God's middleman and it was his task alone to enact the plain will of the Maker. He beseeched Robertson to temper certain frank statements rendered to the press by the War Office: "They do, I feel sure, much

harm, and may cause many in authority to take a pessimistic outlook, when a contrary view, based on
equally good information, would go far to help the nation on to victory."

Perhaps General Charteris was somewhat cleverer
than his chief, but he was more disliked, and the despair of all who tried to impress upon him the misery
and futility of the waning campaign. His habit of remarking absently that war was an ugly thing—whatever the plea or complaint—was infuriating to those
who had to deal with him. Even Plumer was reported
(by the ubiquitous Repington) "rather sarcastic about
Charteris' optimism," and as for the disillusioned General Gough he had made it a point not to talk to the
man at all, if he could help it.

The outlook of General Davidson, Chief of Operations, during these hard times continued to be a replica of Haig's, except that he favored more deliberate
methods.

Rounding out the foursome of inspired gentlemen
who currently directed the British Expeditionary
Force in France and Belgium was Haig's Chief of
Staff, General Kiggell, whose attitude had just been
recapitulated in a luncheon talk with Colonel Repington. The Huns must stand in Flanders, he had said;
"therefore" the British would beat them there. He was
not in favor of taking over one yard of front from the
French. It would be "fatal" to abandon Haig's plan.
This winter they would capture the rest of the ridge,
next April the Channel ports and the rest of the Bel-

gian coastline. The campaign would take two months at most and would, for all practical purposes, end the war. The Germans were already so weakened that they might give way at any moment. All he needed was half a million more men.

Repington was startled, could not agree with these impetuous conclusions, and told Kiggell so. Another who had been hitherto unswerving in his support of the campaign was the Jewish General, Sir John Monash, commanding the 3rd Australians, but by October even he had become distressed over the conduct of affairs, and wrote his wife, "It is bad to cultivate the habit of criticism of higher authority, and, therefore, I do so now with some hesitation. . . . Our men are being put into the hottest fighting and are being sacrificed in hare-brained ventures, like Bullecourt and Passchendaele, and there is no one in the War Cabinet to lift a voice in protest."

After the loss of Broodseinde, Crown Prince Rupprecht had decided to revert to the earlier technique of holding his front almost exclusively by machine gunners—a handpicked collection of hard, murderous veterans—with the bulk of his infantry farther back in position to counterattack. The policy had largely accounted for British defeats during the balance of October, and would continue to prove its worth. The Germans had learned that a new attack was coming on the 30th, and five minutes before zero hour their own bombardment fell heavily upon the narrow Canadian front athwart the Ravebeke. The weather had been cold but dry for three days, and, for a change, rain was not falling when the 3rd and 4th Canadians jumped off, supported on their left by XVIII Corps under Sir Ivor Maxse. It was 5:50 a.m. and pitch dark. Rain had been forecast, and torrents began to fall before noon. Again pillboxes held up the advance. By afternoon many of those farthest forward were still holding out, spitting flame, surrounded by piles of dead Canadians. But the slow advance continued, and gradually some Dominion troops moving northeast found themselves on sandier, drier soil. They were now five hundred yards from the center of Passchendaele. Further attempts to push on were thwarted by a series of enemy counterattacks. On the left flank, XVIII Corps suffered severe casualties and was unable to make headway. Knee-deep in mud, splashing and struggling in the ponds of various streams, they tried all morning to penetrate the enemy zone near Lekkerboterbeke, but could not follow their barrage and were cut down by German guns operating from high ground near Westroosebeke. At dusk it was still pouring. It was of this period that Ludendorff later wrote in a famous passage:

The horror of the shell-hole area of Verdun was surpassed. It was no longer life at all. It was mere unspeakable suffering. And through this world of mud the attackers dragged themselves, slowly but steadily, and in dense masses. Caught in the advance zone of our hail of fire they often collapsed, and the lonely man in the shell hole breathed again. Rifle and machine-gun jammed with the mud. Man fought against man and only too often the mass was successful. . . .

The enemy charged like a wild bull against the iron wall. . . . He dented it in many places, and it seemed as if he must knock it down. But it held, although a faint tremor ran through its foundations.

From faraway Russia Major General Max Hoffmann noted approvingly, "There is heavy fighting in the West, the English mean to win a victory at all costs; which is a good sign." And at 10 Downing Street Lloyd George's mood turned even more wrathful. In meetings of the War Cabinet he paced the floor and startled his listeners with violent comments concerning Sir Douglas. It was easy for Haig and his staff to continue attacking, he exclaimed; *they* did not have to fight; and in his memoirs he writes of "the pencil which marched with ease across swamps and marked lines of triumphant progress without the loss of a single point. As for the mud, it never incommoded the movements of this irresistible pencil."

He received Charteris, who "treated me as a stupid civilian who knew nothing of war." He spoke of the casualties and was told that "you could not expect to make war without death and wounds." He alluded to the weather and the resultant terrain, and Charteris replied that "battles could not be stopped like tennis matches for a shower."

The views of the French had turned sardonic. From

the beginning neither Foch nor Pétain had expected the campaign to succeed—they always would have been satisfied with limited, inexpensive demonstrations and with the British taking over more of their line—and by now they were expressing themselves quite derisively. Lord Rawlinson, wild for something to do, had been sent to Pétain to discuss various matters; in a letter to a friend he quoted the Frenchman as saying "that once the Boche has been given time to bring up reinforcements, the moment has arrived to stop and try elsewhere." Since this point had been reached months ago, Rawlinson had to agree that the Flanders scheme was in a bad way.

Many newspapers had begun to turn against Haig and the general staff. The *Manchester Guardian* and the *Evening Standard* were especially critical, though David Davies had started it around the middle of October in the *Times*. Haig and Robertson were sure that the Prime Minister was the instigator. Colonel Repington agreed that the attacks were ignorant and unjust, "display a common origin," and were a despicable attempt on the part of the politicians to turn public opinion against the top Westerners.

Early in November plans for a Supreme War Council finally jelled. France, England, and Italy agreed to subordinate their war efforts to the Council (Foch was appointed Allied Commander in Chief the following spring), by each nation's sending to Versailles a Military Member. In turn, these gentlemen would then constitute a group empowered to make and change plans without referring to the respective chiefs of staff. "Wully" walked out on the meeting at which this was decided. "I wash my hands of this present business," he grunted, and asked to be summoned when something new was ready for discussion.

Haig hated the decision too, but his reaction was more subtle. By what channel, he asked mildly, was he to receive his orders? And this new Allied Central Reserve—where would it come from? Where would it exist? Surely its components would not be controlled by an external agency. Was such a concept possible, or even legal? There was no question in the minds of the British Marshal and his CIGS that the Supreme War Council would drastically downgrade them to foreigners and civilians. Of course it was too late to affect the Flanders campaign, but by next year (and with the Americans added to it) it was bound to clip their wings.

They were especially annoyed, for Henry Wilson, of all people, was to be the British military member. "The whole future of the war rests on your shoulders," Lloyd George told him. "You must get us out of the awful rut we are in." General Kiggell, that luckless emissary, arrived and pleaded for another eight days of fighting in Flanders to make Haig secure for the winter. He also hinted darkly at another secret operation Haig had in mind "which promised satisfactory results provided no more troops were sent to Italy." But at 10

Downing Street the stock of Haig's staff had fallen very low indeed, and Kiggell was treated with indifference.

On Sunday, November 4, Haig himself traveled to Paris and spoke to the Prime Minister in his room at the Hotel Crillon. It was the civilian's turn to be incensed at attacks against him in the *Morning Post, Spectator, Nation,* and *Globe*. He felt that the military brass were the instigators, and in particular complained of Mr. Spender of the *Westminster Gazette,* who had returned from Haig's headquarters with an article to the effect that the field marshal was upset over Lloyd George's interfering tactics. The general and the civilian exchanged a few sharp words. In his diary that evening, in his usual neat, small handwriting where never a word was ever added or scratched out, Sir Douglas wrote:

> I thought L. G. is like our German enemy who, whenever he proposes to do something extra frightful, first of all complains that the British or French have committed the enormity which he is meditating. L. G. is feeling that his position as P. M. is shaky and means to try and vindicate his conduct of the war in the eyes of the public and try and put the people against the soldiers. In fact, to pose as the saviour of his country, who has been hampered by bad advice given by the General Staff!
>
> At 12 o'clock he asked me to go out for a walk, and I went with him up the Champs Elysées to the Arc de Triomphe. Quite a pleasant little man when one had him alone, but I should think most unreliable.

That week Ramsay MacDonald moved again for a peace by negotiation. He was supported by only twenty-one Members. The man was almost a lunatic, it was felt. Feared and hated, he was held at arm's length even by his own Labour Party colleagues.

On November 6, as if in reply, the final attack on Passchendaele took place. At 7:10 a.m. the 6th Brigade (Brigadier General H. D. B. Ketchen) of the 2nd Canadian Division (Major General H. E. Burstall) was in and around the town and the members thereof were bayoneting German diehards along the main street. Thus (in a typical cold rain) fell Passchendaele, or Passion Dale, or Easter Valley, as it was sometimes called by the English after the event. And of this final five-hundred-yard lunge the Canadian Official Historian found a new way to associate God with war:

> It is not too much to compare the Canadian troops struggling forward, the pangs of hell racking their bodies, up the Ridge, their dying eyes set upon the summit, with a Man Who once crept another hill, with agony in soul and body, to redeem the world and give Passchendaele its glorious name.

It had once been an archaic little crossroads village, like so many others in Belgium or Sussex or Vermont: a few dozen cottages and shops clustered along the main road that straggled north to Westroosebeke. Years ago another narrow country road had intersected it. At the northeast corner a simple church had stood, built of white stone and reddish brick. For three years British soldiers had watched Passchendaele gradually vanish under shell fire. In time nothing stood but the church, and this too was half ruined when the Third Battle of Ypres began. Now Passchendaele was shelled anew, and as time passed, and as the British army inched sluggishly up the slopes of the ridge, it was shelled with increasing ferocity. Soon the only distinguishable ruins blurred; but the soldiers staring upward through the drizzle and mist could still identify a vague scribble of stones several feet high. This they continued to call the church.

The Canadians, smoking cigarettes and trailing their rifles as they walked over the site, could hardly grasp that it had once been a town. The cobblestone and dirt roads had disappeared, and in their place was a muddy maze of German army trails. Not one building remained, other than the feeble remnant of the church. Not one brick stood on another. Sand and mud had drifted over the remains. In a later war atomic bombs wrecked two Japanese cities; but Passchendaele was effaced from the earth. An aerial photograph shows not a ruined town but only pillboxes and shell holes, the latter in such numbers that (from the airman's altitude) it is hard to discern any bit of ground which is not part of a crater.

From the former village, fifty feet above the Flanders plain, the Canadians looked down dully at thousands of antlike men on both sides—British troops below the western slope near Gravenstafel, Germans in the lowland near Moorslede to the east—and watched the flash and smoke of field guns still pounding the ridge and both fronts, as daylight dimmed.

The following day Lieutenant General Sir Launcelot Kiggell paid his first visit to the fighting zone. As his staff car lurched through the swampland and

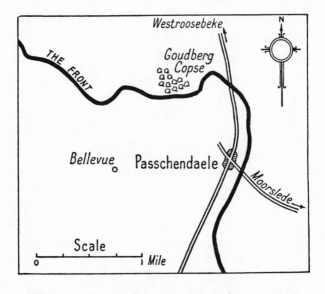

The Passchendaele salient, November 11, 1917

neared the battleground he became more and more agitated. Finally he burst into tears and muttered, "Good God, did we really send men to fight in that?"

The man beside him, who had been through the campaign, replied tonelessly, "It's worse further on up."

The situation that now existed was not a comfortable one. Haig had correctly stressed that a good winter line would have to include possession of the high ground running north to Westroosebeke; since this had not proved possible, the capture of Passchendaele had only created a worse salient, a sore little semicircular thumb a mile and a half across the base and about the same distance to the apex. So it was a miniature Ypres projection into which the entire Canadian Corps was now jammed, facing the prospect of spending several months under German guns ranging an arc of 180 degrees from Goudberg Copse to Moorslede.

GHQ recognized that the position would be vulnerable in the event of a strong enemy attack, and that it was more exposed than the original salient had been; and even as the newspapers were exulting in the capture of the town, staff officers were considering the likelihood of abandoning it. Instead, the field marshal, still probing almost instinctively toward Westroosebeke, called for another attack. In a rainstorm the 1st Canadian Division lunged northward another five hundred yards on November 10. This gain made matters worse, for the new tongue of ground jutted out even more awkwardly and now could be fired into not only from three sides but slightly from the rear as well. A few more costly minor actions took place the following week, and on November 20 Haig decided to close down the Flanders campaign. "It had served its purpose."

One final episode concludes the British operations on the Western Front—a most significant one, for it proved after all that Haig held a trump card irrelevant of head-on assaults and attrition. It will be recalled that the Tank Corps people had been searching for a likely place in which to prove themselves, and this they had found at Cambrai, some forty miles to the southeast. Here the terrain was relatively dry, had not been torn up by shell fire, and presented an ideal downslope. Sir Julian Byng, commanding the Third Army, risked his professional career and (against Haig's judgment) authorized a mass tank attack without the firing of a single preparatory artillery shell. Out of the morning mists on November 20, 381 tanks lumbered without warning against the Hindenburg line and cracked it open like an eggshell. In one day an average gain of four miles was registered (not much less than the entire Ypres campaign over a period of four months), 10,000 prisoners and 200 guns captured —all this against the loss of 1500 British troops. It was one of the most startling and one-sided successes of the war, but since the Flanders fighting had depleted Haig's reserves Byng had none with which to exploit it, other than a few cavalry regiments, notoriously helpless against machine guns and snipers. The attack petered out quickly. On November 30 the Germans counterattacked in strength, won back most of their previous loss in ground, and recaptured the same number of men and guns that had been wrested from them ten days earlier. The score was even. The momentary thrill of an outstanding victory had led to an even greater reaction, and the military year closed in despondency, while an official court of inquiry delved bitterly into the reasons for this final and most embarrassing debacle.

15. War and Peace

IT IS NOW time to summarize the British effort in France and Flanders during 1917.

The purely tactical situation is readily evaluated by quoting GHQ's special instructions for dealing with the Passchendaele sector and the new bulge created after Cambrai, dated December 13, and withheld from the War Cabinet:

> These salients are unsuitable to fight a decisive battle in. It is, however, desirable to retain possession of them if they are not attacked in great force; and in the event of attack in great force to use them to wear out and break up the enemy's advancing troops as much as possible before these can reach our battle zone of defense which will be sited approximately as a chord across the base of each salient.

And, in the event, the Passchendaele salient did furnish target practice for German guns the rest of the winter, and the

men in it suffered heavy losses therefrom for no advantage.

There has never been any argument about the
worthlessness of the few miles of muddy ground captured. Nine thousand yards was the largest gain. The
average was about four miles of terrain which was to

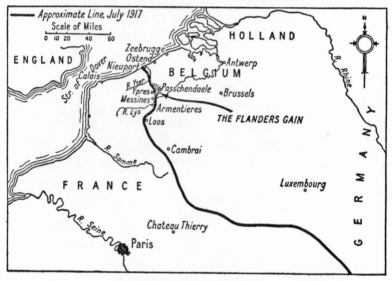

The Western Front

have been occupied three or four days after the main
attack started on July 31. The Channel ports were out
of sight and out of mind. Less than half the ridge was
in British hands—not even enough to make Passchendaele heights defensible, and this by Haig's own admission. The northern end of the Messines–Passchendaele ridge, eastern wall of the Ypres bastion, was still

in German hands. The line of the Yser, flooded from Ypres to Nieuport, had been captured, but by the enemy, and if there had been any possibility of a turning movement it had ended long ago.

Excluding the dubious achievement at Passchendaele, we find no gains of value on the flanks. To the south there had been small and meaningless advances around Gheluvelt. On the north, most divisions wound up crouching and drenched in or near the icy mud of Houthulst Forest, shelled night and day throughout six hundred acres of broken tree stumps, wreckage, and swamps—"the acme of hideousness, a Calvary of misery."

Since the campaign had degenerated into a swamp battle, "nothing can be said," in the words of the tank expert on the War Committee, "in defense of the fatuous employment of machines, weighing over thirty tons, in the liquid mud. . . ." And Baker-Carr, sharp-tongued to the end, remarked that "the tanks had failed in common with all other arms. . . . The cavalry did not even have the melancholy satisfaction of failing."

As autumn dragged on, Haig still clung to his irrational hope of a German collapse and a British breakthrough. It was not until his offensive had come to an ignominious end (and for years thereafter) that in self-defense he began citing attrition and the need for shielding the French Army as justifications for his campaign. There is nothing that can be said conclusively about the latter argument. Demoralization cannot be weighed, measured, or counted. The anti-Haig faction claims that the French were at least capable of self-defense a month or two after the Nivelle fiasco and that they were virtually back to normal military morale by October. Major General J.F.C. Fuller in his *Military History of the Western World* dismisses the entire campaign in one paragraph which ends: "To persist after the close of August in this tactically impossible battle was an inexcusable piece of pigheadedness on the part of Haig, because on the 20th of that month the French had recovered sufficiently to mount an attack at Verdun, which was continued until September 15 with the usual heavy losses." And the French had also fought normally at Malmaison in October and at the northern end of the Flanders line under General Anthoine for four solid months. Winston Churchill considered Haig's argument mythical: "The French Army was no doubt saving its strength as much as possible, but the casualty tables show that during 1917 they inflicted nearly as many losses on the Germans as did our own troops."

On the other hand, there are those who claimed— long after the war was over—that the Flanders campaign saved France. General Davidson, of Haig's staff, flatly says that if and when the Germans had learned fully of the French weakness they would have immediately attacked and would have had "no difficulty in destroying their army and compelling its surrender." The Australian historian Bean is more moderate, but on this issue (if on few others) took Haig's side:

> It is not sufficient to show that French resentment at British inaction *might* not have had fatal consequences, or that the Germans *might* not have attacked the French Army, or that, if relieved by the British on part of its front, that army *might* have shattered a German offensive. The situation was such that Great Britain could not afford to take a risk.

Haig himself, in a later letter to Charteris, stated his case bluntly: ". . . the possibility of the French army breaking up in 1917 *compelled me to go on attacking* . . . on account of the *awful* state of the French troops!" And still later he maintained that he had fearfully kept many facts about the French decay even from Charteris. But the letter was written in 1927.

Today the consensus is that the French argument was an afterthought with Haig, that his plan to attack in the salient was complete long before Nivelle's episode, and that his insistence on continuing the campaign after its initial bogging down was based, at the time, almost entirely upon the theme of attrition.

Since the debate is endless and by its nature cannot lead to a conclusion, let us turn to the repellent but more tangible process of "counting heads." At once a curious problem arises, for it turns out that there are two sets of figures.

In March 1922 the British War Office published its

Statistics of the Military Effort of the British Empire during the Great War. Released as soon as possible after the event, it flatly lists British casualties between July and December 1917 (the Flanders campaign and Cambrai) at 448,614. This does not include French losses on the north flank, which may be conservatively reckoned at 50,000 for the same period. Thus the total Allied loss comes to half a million. The Flanders campaign was normal for the Western Front, in which the proportion of dead to other casualties almost always ran about thirty per cent; therefore, 150,000 approximately were killed.

In the same report German casualties are listed as 270,710.

The figures were not questioned by the Australian official historian, who remarks that "the balance of loss was still strongly against the British," though not as badly as at the Somme in 1916, where British casualties were 481,842 against the German 236,194. In other words, the proportion against the attacker had been greater than two to one at the Somme, and only 1.6 to one in the 1917 campaign. The writer then suggests that both sides were in error; cautiously refiguring the losses, he allocates 52,000 more to the British than to the enemy. Haig, of course, thought it was the other way around; and in all these figures French losses are disregarded. In any event, the arithmetic is in line with experiences on the Western Front throughout the war: the attacker suffers more than the attacked. There seems no reason why the ratio that held good at the Somme should not roughly apply to Flanders. Both campaigns were similar. They were fought over approximately the same length of time. The terrain was similar—though the mud was worse in Flanders and hampered the attackers more. The tactics were similar —pure and simple bludgeoning. The ratio of artillery and infantry was much the same. It is hard to escape the conclusion that the ratio of casualties also must have been similar, and the 1922 report bears this out.

But now comes new arithmetic. In Volume 4 of his *War Memoirs* Lloyd George notes: "I learn that an elaborate effort is being made to gerrymander the casualty returns—both British and German—so as to present a more favourable balance sheet for this adventure." In 1948 the British *Official History*, admitting that "the clerk-power to investigate the exact losses was not available," totals the British casualties at 244,897. Then follows a series of assumptions ending with this sentence: "There seems every probability that the Germans lost about 400,000." So the ratio was 1.6 to one against the defender, rather than in his favor, a rather incredible reversal.

General Edmonds' figures are preposterous; and the offhand way in which he adds a flat 33 per cent (for lightly wounded who did not have to leave their units) to the maximum German casualty figures approaches the fraudulent. (German Supreme Headquarters, incidentally, tabulated only 202,000 casualties for the entire campaign—and these on a front reaching beyond Ypres and all the way to Armentieres.) In the

November 1959 issue of the *R.U.S.I. Journal*, Captain B. H. Liddel Hart demolishes the official historian's house-of-cards; the captain's article, "The Basic Truths of Passchendaele," is devastating in this and other respects, and deserves wide reading.

The case for Haig is further weakened by the statement that British casualties of 244,897 included "normal wastage." Normal wastage in the salient, before the campaign started, was running around 7000 weekly. The Flanders campaign lasted about fourteen weeks, during which time wastage would have totaled almost 100,000, leaving battle losses at less than 150,-000. This figure is far less than reported day by day, and implies that the attackers lost about half as many troops as the defenders. Logic points toward the original 1922 statistics as substantially correct, rather than those announced twenty-six years later by a general officer admittedly on Haig's side of the argument.

But though the 1922 figures seem correct it remains true that the Germans had been badly mauled, that they could less afford their losses than the Allies, and that pragmatically the campaign hurt them more than the British. Let us assume that Tommy has thirteen pennies, and that Fritz has eight. Tommy throws three pennies into the lake each time that Fritz throws two. Soon Fritz will be bankrupt, while Tommy, despite his profligacy, will still be solvent. While in terms of warfare this may be a revolting process, the Germans recognized its effectiveness. General von Kuhl writes:

On this point Field Marshal Haig was right in his judgment—even if he did not break through the German Front, the Flanders Battle wore down the German strength to a degree at which the damage could no longer be repaired. The German sword, heretofore sharp, was blunted.

The German official history says:

Divisions disappeared by dozens into the turmoil of the battle, only to emerge from the witches' cauldron after a short period, thinned and exhausted, often reduced to a miserable remnant.

In his diary, Crown Prince Rupprecht of Bavaria states:

Most perturbing is the fact that our troops are steadily deteriorating.

And the German official history concludes:

Above all, the battle had led to an excessive expenditure of German forces. The casualties were so great that they could no longer be covered, and the already reduced battle strength of battalions sank significantly lower.

It may be observed that these and similar quotations might also have been uttered by British authorities.

The life expectancy of a machine gunner in battle on the Western Front has been computed at thirty minutes. Since the Germans defended their Flanders line largely with machine gunners their losses in these elite troops were enormous. But the flower of the British Army had also withered away: its junior officers. The 1922 report shows that 22,316 of them became battle casualties in the west between July and December, as against only 6913 Germans. Again this reflects the lethal risks taken by men proceeding slowly through mud, led by lieutenants and captains, against barricaded machine guns manned by noncommissioned officers and privates. Sir Douglas Haig claimed that his men "advanced every time with absolute confidence in their power to overcome the enemy even though they sometimes had to struggle through mud up to their waists to reach him." Whether or not they had such confidence, their inability to evade hostile small-arms fire under such conditions is clear.

What Lloyd George thought of the Flanders campaign from the standpoint of casualties can well be imagined. An excerpt from his memoirs will suffice:

> During the whole battle we recovered less ground, we took fewer prisoners, we captured fewer guns (about one fourth) than we did in the despised Nivelle offensive, and that with nearly three times the casualties we sustained in that operation, which was always alluded to by the Staff as a "failure." . . . So much for the bovine and brutal game of attrition on the Western Front.

And in speaking at a Paris luncheon he said, concerning the Passchendaele phase, "When we advance a kilometre into the enemy's lines, snatch a small shattered village out of his cruel grasp, capture a few hundred of his soldiers, we shout with unfeigned joy . . ." and he went on to compare this kind of thing with the tremendous Austro-German triumph at Caporetto. The quoted sentence was given a bad press in London, for it came quite close to saying publicly that the British Army was being incompetently led and that the entire Third Battle of Ypres had been a needless blood bath; nor did the remark sit well with the masses in the Army who had fought desperately and suffered much, nor was it much solace for those back home who had lost their young men in Flanders. The newspapers were not happy, and in Parliament many spoke up bitterly against Lloyd George. Sir Edward Carson, for one, regretted that his chief had seen fit to hold up the high command "to the odium of their countrymen, as though in some way or other they were betraying their country, if not by their corruption, at least by their incompetence."

Gough came in for the major share of blame, and defended himself thus in his book, *The Fifth Army:* "But these battles were not fought on my initiative, nor was I responsible for their continuance, nor was the Fifth Army the only participant. . . ." Harington admitted that perhaps the campaign should have started and ended with Messines, and that perhaps

there was no place where his army could have reason-
ably stopped for the winter, once the fighting had
bogged down. General Davidson regrets that Plumer
had not been given charge from the very beginning,
and implies that Gough ran the offensive into the
ground scarcely before it had time to get under way.
The Australian historian points out that since the
enemy artillery could never be dislocated by the snail-
like nature of the advance, Haig's far-reaching strategic aims were impossible of achievement. Churchill
derided the false god of attrition, in view of the official figures. "If we lose three or four times as many officers and nearly twice as many men in our attack as the
enemy in his defense, how are we wearing him down?"

An Army Commanders' conference at Doullens on
December 7 appears to have been a morose affair. Sir
Douglas pointed out that the manpower problem was
extremely serious; he had little hope of bringing his
divisions up to strength by next spring, whereas it was
now an open secret that German divisions were coming down from the Russian front at the rate of ten per
month, Russia having signed an armistice with the
Central Powers several days previously. General Rawlinson, who attended the meeting, was grim over the
turn of events but blamed it on the civilians:

> . . . by the end of February we are likely to have a
> lively time. Anyhow, we shall be thrown on the de-
> fensive, and shall have to fight for our lives as we
> did at the first battle of Ypres. We have had no luck
> this year. There is something radically wrong with

the general management of the war by the Allies. The politicians insist on butting in just at the wrong time. . . .

General Plumer was assigned to take charge of British forces in Italy, and left remarking that he was glad to be out of the mud and blood of Flanders. His Second Army was handed over to Rawlinson. By this time Gough, a hard-luck commander virtually in disgrace, was in command of only one corps. At the suggestion of General Kiggell, Haig removed Charteris from GHQ; at once a torrent of abuse rained down on the Intelligence officer's head. In turn, Kiggell was replaced by the commander in chief, on grounds of ill health. The old order of command and power in France and Belgium was fast disintegrating. Who would be next?

Long had "Wully," Chief of the Imperial General Staff, been railing over the mechanics of the Versailles Supreme War Council. Not only did he consider that body unworkable, but he insisted that the CIGS could not be made the errand boy of General Wilson and a pack of foreigners. As far as Lloyd George was concerned, Robertson could resign if he wished. Everybody was in step but him—even Sir Douglas, who, to the Prime Minister's surprise, would not fight for his old friend in a personal talk with Lloyd George at Walton Heath. In fact, Haig remarked, he himself had no interest in all these petty quarrels; he would "play up all he could" with the decisions of the War Cabinet.

Since the same could not be said of Sir William, his finish was plainly in sight. But Haig continued to stand apart, and to his wife wrote that Robertson, after all, had never resolutely adhered to the Western Front philosophy. So the only man who might have saved Robertson turned his face away. It was a stunning disappointment for the burly, grumpy, popularly loved chief of staff, and this after years of playing Haig's game. On February 8 the War Cabinet decided that he and Sir Henry Wilson should switch jobs.

A distasteful episode followed. In a ferocious temper at this stage, and almost impossible to talk to, "Wully" refused to resign and flatly declined the Versailles appointment. Haig visited him at the War Office, where he was still moodily holding on, and tried to persuade him to work on the Supreme War Council. "Wully" refused, and in his diary Sir Douglas wrote, "I am afraid that in the back of his mind he resents Henry Wilson replacing him in London, and means to embarrass the Government to the utmost of his power." On February 18 Robertson read in the newspapers that he had "resigned," that Wilson was the new CIGS, and that he—Sir William—had been given the Eastern Command, a minor house assignment in southeast England.

Subordinated to a war council which generally opposed him, the strange bedfellow of a new chief of staff who had gone on record as disagreeing with his Flanders campaign (which he expected to start up again next spring), almost alone against the animosity and

plots of the Prime Minister, mistrusted by the War
Cabinet after the failure of his 1917 plan, Douglas
Haig too seemed at the crossroads. Would it be his
turn next to leave the paths of glory?

December ended and another cheerless New Year's
Day dawned on the Western Front, as rigid and
granite-like as ever. The stalemate still held, despair-
ingly the vast armies continued to face each other, and
peace seemed all too familiarly remote. America was
in but Russia was out, and so, for all practical purposes, was Italy. Many in the War Committee had
come to realize that Haig's promises had led to nothing; one by one his assurances delivered in the spring
had proved empty. Many newspapers formerly sympathetic to Sir Douglas now turned against him. Even
Lord Northcliffe underwent a sudden revulsion and
demanded a "prompt, searching and complete" inquiry into what had happened, and his *Times* roared:

> We can no longer rest satisfied with the fatuous esti-
> mates, e.g. of German losses in men and morale,
> which have inspired too many of the published mes-
> sages from France.

But the dissatisfaction did not spring merely from
distorted communiqués. Behind it was a feeling that
the campaign had been botched and that countless
young men had been butchered for nothing. A new
and nagging realization arose that the generalship on
the Western Front had been something less than inspired. In the words of Mr. H. G. Wells:

the professional military mind is by necessity an inferior and unimaginative mind; no man of high intellectual quality would willingly imprison his gifts
in such a calling. . . . This war after fifty years of
militarism was a hopelessly professional war; from
first to last it was impossible to get it out of the hands
of the regular generals. . . .

Tactics had been on a rather low level, and if there
were those who said that nothing else was possible on
the Western Front there were others who replied that
Napoleon would have found a way. But the British in
Flanders had no Napoleon. Planning could not have
been more routine. Except at Messines and Cambrai,
surprise and deception were neglected. A date for each
attack was decided upon. The staffs glanced at their
maps and decided which divisions would participate.
These were assembled at the front. Guns and supplies
were brought forward. Zero hour was set. Lines were
traced on the map showing the objectives. A bombardment softened up the defenses and completed the job
of tipping the attacker's hand. Finally the assault
brigades went over the top and walked directly at the
prepared, entrenched enemy. Thus France and England had fought the war for three years on the Western
Front; and as to which leadership of the two allies was
the more inept Hindenburg writes, "The Englishman
was undoubtedly a less skillful opponent than his
brother in arms. He did not understand how to control
rapid changes in the situation. His methods were too
rigid." But, he admits, they were indeed obstinate.

Essentially it is Haig that the German describes, and despite his continual attacks Haig must be regarded more attuned psychologically for defense. "He had not a critical mind," writes Charteris, nor was his imagination appropriate for the dash and subtlety of successful offensive operations. Like General Ulysses Grant, his nature was best suited to a calculated process of attrition; and there is a remarkable parallel between the 1917 Flanders campaign and Grant's operations in 1864 from the Rapidan to Petersburg.

Both Haig's supporters and detractors agree on one thing: the timing had been unfortunate. To start the Flanders campaign just before the rains was to invite calamity. If it had to take place at all, spring was the time. Given dry ground and acknowledged superiority in artillery and shells, Haig might have accomplished much more than he did. When Nivelle's plan was given precedence, and when subsequent delays began to pile up, it might have been best to wait for the Americans, for the tanks, and for 1918. Haig had come to the well once too often—at the Somme for 500,000 men, at Ypres for 400,000. And the Australian historian writes:

> When in the near future he pressed for still more men, the War Cabinet felt, not without reason, that, if given another 100,000, he would stake them to gain the next shell-shattered hilltop; he would use up all he had, and his side would not be appreciably nearer to victory. To political leaders, forced to accept his

plans but shocked with the result, the obvious moral was: "Keep back the men."

As a result, incidentally, of this policy of keeping back the men, Haig's skeleton armies were less able to withstand the German offensive that burst upon them in 1918.

The argument that started when the campaign ended has never been settled with finality. Should it have taken place at all? Should it have been stopped after Messines, after the August breakdown, after Broodseinde? Was the gain in ground whatsoever meaningful? Were the Germans hurt more—relatively or absolutely or both—than the Allies? Did the campaign save France, and how weak *was* that nation's army when July 31 dawned? A small but determined minority, mostly army officers, believes that Haig was right from start to finish. But an equal or larger number of military personnel, and almost all civilians, have always felt (in varying degrees) that Haig blundered, or was irrationally stubborn, or was at least misled by his Intelligence advisers.

The controversy is strikingly similar to that which later revolved around Truman and MacArthur. In both cases the general's side was taken by a violent and highly articulate minority. In both cases there seemed to be no neutrals. In both cases the general was looked upon almost as a god by his followers. In Haig's case, the last is hardest to explain. Few men in public service have been more plagued by an un-

attractive personality than he. His inarticulateness
was so severe as to give circulation to a host of anec-
dotes—some affectionate, some malicious—such as the
one concerning his speech when presenting trophies
to an Aldershot cross-country team: "I congratulate
you on your running. You have run well. I hope you
run as well in the presence of the enemy." At mess the
field marshal ate silently. He had no nickname, no
small talk, no sense of humor, no warmth in his deal-
ings with other men. His public speeches were hardly
of the sort to arouse idolatry; written out meticulously
in advance, they dealt always with "Sacrifice" or
"Duty" or "Endeavour." Yet the devotion to the man
and to his 1917 campaign has always been inversely
proportional to the number of devotees, and probably
will always be so.

The analyses of those who have written of Haig and
Flanders naturally reflect their own prejudices. At one
extreme is Bragadier General J. E. Edmonds, the British official historian, in whose eyes Haig could do no
wrong, German casualties almost doubled the British,
the military victory was substantial, Flanders was the
best place to attack, the bad weather was exaggerated,
the mud was routine and not as bad as at the Somme,
the tanks cooperated successfully until October, and
so on.

At the other stands David Lloyd George. In his *War
Memoirs*, Volume 4, 116 pages are devoted to the
"Campaign of the Mud: Passchendaele," later widely

circulated as a separate pamphlet. These are vitriolic pages, hard to answer but intemperate in language (some of which has been quoted in this narrative), in which Haig emerges as a stubborn, fame-hungry, cold-blooded, deceiving oaf, and his campaign a military abortion unparalleled in the history of the western world.

Between these lies Volume 4 of the Australian *Official History,* admirably written by Dr. C. E. W. Bean, in which blame and credit are so evenly apportioned that one cannot enter the result on one side of the ledger or the other.

Haig never wrote his memoirs, but several of his followers later took up the war of words on his behalf. Dewar and Boraston, formerly of his staff, issued their appraisal in 1922—an unfortunate effort showing serious inaccuracies and bias; it was received badly, and even Haig was not pleased by it. His official biography, by Mr. Alfred Duff-Cooper, paints the usual portrait of a master soldier who can do no wrong, and his life as interpreted by General Charteris is scarcely less idealistic. General Davidson's book is largely a résumé of the *Official History.*

On the other hand, the biographies of Lloyd George by Thomas Jones and Frank Owen are laudatory of the Prime Minister, especially the latter; and the various works of Captain Liddell Hart show little sympathy for the field marshal. Hart's books are by far the most widely read, and his point of view has deeply permeated the public consciousness. It is no surprise

to learn that he advised Lloyd George militarily
throughout the preparation of his memoirs, and that
it is his voice which is heard in the many definitive
articles concerning World War I in the *Encyclopædia
Britannica*.

Sir William Robertson's *Soldiers and Statesmen* summarizes his expected attitudes with icy restraint. The
official histories of Canada and New Zealand are critical of Haig to a degree, but generally noncommittal.
Almost all the worm's-eye views of the campaign, such
as those written by Charles Edmonds, Reginald Farrer, Robert Graves, Stephen Graham, Thomas Hope,
and Ralph Mottram, plus a thousand others in this
vein, are shockingly bitter. Sir Arthur Conan Doyle's
fourth volume in his microscopic history of the course
of battles on the Western Front is, perhaps, the most
uninhibited apologia for the tactics pursued by GHQ
and, since it has been superseded by later and more
authoritative technical accounts, may be considered of
meager value. Haig's own published *Despatches* to
the King are somewhat colored by a tinge of propaganda and self-justification. These, along with his
edited *Private Papers*, however, present a convincing
case for the policy he pursued so inflexibly to Passchendaele's bitter end. The writings of Sir Philip
Gibbs vary radically between praise for Sir Douglas
and his wise leadership, horror at the conditions of
warfare and at the concept of warfare itself, admiration for British valor, hatred for the ineptitude of certain British generals, and sheer propaganda to bolster

public opinion. It is hard to classify this distinguished writer, though in public speech and after the war he showed himself to be in opposition to the Flanders plan and execution.

One may turn, therefore, to these and innumerable other sources to arrive at an opinion, or to justify one's preconceived opinion. The face of history is, as usual, blank and imperturbable. This is war, it says; this is life as twentieth-century man chose to conduct it. The Third Battle of Ypres was fought thus and so, and human judgment is inadequate to categorize its ultimate meaning, if, indeed, it has any meaning within the larger surge of life. Broad and turgid, the river of time flows toward an unnamed sea. On it the Flanders campaign survives only for a moment, an eddy of muddy water that convulsively twists and turns and then disappears.

On March 21, 1918, the long-anticipated German onslaught crashed against the British Third and Fifth Armies and within two weeks had penetrated to a maximum of forty miles. The second phase began April 9. In a matter of hours the little strip of ridge won at such cost by Haig's troops the previous year was wiped out. Soon the entire salient was obliterated and twelve more miles gained. In May Ludendorff struck another heavy blow, this time at the French in Champagne; after four days the Marne was reached, thirty miles farther away, and again Paris was threatened. But the sands had run out for Germany. The

Allies had fumbled and almost panicked, but they had held. The Americans were on the scene in considerable force. All surprise was now gone. The last great German attack (in July) fell against a thoroughly prepared and determined opponent; it failed, and three days later Foch counterattacked, using masses of tanks and 100,000 feverishly combative American troops as spearheads.

Throughout all these titanic experiences Haig remained cool, and surprisingly prudent of human life. He, like Gough, had learned much from Flanders. It was a sadder and wiser man who met the enemy juggernaut, skillful in defense, methodical in his dispositions, ready and willing to work with the Supreme Commander, Marshal Ferdinand Foch.

With this offensive the German war machine committed suicide, for in thirteen weeks 688,000 of its men were lost. "They were worn down," says Churchill, "not by Joffre, Nivelle and Haig, but by Ludendorff." On August 8, "the black day of the German army in the history of the War," Haig smashed through on the Somme. There followed a series of sharp punches all along the line, ending with the American victory at St. Mihiel on September 12. On the 29th Haig broke through the Hindenburg line. Bulgaria, then Turkey, then Austria capitulated. German peace overtures were proffered when revolution was sweeping over that land. When her admirals tried to send the fleet on a death-or-glory ride, the sailors mutinied. More alert to impending Bolshevism than to military defeat, the

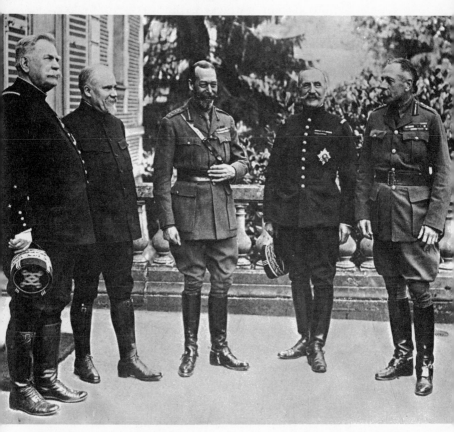

Marshal Joseph Joffre, Raymond Poincaré, King George V, Foch, and Haig

German government rushed a peace delegation to Foch on November 6.

It remains to be said, as usual, that the war ended on the eleventh hour of the eleventh day of the eleventh month of 1918. It had meant nothing, solved nothing, and proved nothing; and in so doing had killed 8,538,315 men and variously wounded 21,219,-452. Of 7,750,919 others taken prisoner or missing, well over a million were later presumed dead; thus the total deaths (not counting civilians) approach 10,-000,000. The moral and mental defects of the leaders of the human race had been demonstrated with some exactitude. One of them (Woodrow Wilson) later confessed that the war had been fought for business interests; another (David Lloyd George) had told a newspaperman, "If people really knew, the war would be stopped tomorrow, but of course they don't—and can't know. The correspondents don't write and the censorship wouldn't pass the truth. The thing is horrible, and beyond human nature to bear, and I feel I can't go on any longer with the bloody business."

But now the thing was over. After a few final shells thrown into enemy lines at 11 o'clock by cannoneers who shall be forever nameless, an uncanny silence enveloped the Western Front. Cautiously, unbelievingly, the men raised themselves above their trenches, shell holes, and dugouts, and stared at the opposing lines. Soon they became very excited, and often regrettably drunk; and, as the once-hostile armies merged, the men exchanged cigarettes, wine, embraces, and souvenirs. Then came the stern, inevitable order forbidding fraternization.

In London madness reigned, a mixture of joy and sorrow almost too poignant to be endured. At the first stroke of Big Ben's chimes thousands poured out into the streets. Now all the bells of the city began to clang. Drivers of busses and military lorries careened in all directions with loads of screaming passengers. Hordes flocked to Buckingham Palace and sang "God Save the King" until His Majesty appeared on the balcony and tried to speak through the cheers, the singing, the sputtering of firecrackers. Flags appeared from countless shops and houses. One crowd hauled out a captured German gun from the Mall and burned its carriage in Trafalgar Square. Soon all traffic choked to a stop. It began to rain, but few noticed, and dancing and singing continued in the open air. Some people climbed into the arms of Queen Victoria's statue. Under an archway in a tiny street near Charing Cross two old women in capes and bonnets danced primly to the music of a barrel organ. That night all the previously darkened streets were lit up like a carnival, and the merrymaking went on—in restaurants (where the food soon ran out), in pubs, on the streets, in night clubs—and there was no end to the confetti throwing. To the shout, "Have we won the war?" the answer came back in a roar, "Yes, we've won the war!" Clerks, factory workers in caps and overalls, a stout colonel beating a dinner gong atop a taxi, wounded soldiers in

hospital blue, girl messengers, sailors, government officials, and many a child—all were caught up in the
maelstrom. And that day a new song was often heard:

"What shall we be
When we aren't what we are? . . ."

A rollicking little thing it was, but there were those
who found it vaguely disquieting.

16. Sequel

AFTER THE WAR the famous generals were allotted great tasks at the seven corners of the earth. Sir Herbert Plumer became governor of Malta and later high commissioner for Palestine. In 1920 Sir Henry Rawlinson was assigned to India as commander in chief. As military adviser of the government, Sir Henry Wilson was active at Versailles, and subsequently entered Parliament as Member for North Down. Sir Hubert Gough was named head of the British Mission to the Baltic States, General Byng became governor general of Canada, General Allenby high commissioner for Egypt. Thus all but one were honored by a grateful Empire for services rendered. Only Sir Douglas Haig was given nothing to do. Fifty-eight, in perfect health, a handsome figure of a man, after stepping ashore at Dover in 1919 he found that his official life was over; he was in effect unemployed.

Innumerable titles and decorations

were conferred upon him by France, the United
States, Italy, Belgium, Portugal, Japan, Serbia, Rumania, even China. He was raised to the peerage as
Earl Haig and Baron Haig of Bemersyde. Parliament
granted him £100,000, and he remained on the active
list as a field marshal. Talk of appointing him viceroy
of India came to nothing. He concealed his emotions
behind a mask of stone, toured the land and made
speeches concerning duty, sacrifice, and service, became active in veterans' affairs, unveiled any number
of war memorials, went to Edinburgh to live, and
toiled daily on the grounds and gardens of his estate.
He entered the local social life, hunted foxes with his
neighbors, and lived quietly with his wife and the son
who had been born in the month of Ludendorff's 1918
offensive. All letters—and they poured in like a stream
—he answered in his own hand. He joined the boards
of several great companies, cultivated an interest in
business, attended their meetings and studied the details of their operations. In connection with the British
Legion he did much charity work for the survivors, the
wounded, and the relatives of those killed in the war.
Always religious, he became active in the Church of
Scotland. But still Lloyd George and the Government
spurned him.

He golfed at St. Andrews, and one may unearth delightful pictures of him in several old golf volumes,
stiffly dressed, a ghost of a smile on his lips as he struggles with the maddening game. We find him photo-
graphed in Andrew Kirkaldy's book while teeing off as

captain of the Royal and Ancient. The ball is on its way, the crowd peers down the fairway, and one learns sadly that his drive was the Flanders campaign in microcosm—very short but very straight; and one may also observe that the field marshal's grip is, typically, far too rigid, his weight piled back on the wrong foot somewhat in the manner of a later distinguished soldier, President Eisenhower.

As the years passed Lord Haig became somewhat more talkative, less abrupt, more tolerant in his judgments. He began to speak humorously of what he would do when the infirmities of age beset him. Always pathetically addicted to weird diets, he now concentrated on oranges. Over and over he relived the war before his fireside, and welcomed people with whom he could discuss it—especially old comrades in arms. On trains he asked the conductor for the names of the passengers; if he recognized one he would seek him out.

The 1920s waned, and Sir Douglas aged quickly in the way of those who have nothing to do. Ignored by the authorities, he turned to dreams of the past and to his family. To meet attacks on his war leadership that had sprung up when censorship was lifted, he provided his friends and former assistants with counter-arguments to use publicly and privately. In addition, the *Official History* would vindicate him, he assured his wife and friends; nothing else mattered. So the people of Britain gradually forgot him and less and less wondered why he was not to be found in the spheres of power and prestige. One winter evening he played cards with his wife and sister, and went up to his room. A cry was heard. He had suffered a heart attack; and on January 29, 1928, the old soldier passed away.

The long road followed by David Lloyd George after the end of hostilities is a familiar one and may be briefly summarized. In 1918 he was returned overwhelmingly to power and at Versailles tried without much success to weaken Clemenceau's ferocious demands on the defeated enemy. In a lukewarm way he took President Wilson's side on the League of Nations issue, but never attended any of its meetings. The general election of 1922 returned the Conservatives to leadership and Lloyd George to the Opposition. From here to the end his political fortunes declined while the Labour Party grew in numbers. In 1929 the Liberals under his ostensible leadership were able to win only fifty-nine seats in Commons.

Increasingly he stayed aloof from the national scene and spent three full years (1931-1934) writing his *War Memoirs*. He became one of the earliest appeasers of Hitler, in a phase which continued almost until the start of the new war. As Germany went from victory to victory Lloyd George waited for a nod from Churchill that would bring him back into the Cabinet. It came in May, 1940, subject to Mr. Chamberlain's approval. Since Lloyd George despised the former prime minister, and had helped force him out of office, he angrily refused Churchill's offer. Also, he doubted if he could work with an antagonistic War Cabinet. So the elder statesman brooded and fretted and almost seemed to welcome some shattering crisis that would cause those in the inner circles to seek out his aid and prestige. This, too, never developed, whereupon he predicted disaster for the Allies under Churchill's leadership. In 1941 the death of his wife, Dame Margaret, left him even more pessimistic, lonely, detached from the new war that he did not quite understand—its origin, its strategy, the aims of its belligerents. His attitude toward Russia alternated throughout the years; at first he welcomed the revolution; then for a long period he fancied Herr Hitler as the man who might mercifully throttle that revolution; but his last speech in Parliament (on June 11, 1942) was to congratulate the Government on its treaty with the Soviets. Next year, at eighty, he married his secretary, Frances Louise Stevenson, and returned to his farm in Wales. By now the old fighter was failing fast, hardly even aware of the war. Each morning he awakened late, strolled down to the village, came back for luncheon, napped, smoked, supped, and talked to old friends. He could no longer run actively for office; yet to make no speeches and conduct no campaign, and then to be defeated by some glib youngster, would be tragic. While debating whether to evade the contest, he was asked by Winston Churchill to have his name submitted to the King for an earldom. He wired the Prime Minister, "Gratefully accept," and became free, in theory, to speak in the Lords. The Great Commoner, to the amusement and resentment of many, thus was named on New Year's Day, 1945, the Right Honorable Earl Lloyd George of Dwyfor.

For three months the wizened, senile Welshman held on, very weak and seldom rational. Occasionally his mind cleared and, for a wonderful hour or two, operated with its old speed and acid clarity; then on March 26 he died in the presence of his wife and two daughters. During his funeral several aircraft roared by, and the villagers asked one another if Mr. Churchill had finally arrived; but they were warplanes bent on other business that cold and foggy afternoon.

It had cost Sir William Robertson dearly to hitch his wagon to Haig during the war years. After being removed as Chief of the Imperial General Staff, the whipping boy of those who had not found it possible to sack Sir Douglas, he never again attained his former glory. In 1919, after receiving a baronetcy and a grant of £10,000, he was given command of British troops on the Rhine, an appointment he soon relinquished when the forces under him dwindled. His military career ended in 1921 and he turned to writing his autobiography and his classic work, *Soldiers and Statesmen*. Later, somewhat surprisingly, he immersed himself in peace propaganda—" a role," in the words of Liddell Hart, "which seemed to some who knew him well as due more to disappointment than to conviction." After receiving many honors of the Empire and foreign nations he died, irascible and shrewd to the end, in 1933 at the age of seventy-three.

After the war Ypres was rebuilt in elaborate medieval style, with only the ruins of the Cloth Hall allowed to lie and molder as war had created them. The venture was an astounding *tour de force* but an unsuccessful one; today the town seems too precious, too self-conscious, and its old-world curiosity-shop flavor is forever gone. Like the commercialized reincarnation of Tombstone, Arizona, it thrives on the tourist trade.

No longer does the Menin road, dreary and squalid, a tragedy of mud, weeds, and shell craters, lead to the Western Front. Now it is a trim provincial highway; and the sweating, heavy-laden, sleepy-eyed men are wraiths of the past. The Menin Gate, too, has been reconstructed: a gigantic memorial of marble, broad, vaulted, Roman in design. Facing the former enemy a stone lion crouches; his paw holds his prey, and he does not intend to let go. Fifty-six thousand names are engraved in gold on the walls, all British dead whose graves or bodies were never found in the salient during or after the war. It was of this that Siegfried Sassoon wrote his biting sonnet, "On Passing the Menin Gate," which begins:

Who will remember, passing through this Gate,
The unheroic Dead who fed the guns?

The remaining British missing are recorded in Tyne Cot Cemetery, Passchendaele, largest British cemetery in the world. And, among others, there is the Canadian Memorial near St. Julien. Here the colossal head and shoulders of an ordinary soldier rises from a tall column and seems to grieve for all soldiers of all lands since time began.

In all, 174 British cemeteries cram the one-time salient, tended by a small army of British subjects under the employment of the Imperial War Graves Commission. All crosses are white and scrupulously neat in arrangement, and brilliantly green is the grass between them, the rows interrupted here and there only by the sawed-off propellers of fliers who fell to their deaths in Flanders. These cemeteries, land "that is forever England," were conceded in perpetuity to Great Britain by the Belgian government in 1917; they contain in the Ypres area forty thousand British graves, while untold thousands still lie under unmarked soil. All are bounded by low walls or fences. Within them trees and flowers grow. The orderly rows are marked by headstones showing the deceased's name, rank, unit, date of death, regimental crest, religious symbol, and any simple inscription that his friends might have cared to add. Officers and enlisted men lie side by side. There is a Cross of Sacrifice at the entrance of each cemetery, and a Stone of Remembrance inscribed with the words, "Their name liveth for evermore." One registers at each entrance gate.

Visitors may learn in advance at 82 Baker Street, London, the location of the deceased, the name of his cemetery, the row, the number in the row. There is a Graves Enquiry Bureau in Ypres where an official map may be consulted. It is all extremely efficient.

Long were the fields of the salient littered with the debris of war, especially near the Menin road. In the "Tank Graveyard" seventeen machines lay embedded where they had been struck down. Tours were conducted around Ypres; the most popular was Number 7, which led through St. Julien, Poelcapelle, and Houthulst Forest. For years the ridge was too trenched, cratered, and mined to be of any value, and nothing grew on it but the coarsest of weeds. On Hill 60 the peasants dug up vast quantities of souvenirs—buttons, badges, pistols, boots, the bones of soldiers, holsters, wooden pipes, cartridges, shell fragments, and the like —and sold their wares out of little boxes to tourists who flowed like battalions across the former battlefield. Everything was priced quite methodically: twenty francs for a Smith and Wesson revolver, one penny for a brass button, and so on.

A former soldier became caretaker of one portion of the ridge maintained as a memorial in its original state. He lived in an army hut, talked to visitors, and for one franc conducted them on his little tour to Death Trench. Each day after tea the caretaker and his dog walked down the communications trench (Princes Street) to the support line (Paradise Alley), up international trench to the mine crater, through formless

Schenken Redoubt, and returned by way of the sap that entered the German dugouts (Piccadilly Buildings). He mended the duckboards, noted where the imitation concrete sandbags were split by frost, and kept the shallow trenches at the summit boarded up; and as he walked his heavy boots rasped against the remnants of rusty barbed wire and occasionally jostled a helmet, or a rifle barrel from which the wood had long since decayed. Only this, and sometimes the barking of his dog, disturbed the deathlike silence where once men had screamed in fear and agony amid the clamor of the guns.

In time the caretaker disappeared, along with his bit of Western Front. Only along the coast, near Nieuport, does another such replica still exist, and this too, it is said, is soon to be abandoned. Time reclaimed the ridge and what was once the salient. But in 1940 war rolled again through Poelcapelle, Passchendaele, Ypres, Poperinghe, Messines. Again this weary land and these familiar towns, soaked with the blood of centuries, were occupied by new armies; and later other legions passed through and drove their enemy back, as the Duke of Parma did in 1584, as the French did in the seventeenth century, as Austria did in the next, as a hundred armies did before them. And again the salient reverted to farmland. Yet today the millions of shell holes have never quite leveled out, and anyone who walks through the fields south and west of the ridge can still sense the undulations caused by shells that blasted this ground in the First World War.

In *Sartor Resartus,* a hundred years earlier, Carlyle wrote:

> . . . there dwell and toil, in the British village of Dumdrudge, usually some five hundred souls. From these . . . there are successively selected, during the French War, say thirty able-bodied men: Dumdrudge, at her own expense, has suckled and nursed them; she has, not without difficulty and sorrow, fed them up to manhood, and even trained them to crafts, so that one can weave, another build, another hammer, and the weakest can stand under thirty stone avoirdupois. Nevertheless, amid much weeping and swearing, they are selected; all dressed in red; and shipped away, at the public charges, some two thousand miles, or say only to the south of Spain; and fed there till wanted. And now to that same spot in the south of Spain, are thirty similar French artisans, from a French Dumdrudge, in like manner wending: Till at length, after infinite effort, the two parties come into actual juxtaposition; and Thirty stands fronting Thirty, each with a gun in his hand. Straightway the word "Fire!" is given: and they blow the souls out of one another; and in the place of sixty brisk useful craftsmen, the world has sixty dead carcasses, which it must bury, and anew shed tears for. Had these men any quarrel? Busy as the Devil is, not the smallest! . . . Their Governors had fallen out: and, instead of shooting one another, had the cunning to make these poor blockheads shoot.—Alas, so it is in Deutschland, and hitherto in all other lands. . . .

Bibliography

Aston, George. *Marshal Foch* (New York: Macmillan, 1929).

Baker-Carr, C. D. *From Chauffeur to Brigadier* (London: Benn, 1930).

Bean, C. E. W. *Australian Official History in the War of 1914–1918*, Volume 4 (Sydney: Angus and Robertson, 1935).

Beaverbrook, Lord. *Politicians and the War* (New York: Doubleday Doran, 1928).

B.E.F. Times: A Facsimile Reprint of the Trench Magazine (London: Jenkins, 1918).

Binding, Rudolph. *A Fatalist at War* (London: Allen and Unwin, 1928; New York: Houghton Mifflin, 1929).

Birdwood, Field Marshal Lord. *Khaki and Gown* (New York: Robert Speller and Sons, 1957).

Blunden, Edmund. *Undertones of War* (New York: Doubleday Doran, 1929).

Boraston, J. H. *Haig's Despatches 1915–1919* (London: Dent, 1919).

Brice, Beatrix. *Ypres* (London: Murray, 1929).

Callwell, C. E. *Field Marshal Sir Henry Wilson; His Life and Diaries* (New York, Scribners, 1927).

Charteris, John. *Field-Marshal Earl Haig* (New York: Scribners, 1929).

Churchill, Winston. *Great Contemporaries* (New York: Putnam, 1937).

——. *The World Crisis* (New York: Scribners, 1949).

Davidson, John H. *Haig, Master of the Field* (London: Peter Nevill, 1953).

Dewar and Boraston. *Haig's Command* (London: Constable, 1922; New York: Houghton Mifflin, 1923).

DeWeerd, H. A. *Great Soldiers of World War I* (New York: Norton, 1941).

Doyle, Arthur Conan. *The British Campaign in France and Flanders,* Vol. 4 (London: Hodder and Stoughton, 1920).

Drew, H. T. B. *The War Effort of New Zealand* (London: Whitcombe and Tombs, 1924).

Duff-Cooper, Alfred. *Haig* (New York: Doubleday, 1936).

Edmonds, Charles. *A Subaltern's War* (London: Peter Davies, 1929; New York: Minton, Balch, 1930).

Edmonds, J. E. *British Official History of the War. Military Operations, France and Belgium, 1917.* Volume 2 (London: H. M. Stationery Office, 1948).

Farrer, Reginald. *The Void of War* (London: Constable, 1918).

Fielding, Rowland. *War Letters to a Wife* (London: The Medici Society, 1929).

Foch, Marshal Ferdinand. *Memoirs* (New York: Doubleday Doran, 1931).

Fox, Frank. *Battle of the Ridges* (London: C. A. Pearson, 1918).

Gibbons, Floyd. *The Red Knight of Germany* (New York: Garden City, 1927).

Gibbs, Philip. *The Struggle in Flanders* (New York: Doran, 1919).

———. *Now It Can Be Told* (New York: Harpers, 1920).

Gough, Hubert. *Soldiering On* (London: Barker, 1954).

———. *The Fifth Army* (London: Hodder & Stoughton, 1931).

Graham, Stephen. *A Private in the Guards* (New York: Macmillan, 1919).

———. *The Challenge of the Dead* (London: Cassell, 1921).

Graves, Robert. *Goodbye to All That* (London: Cape, 1929; New York: Cape and Ballou, 1930; second revised edition, New York: Doubleday Anchor Books, 1957).

Grey, Charles. *History of Combat Airplanes* (Norwich, Vt.: Norwich University, 1941).

Guedalla, Philip. *The Two Marshals* (New York: Reynal and Hitchcock, 1943).

Haig, Douglas (ed. by Robert Blake). *Private Papers* (London: Eyre and Spottiswoode, 1952).

Harington, Charles. *Plumer of Messines* (London: John Murray, 1935).

———. *Tim Harington Looks Back* (London: John Murray, 1940).

Hart, Liddell. *Reputations Ten Years After* (Boston: Little Brown, 1928).

———. *The Real War* (Boston: Little Brown, 1930).

———. *The War in Outline* (New York: Random House, 1936).

———. *Through the Fog of War* (New York: Random House, 1938).

Hoffmann, Max. *War Diaries and Other Papers*, Volume 1 (London: Secker, 1929).

Hope, Thomas. *The Winding Road Unfolds* (New York: Putnam's, 1937).

Horne, Charles (Ed.). *Source Records of the Great War*, Volume 5 (Indianapolis: The American Legion, 1930).

Housman, L. (Ed.). *War Letters of Fallen Englishmen* (New York: Dutton).

Hurst, L. C. *The Silent Cities; Illustrated Guide to War Cemeteries in France and Flanders* (London: Methuen).

Johnson, Douglas. *Battlefields of the World War* (London: Oxford, 1921).

Jones, H. A. *The War in the Air*, Volume 4 (London: Oxford, 1928).

Jones, Ralph E. *Fighting Tanks Since 1916* (Harrisburg, Pa.: Military Service Publishing Co., 1933).

Jones, Thomas. *Lloyd George* (Cambridge, Mass.: Harvard, 1951).

Junger, Ernst. *The Storm of Steel* (New York: Doubleday Doran, 1929).

Lloyd George, David. *War Memoirs*, Volume 4 (Boston: Little Brown, 1934).

London Times History of the War, Volumes 15 and 16.

Luard, K. E. *Unknown Warriors* (London: Chatto & Windus, 1930).

Ludendorff, Erich. *Ludendorff's Own Story*, Volume 2 (New York: Harpers, 1919).

Lytton, Neville. *The Press and the General Staff* (London: Collins, 1921).

MacDonagh, Michael. *In London During the Great War* (London: Eyre & Spottiswoode, 1935).

Maurice, F. *Life of Lord Rawlinson of Trent* (New York: Houghton Mifflin, 1928).

Monash, John. *War Letters* (Sydney: Angus & Robertson, 1935).

Mottram, Ralph. *Through the Menin Gate* (London: Chatto & Windus, 1935).

———. Easton, John; and Partridge, Eric. *Three Personal Records of the War* (London. Scholartis Press, 1929).

Muirhead, Findlay. *Belgium* (New York: Macmillan, 1924).

Nichols, G. H. F. *The 18th Division in the Great War* (London: Blackwood, 1922).

Owen, Frank. *Tempestuous Journey: Lloyd George, His Life and Times* (New York: McGraw-Hill, 1955).

Pankhurst, Sylvia. *The Home Front* (London: Hutchinson, 1933).

Peel, Mrs. C. S. *How We Lived Then* (London: The Bodley Head, 1929).

Pierrefeu, Jean de. *French Headquarters, 1915–1918* (London: Bles, 1924).

Playne, Caroline. *Britain Holds On* (London: Allen and Unwin, 1933).

Pulteney, William. *The Immortal Salient* (London: John Murray, 1925).

Purdom, C. B. (Ed.). *Everyman at War* (New York: Dutton, 1930).

Quigley, Hugh. *Passchendaele and the Somme* (London: Methuen, 1928).

Repington, Charles A'Court. *The First World War* (New York: Houghton Mifflin, 1920).

Reynolds, Quentin. *They Fought for the Sky* (New York: Rinehart, 1957).

Robertson, William. *Soldiers and Statesmen* (New York: Scribners, 1926).

Rupprecht, Crown Prince. *Memoirs of the Crown Prince of Germany* (London: Butterworth).

Shaw, Bernard. *What I Really Wrote about the War* (New York: Brentano's, 1932).

Simonds, Frank H. *History of the World War,* Volume 4 (New York: Doubleday Page, 1919).

Spears, Edward. *Prelude to Victory* (London: Cape, 1939).

Stallings, Laurence. *The First World War: A Photographic History* (New York: Simon and Schuster, 1933).

Steele, Harwood. *The Canadians in France 1915–1918* (London: T. Fisher Unwin, 1920).

Stewart, H. *The New Zealand Division* (London: Whitcombe and Tombs, 1922).

Von Hindenburg, Paul. *Out of My Life,* Volume 2 (New York: Harpers, 1921).

Von Kurenberg, Joachim. *The Kaiser* (New York: Simon and Schuster, 1955).

Williamson, Henry. *The Wet Flanders Plain* (New York: Dutton, 1929).

Willis, Irene. *How We Got on with the War* (London: National Labour Press, 1919).

Witkop, Phillip (Ed.). *German Students' War Diaries* (London: Methuen, 1929).

Notes

The majority of direct and indirect quotes in this book are accompanied by their sources, and since the sequence is fairly chronological it has not seemed necessary in most cases to relate them to exact dates and page numbers. The following notes will substantiate other quotations not identified in the narrative, as well as factual statements requiring verification. Except where indicated, references are to the bibliographical material that follows these notes.

Chapter 1.

The episode of the seventeen shells was derived from Gibbs' *The Struggle in Flanders,* p. 39. For my portrait of the Western Front, I drew heavily on Mottram, Williamson, Charles Edmonds, James Edmonds, the Mottram—Easton—Partridge volume, Graves, Purdom, and from a multitude of other accounts of this kind—especially the two books by Gibbs, who was far and away the most gifted lay reporter of the war. Stallings' pictures were also extremely useful. The various quotations from Foch, Napoleon, etc. appear in the introduction to Hart's *Through the Fog of War.*

Chapter 2.

Curzon was quoted in the *Times* January 1; the peace rebuff and Pankhurst uproar are also reported on that date. While I collected many fragments from many places concerning the home islands during the war, the majority in this and later chapters may be credited to Peel, Playne, and Willis. Peel, for example, quotes the child's plaintive "Mummy . . ." phrase. The conversation with the worker is recounted by Playne, who also writes of the rush-hour jam. Pankhurst tells of Conan Doyle's suggestion concerning fallen women. See Peel, p. 58, for the German lady's letter. Strachey is discussed by Graves, p. 249, second revised edition. I discovered the Smuts remark in Playne. Lloyd George's gloomy greeting to

Lord Hankey in November is quoted by Thomas Jones, p. 78. Primarily I leaned on Thomas Jones, Owen, Robertson, Churchill's *The World Crisis,* and Bernard Shaw for the general political background of the day, and on these plus Hart's books, Callwell, and Bean for summaries of the East-West controversy. Duff-Cooper tells of newspaper attitudes and the "twenty-three ropes" placards. Mr. Asquith's comment appears in Beaverbrook. See Charteris for a summary of Haig's post-Somme memorandum. Bean, p. 12, and Thomas Jones, p. 76, refer to Lord Lansdowne's letter, and Duff-Cooper quotes Robertson in reply. Mostly I used Bean, James Edmonds, and Owen on the Chantilly conference.

CHAPTER 3.

Charteris, Duff-Cooper's official biography, and Hart's *Reputations Ten Years After* and *Through the Fog of War* tell of Haig's life and character to date. See Duff-Cooper and *Through the Fog of War* (p. 36) for excerpts from the marshal's early correspondence, and the latter, p. 37, for the comment on his operations in the Boer War, plus the subsequent phrases and quotations. The quotation "The British cavalry officer seems to be impressed . . ." was reported by Gronow from the Frenchman, Excelmann; I extracted it from Cecil Woodham-Smith's *The Reason Why* (McGraw-Hill, 1953). Shaw's opinion appears on page 216. Haig's spiritual and religious attitudes are noted in Hart's *Fog of War,* p. 43. The Churchill extract appears in *Great Contemporaries;* this essay has also been reprinted in *Famous British Generals* (Barrett Parker, Ed., Nicholson & Watson, 1951). I followed Duff-Cooper, Thomas Jones and Robertson, among others, for details of the Rome conference. Thomas Jones, Owen, and Hart's *Through the Fog of War* tell of Lloyd George's career and nature. See Thomas Jones, p. 15, for Gladstone's plea of April 28, 1892. From Duff-Cooper I extracted Lloyd George's monologue in the train after the Rome meeting, and Kiggell's letter to Haig. The various Nivelle assurances may be found in Churchill's *The World Crisis,* pp. 712 *et. seq.,* and Hart's *The War in Outline,* pp. 173–74. See diary entries of January 16 for Haig's counter-views. Wilson's entry ("an amazing speech") was written January 24. Lloyd George's argument in favor of a single army command is quoted by Owen, p. 392. Haig's reaction appears in his diary for February 26; and the letter to his wife was derived from Duff-Cooper. Again, Duff-Cooper provides the reference for Robertson's comment on the Prime Minister ("I can't believe that a man such as he . . ."), for Haig's next diary entry, and for his letter to Nivelle concerning "unity of effort." The dialogue between Sir Douglas and Gough is recounted by the latter in *The Fifth Army*. See Haig's published diaries February 28 for the letter to Robertson: "Briefly it is the type of letter . . ." The technicality over the Haig-Nivelle grade differential is commented upon by Hart in *The War in Outline*, p. 171. Repington in his diary for April 13 tells of Sir William's sour views on the Russians. I have borrowed from Willis concerning the various quotations by Haig, by the *Daily News*, and by Lloyd George prior to America's entry. The poem, "I hear a noise of breaking chains . . . ," appeared April 9 and was written by James Douglas. This, too, is from Willis, as well as the report on the Savoy luncheon.

CHAPTER 4.

Winston Churchill in *The World Crisis*, pp. 705 *et. seq.*, has written a fascinating appreciation of the inception and unfolding of the French spring offensive. This, Owens and Duff-Cooper are my major sources for the present chapter. See the first, p. 724, for the quotation beginning, "So Nivelle and Painlevé, these two men . . . ," and pp. 718–19 for Rupprecht's words. The increase in German divisions from nine to forty is verified here, p. 720. See various sections of Bean and James Edmonds *re* facts and figures on the German withdrawal. Ludendorff's "decision to retreat" was taken from Gibbs' *Now It Can Be Told*, p. 454, and the statements of the villagers from the page following. See *The World Crisis*, p. 717, for the text of Nivelle's March 6 directive. The astounding claims of Nivelle prior to the attack are derived also from Churchill's chapter, and from Hart's *The War in Outline*, pp. 173-74. Again see Churchill, pp. 721-22 for Nivelle's order to Micheler, and the next page for an account of the meeting on April 3. Wilson's diary excerpt, a typically lively one, is dated April 8. "The effect of the Nivelle alterations . . ." is on p. 713 of *The World Crisis*. Another absorbing account of the Nivelle episode appears in Pierrefeu's volume; the conversation between d'Alenson and the general is reported here. I found Hart's summary in *The Real War*, pp. 321-29, sufficient for telling briefly the Arras story. The bitter passage concerning Bullecourt was written by Bean, pp. 349-50, as well as the phrase about Haig and Gough (p. 352) which follows. See Haig's *Private Papers* under date of April 18, 1917, for the excerpt from Wilson's letter, and Callwell for Wilson's diary note of the day before, which begins, "Nivelle will fall. . . ." By far the best source for what little is known about the French mutinies is the famous article, "The Bent Sword," by A. M. G., published in *Blackwood's Magazine*, January 1944. It is, by the way, reprinted in its entirety as Appendix I, pp. 139 *et. seq.*, by Davidson. I have used it liberally, as well as similar related material in Churchill's aforementioned chapter on Nivelle. Quotations from the French troops, however, were found in Hart, *The Real War*, pp. 300-301. Concerning Lloyd George's note to Haig after the imbroglio, Painlevé's visit to the latter, and Haig's replies, see Duff-Cooper. The occurrence at French GHQ is recited by Pierrefeu. The final quotations from Haig's papers, dealing with Nivelle, Ribot, and Robertson, are dated May 3, April 26, and April 29 respectively.

CHAPTER 5.

I am indebted to Bean and James Edmonds for their recapitulations of the gradual evolution of Haig's Flanders plan. Broadly speaking, these appear in Edmonds, pp. 1-32, and in Bean, pp. 546-60, although there are many other references to its theory and growth: for example, in James Edmonds' final chapter, "Retrospect." Simonds, pp. 194-217, concisely reviews the U-boat problem. Henry Wilson's "case for Haig" will be found in Callwell; this is a diary entry dated April 22, 1917. See Dewar and Boraston for the means by which Ypres was selected "by a process of exclusion." Lloyd George quotes Asquith's memo to Robertson on p. 327, and Robertson's letter to Joffre on pp. 325-26. For the May 1 conference see Callwell, p. 345. The meeting held on May 4 was more important and is reviewed in many books. Thomas Jones, among others, reports Lloyd George's statement, "We must go on hitting . . ." on pp. 117-18. See also Bean, pp. 547-53, from which the next quotation ("It is no longer a question") is derived. Lloyd George, p. 335, mentions his exchange with Pétain. I used Maurice for the following week's conference at Doullens, and James Edmonds, p. 26, for Robertson's warning to Haig concerning the unlikelihood of French cooperation. Pétain's fateful prediction to Wilson about Haig's certain failure appears in Callwell, Vol. 1, p. 355. The fragment from Hoffmann's diary is dated June 1. In describing the Flanders terrain I made much use of Johnson and Muirhead. The pregnant reference of Charteris, "Careful investigation of the records. . . ," appears in his published diaries, p. 272. Johnson is also the background for the sundry quoted remarks about the

Flanders mud. Poignant pictures of Ypres itself have been sketched by many a wartime writer. From our bibliography I refer the reader to Beatrix Brice, Farrer, Hurst, and especially Mottram. From these sources I have done my best to reconstruct the pathetic, almost fabulous reality of 1917.

CHAPTER 6.

The best sketch of General Plumer is perhaps to be found in Harington's *Plumer of Messines*, and for the general background of Messines I have consulted Bean, James Edmonds, and Johnson. The conversation concerning the mines at Hill 60 is reported by Harington in *Tim Harington Looks Back*. Bean, p. 599, verifies von Kuhl's suggestion for a withdrawal, and on the same page quotes the XIX Army Group's order to stand fast. See this reference, also, for the long excerpt concerning the drama May 9. It appears on pp. 958–59. In the same section appear the sections about Captain Woodward and Sapper Sneddon. I obtained the next bit ("He had been working underground . . .") from Gibbs' *The Struggle in Flanders* (which was earlier titled *From Bapaume to Passchendaele*), p. 214. The details and technicalities that follow, prior to the attack at Messines, are mostly drawn from James Edmonds, pp. 32 *et. seq.* Bean on p. 579 relates the detail about Monash and his circular. The quotations in the next paragraph have been taken from Gibbs, *The Struggle in Flanders*, p. 193. Consult Lytton for the trials and tribulations of war correspondents of the day, including the statement made to them by Harington on June 6. Fox's small volume tells of the attack in journalistic terms; and James Edmonds, pp. 54 *et. seq.*, follows it through in his usual pedantic style. But see Bean, pp. 588 *et. seq.*, for a more dramatic account, including the Australian lieutenant's quotation. *The Real War*, Hart, p. 330, calls Messines a "siege-war masterpiece" and is also responsible for the phrase which follows.

CHAPTER 7.

Sir Williams's pungent letter to Haig is reprinted in the latter's *Private Papers* on the same date. The latter's reaction was developed piecemeal from his diary entries. The fact that the War Office disagreed with the optimistic views of Haig and Charteris concerning Germany's weakness is documented in James Edmonds, p. 98. Here we find that the Director of Military Intelligence, Brigadier General G. M. W. Macdonogh, opposed GHQ Intelligence right down the line. It is also noteworthy that Robertson cautioned Haig to avoid contradicting the War Office on this vital point, writing, "It would be very regrettable at this juncture if different estimates of Germany's resources were presented to the War Cabinet." See the marshal's diary on June 7, 1917, for Pétain's quoted assurances. Lytton is one of many who, at the time, wondered whether the time element would not work against Haig's projected campaign. German awareness of the impending assault is noted by Bean, p. 699. The following page of his *Australian Official History* tells of Rupprecht's preparation, his reaction to the Lens feint, etc. Footnoted on p. 699 (Bean) one may locate the diary entry of the Australian on leave. Lloyd George tells, p. 390, of encountering the *Frankfurter Zeitung* story. It would not be useful to document the entire proceedings in London during the momentous days of June 19–20–21. These three conferences are dealt with in Davidson, Haig's published diary, Lloyd George, James Edmonds, Robertson (Vol. 2), Thomas Jones, and Duff-Cooper; however, the more arresting quotations will be cited. Haig's demonstration at the conference map is described by Lloyd George, p. 359. James Edmonds' admission ("the outline of the campaign may seem super-optimistic") is on p. 101. See Lloyd George, p. 359, for "the aerial tower" phrase. Churchill's labeling of Jellicoe's claim as "wholly fallacious," and his reasons, appear in *The World Crisis*, p. 734. Lloyd George's summary, after the June 19 meeting, is in turn summarized in his volume, pp. 363 *et. seq.* For Robertson's June 20 memo see Lloyd George, pp. 581–85, and pp. 586–90 for Haig's memo of the same date. The entire exchange that day is outlined in brief by Lloyd George, pp. 379–81. His long speech of June 21 is recapitulated on pp. 387–97. I derived the detail of the Germans shelling Dunkirk from Leugenboom from Dewar and Boraston. James Edmonds, p. 132, records Anthoine's tardiness on July 2. See Robertson, Vol. 2, p. 247, for his July 6 letter to Haig. Gough's request for a five-day delay is substantiated by James Edmonds, p. 132. See Robertson, Vol. 2, p. 248, and the British historian, p. 105, *re* Sir William's July 19 letter to Haig, the latter's reply, and the War Cabinet's long-delayed approval of his Flanders attack.

Chapter 8.

Much of interest concerning the Eastern Front from the Bolshevik point of view exists in Leon Trotsky's *History of the Russian Revolution* (Simon and Schuster, 1937). See Vol. 1, p. 356, for his reference in the second paragraph of this chapter, and page 387 for the phrase reported by the Russian Eleventh Army. The incompetence of Gough's staff was common knowledge. Haig's later diary entry for September 10 is a typical source. Gibbs' *Now It Can Be Told*, pp. 476–77, is another, vastly more forceful. Lytton refers to the matter, and the *Australian Official History* often does the same. Haig himself comments (diary, October 5) rather mildly, "I think Gough's Staff Officer (Malcolm) is partly the cause of this feeling." As for the dubious composition of the Fifth Army, Gough appraises it frankly in *The Fifth Army*. I consulted James Edmonds, pp. 126–28, for Gough's intention to advance to the theoretical limit, and Haig's approval of same. Davidson's objections are aired in his own book, pp. 28 *et. seq.*, and his record of Plumer's outburst en route to the conference is found on p. 31. I extracted Churchill's suggestion to Lloyd George ("It is clear however that no human power . . .") from *The World Crisis*, p. 735. Bean is credited on p. 698 for the "mixture of motives" phrase; and there is much more concerning the ambiguous planning, lack of surprise, and the German side of the cóin in pp. 685–701 of his history. Regarding Uniacke's warning, see Hart's *The War in Outline*, p. 193. Baker-Carr comments drily on the cavalry preparations. The aerial background is discussed in immense detail by H. A. Jones. Haig's instructions to Rawlinson were dated July 5 and may be verified in Maurice, who also describes Fourth Army training. See James Edmonds generally concerning the German defensive dispositions, and p. 142 for von Lossberg's role. Nichols' is one of the better divisional histories, and I have drawn upon it for the situation "during the latter half of July." Rupprecht's notation, "My mind is quite at rest . . ." is derived from Hart's *The Real War*, p. 340. The sentence about "ridiculous maps" is mentioned by Lloyd George, p. 385. I have quoted Arthur Conan Doyle concerning "a tract of ground which was difficult when dry. . . ." See Repington's diary for June 24 concerning his talk with Sir Douglas. The "sunny days before the attack" are portrayed by Hope, by Gibbs in both his books used in the present narrative, and by Bean. I am in debt to these sources in my attempt to recapture this wistful phase. The verbatim scraps of conversation arise out of Hope's mordant book. See MacDonagh for the July 7 air raid, Playne for the *Swift* and *Broke* naval episode. I derived Mr. Pringle's protest from *The War Magazine*, June 21. Note Haig's diary for his July 30 visit with Gough. See the account by Alfred Willcox in Purdom's book concerning the firing just before the July 31 dawn assault.

CHAPTER 9.

The problem of the 30th Division is discussed by James Edmonds, p. 153, and German defenses on pp. 141–46. Churchill's caustic phrase, "the hopes of decisive victory . . ." derives from *The World Crisis*, p. 733. See Vol. 2 of Hindenburg's memoirs for his quoted paragraph. I acquired the background for the attack itself almost entirely from Conan Doyle, Gibbs' *The Struggle in Flanders*, and the *British Official History*. Baker-Carr is the source for the two messages concerning tanks; the following paragraph, also having to do with the tank failure, is a composite of the narrative by Ralph Jones and Nichols. The 10:40 message was sent by Major General W. de L. Williams and is noted by James Edmonds, p. 155. The officer who found himself "suddenly threatening a sergeant-major" was Edmund Blunden, who on p. 223 describes the state of affairs at this juncture. The death of Artillery Lieutenant Shelley of the 18th Division near Zillebeke is reported by Nichols. I obtained facts about Haig's visit with Gough that afternoon from Duff-Cooper and Haig's diary of July 31. Gough's instructions to his two corps commanders are summarized in *The Fifth Army*. See James Edmonds, p. 177, for Haig's August 4 note to the War Cabinet, and p. 181 for Rupprecht's opposite views. I located Gough's appraisal of Charteris in the former's *Soldiering On*, and Lloyd George's similar estimate in his own memoirs, p. 413. The date of Charteris' diary entry, "Every brook is swollen," is August 4; it is quoted in Hart's *The War in Outline*, p. 193. The description of the terrain forwarded by Haig to the King emanates from Boraston, p. 116. At this time Colonel J. F. C. Fuller was Chief General Staff Officer of the Tank Corps, and it was he who wrote the memorandum ("From a tank . . .") quoted in Hart's *Reputations*, p. 135. The German burial scene appears in Binding. Father Doyle's first passage is dated August 5. I am indebted to Miss Luard for her various diary entries of August 1 and 2, and for other items concerning the handling of casualties. Father Doyle's next note is to be found in the August 7 issue of the *Dublin Review*. For James Edmonds' summary see pp. 177–80. The *Spectator's* paean of praise is dated August 4. I discovered Charteris' revealing protest ("D. H. has not only accepted . . .") footnoted on p. 724 of Bean. Lloyd George, pp. 410–13, requotes the various allegations as to German weakness, and there comments further on Haig ("It naturally pleased Haig . . .") and Kiggell. Robertson's letter to Haig is reproduced at length in the latter's *Private Papers,* pp. 251–52. I extracted Haig's comment ("I could not have believed . . .") from Hart's *Through the Fog of War,* p. 47. My primary source for the section concerning the switch to attrition, and Rawlinson's paper in this connection, was Bean, pp. 725–26. In *Soldiering On* Gough relates his suggestion to close down the campaign in August, and in *The Fifth Army* he also tells how and why Plumer was handed the key assignment on the 25th. More about this may be noted in James Edmonds, p. 206. See Gibbs' *Now It Can Be Told,* p. 477, for his conversation with the officer leaving Flanders. The continuation of the attacks in August, the phrase "these strokes . . . ," the reports received by Rupprecht, and Ludendorff's transfer of nine divisions away from the salient are all recorded by Bean, p. 728. Baker-Carr's book substantiates the passages that follow. Again I have quoted from Ludendorff, Vol. 2, regarding his reaction to the August fighting. The *Daily News* carries the full text of H. G. Wells' plea in its August 14 issue; and Lloyd George uses much of the Pope's note two days later on p. 278. Gibbs' dispatch concerning Inverness Copse was dated August 30, and is reprinted in *The Struggle in Flanders,* pp. 310–15.

CHAPTER 10.

Sir Douglas' September 2 report is on record; for a brief summation see James Edmonds, pp. 232–33. I derived Lloyd George's "blood and mud" citation from Spears, as well as Joffre's "nibbling" phrase. Playne has furnished the background for the section concerning the flood of rumors and the young ladies from the East End. Carson's warning about peace talk is cited in the *Evening Express,* and Thomas Jones, pp. 121–22, tells of the whispering about changes at the helm. Robertson's remarks to Repington may be noted in the latter's diary for August 20; his September 3 wire to Haig appears in the field marshal's *Private Papers* of the same day. For my account of the conference on September 4 I have used Haig's diary of that date, James Edmonds, pp. 233–34, and Davidson, pp. 42–43. The quotation from Sir Henry Wilson ("This is unfortunate . . .") is a combination of his diary entries September 4 and 5. At this time the military was complaining incessantly about manpower shortages on the Western Front; for one of many examples in dozens of sources, the reader may note James Edmonds, p. 234. In this vein, and for Wilson's remark ("to take troops away from France . . ."), check his diary for September 15. Pétain's specious argument which follows is discussed by Davidson, pp. 42–43, who also outlines reprovingly (pp. 22–23) the weird episode of the Russian division which mutinied in France. I borrowed from several passages in Bean, such as the one on p. 748, to write of the dry September interim. See also pp. 757–58. James Edmonds cites von Kuhl's "inmost conviction," p. 244. I unearthed the "Admiral" sketch from Williamson, and the paragraph about the Hotel du Sauvage from Gibbs' *Now It Can Be Told*, pp. 482–83. See Witkop for Corporal Zschutte's letter, and Bean, pp. 730–31, concerning the Australians for whom "time was running out." Many parts of Reynolds' book furnish the background for my aerial material. Von Richthofen's report is quoted by Gibbons. I used James Edmonds, pp. 236–39, for the analysis of Plumer's scheme, and p. 251 for Sixt von Armin's view on the 17th. Bonar Law's letter to Lloyd George was used by Owen, p. 401. See Bean, pp. 753–54, for "the usual comments from onlookers." James Edmonds verifies, pp. 250–51, that Gough wanted the impending attack stopped. The capture of the Australian officer is detailed by Bean, pp. 758-59.

CHAPTER 11.

I have referred mostly to Bean, Edmonds, and Arthur Conan Doyle for my description of the attack on the 20th. The various heroisms sketchily noted are indexed in Bean and Edmonds. It was J. D. Rogers who reported, "I have just returned . . ." according to Bean, p. 767. Again, see Bean, pp. 788–89, for the comment on casualties, the German requote ("The new English method . . ."), and on p. 790 the words of Lord Bertie. Robertson, who "had to knock out a scheme . . . ," writes of it on pp. 253–54, Vol. 2. Regarding Lloyd George's dilemma *re* dismissing Haig, note Owen, pp. 399–400, and the Prime Minister's own memoirs, pp. 446–55. He tells on pp. 412–14 of his visit to the front; Gough also writes of it in *The Fifth Army*. "The usual stuff" from Charteris is derived from Lloyd George, pp. 415–16, and on the latter page also appears the quote: "G. H. Q. could not capture the Passchendaele ridge. . . ." Rupprecht's expression ("It is to be hoped . . .") is used by Bean, p. 803. Ludendorff's words which follow were picked up in James Edmonds, p. 294. Shaw, p. 240, writes how "the war dragged on. . . ." Robertson's well-known and revealing admission to Haig— "My views are known to you"—has been noted in many sources; e.g., his own work, Vol. 2, p. 255. The essay, "Two Appreciations," is in Hart's *Through the Fog of War*. Churchill's attitude toward attrition is reprinted from *The World Crisis*, p. 563, and Lloyd George's similar view from his memoirs, p. 408. I used Gibbs' *Now It Can Be Told*, p. 485, for the episode about the officer sentenced to death. Four sources were consulted for the September 28 conference: Gough's *Fifth Army;* James Edmonds, pp. 296–98; Davidson, p. 51; Bean, pp. 878–80. See Bean for Haig's ebullient estimate *re* German casualties, p. 943. As for the meeting held on October 2, I went to Haig's diary of that date; Davidson, p. 51; and Bean, p. 880. I am under obligation to Caroline Playne for my material on the home front. Finally, see Haig's diary, October 3, for the "great bombshell" about taking over more of the French line.

<h3 style="text-align:center">CHAPTER 12.</h3>

All the German quotations in the first paragraph are in Davidson, p. 55, except the last, which was taken from Bean, p. 876. For Charteris' exclamation, see Bean, p. 908. "An overwhelming blow" is claimed by Bean, p. 875; and Gibbs' sentence is from *The Struggle in Flanders*, p. 379. I used Stewart for the passage, "Long ere now. . . ." Haig's dispatch may be examined fully in Boraston, p. 127. Duff-Cooper reports the congratulations from Pershing and Lord Derby. Repington's diary entry—"nations counted money no more than pebbles"—is dated October 4. The Charteris note of the 7th is from his own published diary. I hesitated about using Foch's almost too-familiar warning (*"Boche* is bad . . ."), but succumbed; it may be noted in Churchill's *The World Crisis*, p. 739. Davidson, p. 58, has summed up the October 7 conference. The need to "tranquilise public opinion" is stated by Stewart. For Haig's memo to Sir William and the politicians, see his *Private Papers* under date of October 8, and Hart's *Through the Fog of War*, pp. 264 *et. seq.* "Still another smashing triumph . . ." is quoted from Lloyd George, p. 417. *The Struggle in Flanders*, p. 386, is the source of the Gibbs excerpt. Pétain's remark to Repington about Charteris was confided to the colonel's diary October 7, along with the one about British generals. Shipping losses were derived from Simonds. Lloyd George has written at length, pp. 262 *et. seq.*, concerning Baron von Kuhlmann's peace overture. I also derived some material about it from Thomas Jones, pp. 129–30. Churchill's appraisal of Haig, who "acted from conviction," and Robertson appears in *World Crisis*, p. 739. The almost unbelievable statement by Charteris ("With a great success tomorrow . . .") causes one to wonder if, after all, this otherwise brilliant officer was quite balanced; it is drawn from Bean, p. 908. Also see Bean, pp. 884–85, for an account of Harington's press conference.

CHAPTER 13.

The section "through what might have been a porthole" has been requoted from Housman. All military details about the attack on October 9 may be verified in Bean and James Edmonds. See Davidson, p. xix of his Foreword, for the little formula $D = \dfrac{W}{2}$. The remarks of the Australian subaltern ("Ah doan' know what our brigade was doin'") are chronicled by Bean, p. 887, and the recollections of soldiers struggling to reach the jump-off line appear in Gibbs' *The Struggle in Flanders*, p. 399. I noted the picture of the bogged mule in Stewart's official history. Again see Purdom, quoting George Brame, as to the corporal who failed. The phrase "there was no curtain of fire at all" is Bean's, p. 888. Two pages later this historian comments on the pre-battle decimation of the 6th and 7th brigades, 2nd Australian Division. I used Hope's description of an attack on a pillbox ("Suddenly his helmet seems to be knocked off. . ."). The forlorn encounter of the eighty-five men who raided Celtic Wood is told by Bean, pp. 899–900. The admission that the Germans won a "comparative success" that day is James Edmonds', p. 337, where one also finds the German complaint concerning "the sufferings of the troops." My reference for the paragraph beginning, "In England and the U.S. the newspapers . . ." is Lytton. Gough's expressive and much-quoted passage ("Still the guns churned this treacherous slime . . .") is from *The Fifth Army*, and the citation immediately thereafter was taken from Bean, p. 890. See Charles Edmonds for the episode about the British officer and his men who could not bring themselves to shoot the wounded German. The appalling photo of the six stretcher bearers may be found in *The Times' History of the War*, Vol. 16. There is much in both Gibbs books which deals with casualties after the battle; for example, see *Now It Can Be Told*, p. 482. Hope, p. 138, depicts those who died in shell holes; and Housman tells of the little German dog.

CHAPTER 14.

The artificial aspect of life in the metropolis during the war years is recalled in many a contemporary account; generally I referred to Playne and Peel. Lady Wilson's query is dated October 20. I was also aided by Pankhurst's classic autobiography of the embattled pacifist. See the *Nation* August 25 for the incantation on the "symbolic Statesman." Robertson's letter to Haig is published in the

latter's papers October 9. Lloyd George's quote ("the patient . . .")
appears in Callwell, Vol. 2, p. 17, and Sir William states his reaction
in *Soldiers and Statesmen,* Vol. 2, pp. 256–58. Haig's comment on
Lord French ("Never before, perhaps . . .") was derived from
Duff-Cooper, as well as the next sentence about Wilson. "A poor
production . . ." comes from the commander in chief's diary for
October 31. See Stewart's fine account of the menacing phase on
October 10 and 11, including the passage, "We all hope for the
best. . . ." I used Haig's diary for October 10 and 11 for his meetings with Gough and Poincaré respectively, and James Edmonds,
pp. 338–39, concerning Plumer's problems with German wire and
British wounded. Note Bean, pp. 906–907, for the misapprehension
as to the 66th Division's front. The state of New Zealand artillery
is conveyed by James Edmonds, p. 339. I got Charteris' quote ("He
was still trying to find some grounds . . .") from Bean, p. 908, on
which page one may also find Haig's interview with the newspapermen. Gough's phone call to Plumer that evening is cited by Bean,
p. 910; and it is Bean, p. 912, who observes that the infantry "attacked virtually without protection." The diary entry, "My opinion
is . . . ," was dated October 12 and appears in Stewart. The
Australian who patrolled the line near the Ravebeke was Lieutenant
W. G. Fisher; his reports are given by Bean, pp. 906–907, 927, 931.
See Haig's diary October 16 for Lloyd George's message of praise.
I used Churchill's *World Crisis,* pp. 739–40, anent Caporetto. Sir
Henry Wilson's diary entries: "We may lose . . ." and "I quoted
also . . ." are dated October 29 and 30; see Callwell's Vol. 2, p. 19.
Birdwood, p. 318, tells of the effect of mustard gas on his men. I ex-
tracted Gough's words about "the state of the ground" from *The
Fifth Army.* See Graham, *A Private in the Guards, re* souvenir
hunting. The *Spectator* note is under date of October 20. Binding is
the Bavarian officer who deprecated the British effort; this is in his
diary October 18. I learned of General Sixt von Armin's press interview via *The Times' History of the War,* Vol. 16. The last in Gough's
long series of pleas "to stop the attack" is verified in *Tim Harington
Looks Back.* It is James Edmonds, pp. 351-52, who writes, "Here,
too, the mud. . . ." Haig's dispatch ("The persistent continuation
of wet weather . . .") is reproduced in Boraston, p. 130. Duff-
Cooper cites the marshal's request that Robertson's people issue
more optimistic reports. See Lytton for his rebuke of Charteris;
Repington (October 14) for Plumer's related opinion; and Repington (October 15) concerning his talk with Kiggell. The citation

from Monash combines his letters of October 15 and 18. Ludendorff's "horror of the shell-hole area" derives from Vol. 2. See Hoffmann, October 28, for his extract. Turning to Lloyd George on "the
pencil" and Charteris, we find these comments on pp. 424–425.
Maurice quotes Rawlinson re Pétain: " . . . once the Boche has been
given time. . . ." The press revolt against the military is noted by
Repington, November 2 and 3. I drew upon Callwell, Vol. 2, p. 20,
for the paragraph about the Superior War Council and Kiggell. The
meeting between Haig and Lloyd George November 4 is described
in the former's diary that date. I referred to MacDonagh concerning
Ramsay MacDonald's peace move. The passage on Kiggell tells
again the incident related by Owen, p. 402, Hart in his *The War
in Outline*, p. 199, and Hart in *The Real War*, p. 343, where an
expanded version is given. The new difficulties inherent in the
Passchendaele salient are pointed out by Bean, p. 936.

CHAPTER 15.

See Lloyd George, p. 427, for GHQ's December 13 instructions,
"These salients are unsuitable to fight. . . ." Nichols writes mor-
dantly about conditions in and near the Houthulst Forest. The
quotation "Nothing can be said in defense . . ." is by Ernest Swin-
ton, tank expert on the War Committee, and is taken from *Eyewit-
ness* (Doubleday, 1933). I next used Fuller's *Military History*, Vol.
3 (Funk and Wagnalls, 1956). Churchill's statement re the French
Army in 1917 appears in *The World Crisis*, pp. 733–34. Davidson's
estimate is on p. 19. Bean, p. 938, writes, "It is not sufficient. . . ."
Haig's reason why he had "to go on attacking" appears in Duff-
Cooper. See Churchill's *World Crisis*, p. 567, for casualty statistics,
and Bean, p. 943. Lloyd George, p. 421, alleges that the figures
may in time be gerrymandered. James Edmonds, pp. 360–63, enun-
ciates the new statistics. I quote Bean, p. 941: "On this point Field
Marshal Haig was right. . . ." The three German complaints that
follow may be checked in Davidson, pp. 71–72. Haig's phrase about
men advancing "through mud up to their waists" is from a dispatch
to the King; see Boraston, p. 133. The Prime Minister's comparison
between Haig's offensive and Nivelle's is on pp. 420-21. Charteris is
one of many sources for Lloyd George's rather unfortunate speech,
"When we advance a kilometre . . . ," and this general also quotes
Carson in rebuttal. The retrospective views in the next paragraph
emanate respectively from *Tim Harington Looks Back;* Davidson,
pp. 72–73; Bean, p. 941; *The World Crisis*, p. 569. I consulted
Maurice for the Doullens conference and Rawlinson's cited passage.

For a broad picture of the fall of "Wully," see Hart's *Through the Fog of War*, pp. 108–110. Owens verifies (p. 462) that Haig virtually abandoned his CIGS. The marshal's diary entry, "I am afraid that in the back of his mind . . . ," was inscribed February 11, 1918. Owen, p. 401, tells of Northcliffe's "sudden revulsion." Note Wells' *Outline of History* (Doubleday, 1949), Vol. 2, p. 1087, for his views on the military mentality. Hindenburg's appraisal of British generalship appears in Vol. 2. Charteris *re* Haig's uncritical mind is quoted by Hart, *Through the Fog of War*, p. 48. See Bean, p. 946, for the excerpt, "When in the near future. . . ." The tale of Haig's presentation at Aldershot was derived from Hart's *The Real War*, p. 388. I found Churchill's remark "They were worn down . . . ," referring to the German spring 1918 offensive, in *The World Crisis*, p. 571. My figures on total war casualties were acquired from *The Encyclopædia Britannica*, 1953 edition, Vol. 23, p. 775. Owen, p. 442, has recorded Lloyd George's words, "If people really knew . . . ," to the newspaperman. My sketch of London at the Armistice was drawn from material in *The World Crisis*, H. G. Wells' *Outline of History*, and especially Mrs. C. S. Peel's published recollections.

Chapter 16.

My facts about Haig's declining years were culled from Charteris, Duff-Cooper, and Churchill's *Great Contemporaries*. The golfing photo of Sir Douglas faces p. 32 of Kirkaldy's *50 Years of Golf* (T. Fisher Unwin, 1921) wherein the famous Scotch professional has much to say about his idol, Sir Douglas, under carefree conditions so unlike his military environment. My references for Lloyd George's "long road" are Owen and Thomas Jones. See Hart's *Through the Fog of War* and *The Encyclopædia Britannica* concerning my passage on Sir William Robertson. Finally, I owe much to Brice, Farrer, Hurst, Mottram, Muirhead, Pulteney, and Williamson, from whom I composed the medley on Ypres, the cemeteries of Belgium, and the former battleground.

Index

(*When a person is quoted in the text but not named, the Index gives, under that person's name, the page on which the quotation appears; quotations may be checked in the Notes.*)

Library of Congress Cataloging in Publication Data

Wolff, Leon.
In Flanders Fields.
(Time Reading Program)
Bibliography: p.
Includes index.
1. Ypres, 3d Battle of, 1917. I. Title.
[D542.Y72W64 1980]   940.4′31   80-20894
ISBN 0-8094-3590-X (pbk.)
ISBN 0-8094-3589-6 (deluxe)